# BENEATH THE SURFACE: RACIAL HARASSMENT

*A civilization that is incapable of solving the
 problems it creates is a decadent civilization.
A civilization that chooses to close its eyes to its most
 crucial problems is a stricken civilization.*

*- Aime Cesaire, 'Discourse on Colonialism'*


  *But dost thou not remember
What the great Rumee hath said:
When the architect plans
To build anew a house
That has fallen into ruins,
He clears away the debris first,
And levels up the ground;
Then he lays the foundations
Afresh.*

*- Muhammad Iqbal, ' Khizr-I-Raah'*

# Beneath the Surface:
# Racial Harassment

BARNOR HESSE
DHANWANT K. RAI
CHRISTINE BENNETT
PAUL McGILCHRIST

# Avebury

Aldershot · Brookfield USA · Hong Kong · Singapore · Sydney

Published by
Avebury
Ashgate Publishing Limited
Gower House
Croft Road
Aldershot
Hants GU11 3HR
England

Ashgate Publishing Company
Old Post Road
Brookfield
Vermont 05036
USA

*HT*

*1521*

*B43*

ISBN 1 85628 315 1

Printed and Bound in Great Britain by
Athenaeum Press Ltd., Newcastle upon Tyne.

# Contents

## Part 1 : Contextuality

## Part 2 : Cartography

# List of Tables

# List of Figures

# Acknowledgements

The research undertaken here owes debts of gratitude to a number of people who made important contributions, whether small or large, to its development. We would like to acknowledge the assistance of Alan Burgoine, Amarjit Devgun, Shahbaz Khan, Monica Lassalle, N.D. Mahmood and Graham Olsen. Thanks are due to Endswell Productions, Nigel Fielding, Juliana Frederick, Tony Jefferson and Bobby Sayyid. Special thanks are due to Bunmi Alemoru, Ike Aneke, Kwamla Hesse, Karim Murji, Ionie Richards, Martin Walker and Merryl Wallace. We have nothing but praise for the respective efforts of Lezma Allison, Joanne Cummings and Cathy Louis who typed and re-typed many versions of the manuscript during extremely inconvenient hours. An extra special mention must also be made of the significant research and development work initiated by Masood Lone. Finally, we are deeply appreciative of the contributions of all those, especially the victims of racial harassment, who submitted evidence to the Inquiry. We hope this proves worth all our efforts.

# Foreword

The word racism has become too easy to say and too difficult to explain. During the 1980s, the antics of anti-racism inside and outside the local state confirmed its debasement. Beaten back, further outside the realm of respectable public politics by the gains which the Right made during that decade, the concept must now be almost impossible to utter in the still, serious places where formal governmental processes operate. Its use reflects badly on the credibility of those who invoke it and yet, in view of the jeopardy in which Blacks still live, its use remains imperative. A theoretically informed and sophisticated understanding of racism is a necessity if we are to interpret and explain the experiences of Blacks in this country and to illuminate the contemporary workings of a political system in which the issue of race and the related questions of nationality and belonging remain central even when they are submerged. One of the principal virtues of this innovative book is that it may help to break the bitter deadlock which has engulfed the crucial term - racism. *Beneath the Surface* demonstrates one important way in which the force and clarity of this essential concept might be restored, enhanced and eventually set to work afresh in the changed circumstances through which struggles around race will develop over the next ten years.

*Beneath the Surface* is valuable for other reasons. It contains an implicit but timely rebuke to the anti-theoretical cast of mind that is often so regrettably evident in discussions of racial politics. The report's tough character and distinctive scholarly orientation have been constructed from several sources which might not, at first, appear to be compatible. A well tuned sense of urban ecology and rigorous attention to the spatial characteristics of areas where harassment happens have not, for example, been prominent in previous discussions of racial violence. This concern with the dynamic, social geography of territoriality and its symbolism is more than a novel academic import. Particularly when taken together with the book's strong sense of how the British nativism associated with racial harassment is already being changed by the cultural and economic proximity of Europe, it indicates the originality of a perspective that points emphatically towards the future where worn out concepts and tired sociological generalizations will have nothing to offer.

However, the foundations on which the project stands also demand that we think in a much more disciplined way about the past than is customary in this vexed area of research and publishing. *Beneath the Surface* asks its readers to pay attention not only to the evasive histories of racism itself but more specifically, to the honourable and little known record of interventionist research and agitational writing around questions of race and the criminal justice system. This type of activity preceded the eighties and was moving in step with popular campaigning around race issues long before what might be called the high period of municipal anti-racism. It was however, changed and given additional momentum by the openness of some local authorities to the demands made upon them by autonomous, defensive organizations rooted within the Black and other Ethnic Minority communities. A layer of activism based on religious institutions, schools and other everyday organizations had been mobilized in the intense local conflicts that clustered around the central, nagging aspiration for racial justice. After the urban disorders of the early eighties, elements in local government saw that the behaviours and processes for which the term racial harassment provides an inadequate shorthand were serious matters that merited the attentions of the local state. Their sense of this problem may have been fleeting and their involvement in it may have been expedient but this precious moment should not now be forgotten or hastily erased from respectable histories of municipal socialism in order to hold the damaging charge of loony leftism at bay. Seeing racism as part of the legitimate brief of local government meant taking it out of the private, personal realm and making it a problem of civil and political society. This revolutionary development underpins the origins of *Beneath the Surface* and it is worth celebrating because of the notable way in which it brought parts of the state into alignment with forces outside their own institutional stuctures. The important lesson here cannot be contained under the narrow heading of anti-racism. It ought to be emphasized because it has a bearing on the wider problem of how radicals understand the relationship between the state and those social and political movements that sometimes challenge its legitimacy and its authority.

The authoritarian transformation of the British state and the sustained assault on local government which has accompanied it are well known topics that serve to frame our understanding of the current political conjuncture. Another useful aspect of *Beneath the Surface* is the way it underscores the place of racism and anti-racism in the steady shift towards a different type of political culture. More than this, the book suggests that the growth of those authoritarian and sometimes populist, modes of political administration did not pass unanswered. It was challenged by the practice of a radical democracy that was signalled in diverse initiatives. In this case, the outcome of these democratic demands was the courageous municipal inquiry which formed the basis of the book.

The pseudo-judicial strategy embodied in inquiries of this type is an interesting political tactic which remains unexplored and largely undersold. It was first deployed by the movements of prisoners, Blacks, women and other marginalized social categories. Its enduring potency resides not just in the expansive forms of democracy contingent upon the loosening of the institutional moorings of the local state. It also articulates a coherent, alternative model of popular justice which has enjoyed a special moral authority particularly when the conspicuous failings of the criminal justice system and the police service are brought to light.

Pointing out these strengths in *Beneath the Surface* is not to undermine the substantive value of the work as a critical resource for policy development around the causes and consequences of racial harassment. It should be obvious that this book will completely transform the ways in which racial harassment is perceived as a policy issue and as a unique cultural and political process. *Beneath the Surface* is doubly significant because it also offers a small but extremely significant step towards producing the sustained and detailed micro-history of local government which will be needed if the political agency local state is to be restored and the promise of democracy and popular justice to be consolidated. *Beneath the Surface* is a vital demonstration of how those goals can be linked. The critical perspective on the dilemmas of local authority practice which it provides may be its most significant contribution. It is certainly unmatched by any other piece of serious research and that alone should guarantee the wide readership which this excellent work merits.

*Paul Gilroy*
*Goldsmiths College*
*London University*
*August 1991*

# Introduction
# Racism : Further notes from the underground

*Barnor Hesse*

> There is really nothing more to say - except why. But since why is difficult to handle, one must take refuge in how .
>
> (Toni Morrison, 1970; The Bluest Eye)

It is remarkable, given the many and varied texts which examine racism in Britain, how very few of them discuss directly the phenomenon of racial harassment. It has almost become a specialist subject in the literature where only a few people specialize. Generally there are three categories of specialism. The first could be described as the 'documentary method' (see Thompson, 1988;Gordon, 1990a). This attempts to expose and codify case histories reported in various types of news coverage or made available from the files of community organizations and advice agencies. It brings to the surface the raw experience of racial victimization, placing in the public domain what might have been disparaged as anecdotal (see Chapter 1). The second belongs more to the tradition of 'survey research' (see Brown, 1984). This assumes the mantle of 'scientistic intervention' whether through a secondary analysis of incidents reported to the police or a randomly selected 'ethnic sample' of the population it attempts to estimate the size of the problem. This is seen as providing a 'legitimate' basis for the attention of public policy (see Chapter 4). While the third is a loose amalgam of 'policy analysis' (see CRE, 1987a; Forbes, 1988). As a research approach this is more concerned to examine what 'local' public agencies are doing as a response to racial harassment. It attempts to develop arguments and proposals for policy interventions of various kinds (see Chapters 2 and 3). These respective approaches are usually only related in so far as one may give credence to or criticize the findings of the other(s). But often there is little systematic discussion of the different findings or any attempt to develop an integrated analysis. In all this it needs to be said, survey and statistical research is by far the dominant influence in the construction of 'official' or 'public' knowledge of racial harassment. It has set the terms and focus of the debate: how much racial harassment really takes place, and to a slightly lesser extent, where it takes place. This has generally resisted any attempt to be linked to a wider concept of racism. Alternative repertoires of knowledge have been formed at the juncture of these observations and others which question the 'official' neglect of racial harassment and its traditional image as the irresponsible or lunatic activities of a 'small minority'. They have emphasized its entrenchment and seriousness albeit with an untheorized connectedness with societal racism. Initially this 'double' framework of knowledge was used by us to design the research described in this book. But it was one we increasingly felt constrained by and were eventually compelled to transform through a sort of paradigm shift. One major premise had to be challenged - this was the notion that racial harassment was random. Ironically despite the apparent opposition between the 'official' and 'alternative' accounts of racial harassment in Britain, that very opposition shared the same premise. Where they differed significantly was in terms of how much occurred and how seriously public agencies were responding. For us the 'randomness premise' required interrogation not merely to show how it obscured patterns in racial harassment. The premise itself (including the oppositional relation between official and alternative accounts) had to be removed in order to see what it occluded, what it assumed without providing the opportunity for assuming otherwise. Principally these assumptions were: the 'content' of racial harassment was known and this was sufficient to analyze it, even though its dynamics were largely unexplained; and also that, it was possible to define racial harassment without explicit theorization of the specific experiences of those communities victimized by it. As we hope is evident from the arguments presented in this book, a combination of methods and analyses are necessary to weaken the 'ground' of these assumptions. In this introduction we can only summarize the significance and implications of some of the ideas which can assist the move in this direction.

## Inquiry into racial harassment

The contextual focus of the research which provides the basis for this book was the Borough of Waltham Forest situated in the environ of London's 'East End' (see Appendix 1). Highlighting this at the outset simply enables us to begin by reflecting on the (in)significance of (this) location for our analysis of racial harassment. This perhaps is especially relevant given the circumstances in which our research emerged and was conducted. As local government researchers we were obliged to be particularly concerned with empirical policy questions - how and why local agencies were failing to tackle racial harassment? what were the experiences of local racial victimization? The research we designed was based on a method of 'local inquiry' under the guidance of a specifically constituted 'Council panel' (see Appendix 2). The inauguration of the Inquiry in November 1988 was a highly publicized affair in the Borough and the bulk of the social research, including the analysis of local 'oral and written evidence' (see Appendix 3), was completed for public presentation by October 1990. Subsequently a comprehensive research document, together with its sixty recommendations (see Appendix 4), was disseminated throughout the Council and the Borough and also made available to various other interested parties. Undoubtedly this was as it should be. However, against the grain of this procedural logic, directly emanating from the research we had initiated, we found ourselves asking, to what extent was this just another commentary on racial harassment? and what, if anything, was significant about Waltham Forest or indeed our analytical approach?

In its own terms Waltham Forest is no more or less remarkable than any other similarly bounded local jurisdiction[1] which is mostly urban landscaped and in various ways 'spatially inscribed' by a profound 'racialized' and 'ethincized' sense of communities. It is likely that in any inventory of racial harassment 'flash points' in London, Waltham Forest would be ranked somewhere in the middle range. Certainly whenever racial harassment in East London is projected in the national media, Waltham Forest hardly ever figures as a recurring image. But it would be wrong to think that the significance of our research somehow lies in an attempt to place this London Borough in the top rank of locations where racial harassment is perceived as acutely problematic. If this bore any resemblance to our initial purpose it was soon discarded once the momentum of our analysis got underway. As is usual in research, the 'handle on' significance is invariably only grasped retrospectively. It was the preparation of the material for *this book* which offered us the welcome opportunity to revise and re-position the structure and presentation of our analysis. It is also worth acknowledging that sometimes the process of (re-)writing itself involves being swept up in the alternating currents of recovery and discovery of insights, self-criticisms, arguments and emphases only to find ultimately that what you are saying is still much less than what can or, more importantly, should be said. The coherence of our eventual perspective reflects this insofar as the point at which we finished is precisely where we think it is crucial to start. Hence one of the central propositions of this book is that it is only when we begin to dig beneath the surface of what is conventionally termed 'racial harassment'[2] that we are able to expose the contemporary roots

xvi

of racism in Britain. It is in this sense alone that Waltham Forest is significant, that is, as a case-study, and also in this sense that what we provide here is more than another commentary. As we argue in the rest of this introduction social research on racial harassment can no longer remain immune to the conceptual rigours required in a contextual theorization.

## Either/or

How do we begin to theorize racial harassment? For us this immediately raises two considerations - first the relatedness of racism to harassment, and second, its spatial conditions of existence, that is its context. When our research for the Inquiry began, its initial publicity attracted many racially abusive telephone calls and letters. One letter was highly remarkable, not simply as a virtual exemplar of racial hatred, but in its articulation of three interactive themes common to the discourse of racial harassment and integral to the focus of our research. We reprint the letter below.

> *Dear Nigger Lovers,*
>
> *If the wogs and niggers do not like being 'racially harassed' there is something they can do - go back to their own countries. Nobody invited them here and nobody wants them here except perhaps a mob of vote-grabbing left wing politicians.*
>
> *I often think it is a pity the Germans did not win the war. They at any rate are white and we would not have been engulfed in the black tide if they did rule this country.*
>
> *Do you live amongst the filth, noise and crime that our coloured cousins wallow in? I bet not or you would not be so fond of advancing their cause.*
>
> *Kill the black swine or at any rate segregate them as they are supposed to do in South Africa.*
>
> *Yours with hatred,*
>
> *One of the white sufferers.*

Through a codification of the themes represented here it is possible to highlight the implications of racial harassment. The first theme expresses the idea that it is illegitimate for public policy to respond to the specific concerns and problems of the Asian or Black communities.[3] The second suggests that Asian and Black people should not complain about being racially harassed because they are an illegitimate presence in this country. While the third, in effect a conclusion to the previous two, simply asserts that Britain or England is a white country which is being 'over-run' or 'swamped' by 'alien', non-white cultures. Arguably these themes are fundamentally racist. They point to a rejection of Britain as a pluralist society and advocate the principle of exclusive white rule and white domination. Here in 'essence' lies the 'ground' of racial harassment and the basis of a public policy response. Or does it?

We pose the question awkwardly at this point in order to subvert the complacency and reactive unthinking of much that informs initiatives however loosely or tightly entwined with Anti-racist policies.[4] Arguably it is possible that the letter we have imbued with our analysis is as exceptional as it is extreme and that there is less of a ground to racial harassment than we imagine, that it is perhaps more 'harassment' than 'racial'. This view must be addressed not only to enable us to conceptualize the contextual relation between racism and harassment but also to force us to recognize that the 'raison d'etre' of racial harassment policies, the imperative of Anti-racism, is currently the subject of a profound and protracted theoretical audit (see Ball and Solomos, 1990).

## Anti-racist revisionism

Arguments for the development of policy responses to racial harassment by local authorities and police forces were among the key elements of Anti-racist discourse during the 1980s. Consequently any renewed efforts, like ours, to re-think the design of these responses cannot ignore the fact that Anti-racism, as a critical social policy initiative, if not run aground, is in serious need of a less wayward and more purposeful direction. Partly due to some of its excesses and flawed efficacy, but also due to relentless mass media opprobrium and the central government driven financial and legislative contractions of local government possibilities, the forward surge of Anti-racism stumbled irrevocably somewhere around 1986-1987 (Gordon, 1990b). Since then a number of revisionist strategies have emerged which despite their differences are ultimately connected with the potential or otherwise for evaluating the tenability of Anti-racist policy initiatives. These revisions are important to consider since they entail a theoretical and political 'struggle over the concept, as well as the extent of racism' (Miles, 1989:7).

It is possible to identify at least three currents or positions in this theoretical maelstrom of realignment.[5] The first describes a conservative version of 'Anti-anti-racism' (Gordon, op. cit.; Solomos, 1989). Emerging in the middle 1980s principally through the mass media and academic discourse it helped to develop a sustained critique of various local authorities and agencies like the Commission for Racial Equality. Its critique was resourced by a perception that 'anti-racism (is) an intrusion on individual freedom and a threat to the interests of the white majority' (Solomos, op. cit.:137). Two of its more coherent criticisms which are central to our concerns have been summarized by Miles (op. cit.). Firstly, this perspective argues that Anti-racism damages and undermines community relations because its interventions cause suspicion and resentment on all sides. The second contention is that 'anti-racists fail fully to examine the available evidence and therefore advance their claims without adequate support' (ibid.). Hence this particular perspective embraces a conclusion which suggests that Anti-racism is a 'foreign ideology' antithethical to a 'traditional' and tolerant British culture which is itself in need of rejuvenation if not restoration. Thus in arguing for the disbandonment of Anti-racist initiatives, 'conservative Anti-anti-racism' dispenses with any notion of racism as a sedimented social practice.

In an emphatic contrast to the above, a second response to Anti-racism takes a more radical position, articulating a perspective 'beyond Anti-racism'. For example, Gilroy (1990:14) has advanced persuasive criticisms of what he describes as 'statist conception(s)' in which the local state is considered as the 'main vehicle for advancing anti-racism'. In addition he argues that key among the deficiencies of 1980s Anti-racism was the particular conception of its project which not only 'trivialized the struggle against racism' but isolated it from other forms of 'oppression' and social subordination. This suggested falsely that 'race' and racism were 'readily extricable from everything else' and paradoxically conveyed the impression it was 'peripheral to the substance of political life'. The radicalism of a perspective 'beyond Anti-racism' insists that a commitment to Anti-racism is deepened and transcended through a revaluation of its conceptual apparatus and a broadening of its public emancipatory appeal to include 'other' subordinated social 'differences' (e.g. women, Lesbians and Gay men).

The third position is harder to pin down. At one glance it appears to be a derivative of the conservative perspective and from another a modification of the radical one, furthermore it appears to be but is not quite a 'middle-term' between these opposing positions. We refer to this as 'liberal Anti-anti-racism'. It draws widely on the various critiques of Anti-racism and offers an evaluation which seeks not to dispense with it or to deepen it, but to retain it in a diminished version. Under-pinning this is its subscription to a social theory which considers 'racial' or cultural differences to be reconcilable (in contrast to the conservative perspective) and seeks to minimize recognition of these differences (in contrast to the radical perpective). Typical of this is Nanton and Fitzgerald's (1990:170) recommendations of a 'new conceptual framework for "race" policies' in order to avoid a 'reified concept of "race"'. This leads them to argue in favour of 'social analysts' who have:

> approached the discussion of race *indirectly*, applying to their analysis of race and ethnicity a broader conceptual framework based on ethnic boundaries, ethnic composition, class analysis and a view of race as a process of political formulation and reformulation.

> (emphasis retained)

Leaving aside the fact that reified social categories are the 'sine qua non' of survey research and policy analysis, the idea of an indirect analysis of 'race' is to say the least, mystifying. The resulting position or 'non-position' of this perspective has the quality of what has been described as an 'undecidable'.[6] In the words of Bauman (1991:145) 'undecidables are all neither/nor, that is simultaneously, either/or'. Liberal Anti-anti-racism is thus infinitely pragmatic. Below we summarize our sketch of the three perspectives currently embroiled in 'Anti-racist revisionism'.

| Nature of revision | Short term | Long term | Policy perspective |
|---|---|---|---|
| Anti-anti-racism | Dispense with policy commitment to Anti-racism | Narrow range of social policy focus | Conservative |
| Beyond Anti-racism | Extend policy commitment to Anti-racism | Broaden range of social policy focus | Radical |
| Anti-anti-racism | Weaken policy commitment to Anti-racism | Generalize range of social policy focus | Liberal |

Any public or social policy commitment to tackle racial harassment will need to choose between the radical and liberal perspectives (see above). In so far as the approach adopted in this book suggests a radical orientation, we will discuss the specific difficulties posed by the liberal perspective on racial harassment policies, this is our purpose in the following section

## Burying race

The research described in this book commits us to an endorsement of the value public agencies have in developing policy responses to racial harassment. Although we analyze the ways in which these have been 'underdeveloped', conceptually unfocused and unsystematic in application, we do not question their rationale or usefulness in principle. However, not all researchers take the same position. In this respect Nanton and Fitzgerald (op. cit.) provide a particularly robust example of 'liberal Anti-anti-racism' which needs to be considered at some length. Their thesis is that local authorities policies on racial harassment generally fail to tackle the problems they purport to address. This thesis is anchored in a theoretical strategy which attempts to critique the category of 'race' in Anti-racist policy thinking by revealing it as a 'static' (reified) concept which both distorts the dynamics and changing aspects of social relations and is counter-productive to the development of a common public interest. However, many of the criticisms they deliver, are couched in terms which subvert the effect they are trying to achieve. For heuristic reasons in the following sections we illustrate how liberal Anti-anti-racism diminishes as it advances the theoretical significance of 'race' in policy terms.

### Conceptual antinomies

Nanton and Fitzgerald (op. cit.:161) contest what they see as unwarranted assumptions in Anti-racism. Firstly they argue one idea under-pinning its concept of 'race' is that fundamental differences exist between 'black groups and the white British population'. The difficulty with this is not that they are wrong but that they themselves assume it is possible to use the category of 'race' in analysis without imputing this significance to a particular dimension of social relationships. Whatever meaning is attached to 'race' its retention in analysis implicates that analysis in the accentuation of differences along that dimension. The idea of 'race' is after all the product of antagonistic racist formations.

Secondly they criticize the proposition that it is possible to 'quantify the extent of racism and the extent of racial inequality' and to use the data to develop policy interventions. Yet whatever the plausibility of this criticism, it belongs not to the domain of 'race' analysis as such but to the application of *policy analysis* to 'race'. In other words concepts entailed in the continuum *social indicator-policy category-policy proposal-performance measure* are unavoidable standard fare in the social policy field. For all its short-comings as long as this lexicon frames policy discourse the visibility (or viability) of 'race' as a policy issue will be reliant on its capacity to be intoned by that discourse. Thirdly, where Nanton and Fitzgerald (ibid.:160) question the assumption that a 'race dimension' can be applied in the 'provision and development of services', they fail to explain (if this is not so) how they are able to speak of 'racial disadvantage' (as they do) in any instance let alone place this in the context of other disadvantages. What is this but the 'race dimension' (renamed)? It is antinomies like these which 'screen out' rather than broadcast the possibilities for strategic re-thinking in liberal Anti-anti-racism. We can demonstrate this more effectively by examining two key aspects of their analysis of local authority racial harassment policies. In this they convincingly question the viability, if not validity, of current racial harassment policies, yet also manage to undermine the very premises from which they speak.

*Detaching 'racial' from 'harassment'*

In a curious way Nanton and Fitzgerald construe a notion of racial harassment which under-cuts any significance previously attached to the victimization experiences of Asian and Black people. Their argument seems to be that *usually* the 'racial' element of harassment is not that significant:

> In reports and the political language used on the subject, racial harassment is depicted as an extreme form of naked hostility manifest for example, in unprovoked attacks on people and property. *But the daily reality consists in 'low level' verbal abuse and insults, most of which go unreported.*
>
> (ibid.:164; emphasis added)

This is a key formulation in their argument since if we accept this dichotomy then the thrust of their approach requires us to abandon the idea of racial harassment as socially constructed across an uneven continuum of sequential and simultaneous experiences. This is what is at stake. Of course many questions arise here, what kind of harassment are we talking about? is it racial, that is, racist? or is it simply the vagaries of individual prejudice, part of general

xxii

rowdiness or the 'anti-social behaviour' of youth? The institution of the dichotomy (i.e. high level, low level) in this formulation directs Nanton and Fitzgerald's critique of the 'emphasis on the distinctiveness of 'race' issues and on treating them discretely from others' (ibid.). This suggests that the majority of racial harassment incidents are not sufficiently serious or distinct to merit so-called 'special' treatment. There are however many problems with this thinking. Firstly the grounds they have for positing a sharp distinction or cut-off point between so-called 'low' and 'high' levels of (racial) harassment seem to be arbitrarily 'quantitative'. They construe racial harassment in terms of unrelated discrete events rather than as a broad span of connected violations. The problem here is that they make no attempt to conceptualize the qualitative relation between these two so-called levels (are there really levels?) and therefore reduce the experience of racial harassment to a random rather than a recurrent 'logic' the significance of which seems determined by whether it is reported. Not only does this obscure the notion of patterns in racial victimization, it invokes a hierarchy of seriousness which completely distorts the cumulative impact of that experience (we discuss this fully in Chapter 5.) Secondly, Nanton and Fitzgerald's criticism of the distinctiveness of 'race' issues ironically dovetails with the views of those private sector companies and public agencies whose parochial visions are self-consciously 'colour blind'. Their approach leaves us with no conception of (white) racism or indeed of the emphasis required to respond to its distinctiveness. In order to position 'race' alongside 'other' issues (which is what they desire), what is required is not less distinctiveness, but more, particularly where other comparable issues are also specific community safety concerns (see the Conclusion).

What perhaps is most bizarre in Nanton and Fitzgerald's (ibid.:165) approach occurs where they suggest that racial harassment policies may be contributing to the very thing they are trying to deter. Despite the potential value of this observation it has *less utility* than at first appears particularly as the alternative seems to be to eject the policy altogether. For example they cite the idea of a 'racial harassment tenancy clause'[7] which they argue 'might be seen as the authority giving priority to the nuisance experienced by black tenants' (ibid.). It is enough to mention in passing how in one swift rhetorical move racial harassment is transliterated into the terms of 'nuisance'. This also displaces the question of whether racial harassment is a serious public concern. It 'toes' the 'undecidable' line of their whole approach. Nanton and Fitzgerald's apparent project to expose the reification of 'race' turns in on itself to obscure the conception of racism - it simply has no currency in their analysis. This point is worthy of further examination. For example, the idea that Asian or Black people are treated better than white people seems only to emerge when any public policy or legal initiative is introduced to redress some of the effects of racial subordination; it has its locus in contemporary racism. When measures like the 1976 Race Relations Act are enforced it is often argued in the 'popular press' that the (English) law is protecting Asian or Black people to the detriment of white people. It is as if 'legality, the ultimate symbol of national culture, is transformed by the entry of the alien wedge' (Gilroy, 1987:85). The social policy terrain is similarly affected by these defensive, proprietorial protestations. The point is we need to be alert to the fact that this is one of the ways in which racism 'works', any Anti-racist intervention will always be a matter for contestation and is therefore vulnerable to Nanton and Fitzgerald's objections. This is not to say that interventions cannot be improved or do not sometimes have negative consequences. But public policy must make choices. This means we are faced either with abandoning a specific public commitment to tackle racial harassment and collapsing the issue into the generic category of nuisance and harassment as Nanton and Fitzgerald seem to imply; or maintaining this commitment, improving the policy and the public explanation of its rationale, and also developing it in a broader remit to encompass other specific forms of violation and crimes against specific persons (e.g. violence against women, anti-Gay violence; see the Conclusion).

## Mystifying (racial) victimization

Developing their critique of racial harassment policies, Nanton and Fitzgerald indict them for treating 'black people in general as victims', they also argue it follows from this that 'black people are not considered to be in the wrong and that white people en masse are considered as potential perpetrators'. An initial response requires that we think about what victimization means. There are at least two senses in which we can think of a 'victim', the first identifies the experiential status of violation, the second refers to the process through which one is duped or tricked, both have their passive and active dimensions. Given the prevailing ineffectiveness of racial harassment policies it is arguable that they can and do encounter the 'victim' in both senses. Yet, it is important to contextualize what is specifically meant by racial victimization. It is the experience of a calculated violation directed at particular communities through associated individuals or families. The unprovoked episode may appear random in so far as it is not always clear why this individual rather than another was targeted. But beneath this surface level the choice is not random, it is strategic since it is the community the individual is perceived as representing which is chosen. Racial harassment policies do not create these conditions, if they disappeared today, Asian and Black people would not cease to be victimized tomorrow. Furthermore it would be wrong to think that racial harassment

xxiv

victims are simply passive objects because it is precisely their continuing resistance to violation which has projected racial harassment to the status of a social crime.[8] What needs to be avoided of course is a general propensity to see the Asian and Black communities solely in these terms. This is not achieved by dispensing with direct references to the dehumanizing experiences of victimization.

But what of their charge that Black people are 'not perceived to be in the wrong'? If the results of our research are anything to go by this was not a view shared by housing officers and police officers in Waltham Forest. We would be more inclined to argue this the other way: Asian and Black people are often considered to be either exaggerating racial harassment or fabricating it (see Chapters 2 and 3). The difficulties still experienced in getting racial harassment accepted as a serious item on local and national public agendas is surely an undeniable testimony to this. While the idea that racial harassment policies necessarily consider white people 'en masse' to be potential perpetrators seems to ignore the fact that policies cannot properly be analyzed outside the instances of their implementation. In other words how do Nanton and Fitzgerald explain the current reality where very little action if any appears to be taken against actual perpetrators of racial harassment? What they fail to see is that if the difficulty is really about how to avoid treating white people as a homogenous category in terms of racism, then the key task is to recognize that it is a particular assertion of white identity which is the problem. This returns us to the task of defining the specificity and context of racial harassment:

> How racial attacks are defined is not therefore an academic point but one with serious practical consequences, since it is only by recognizing the nature of racially-motivated attacks on black people that we can even begin to tackle the problem. To confuse such attacks with ordinary criminal attacks, or to claim, in the absence of any evidence, that attacks by black people on white people are 'racial', is to render the concept of racism quite meaningless.
>
> (Gordon, 1990a)

It is only once we have come to terms with the specific nature of racial harassment that we can take a radical turn and attempt to move beyond the conventional Anti-racist ethos or indeed its liberal revision. But first we must dig a little further in this discusssion in order to survey again the underground of racism.

## Unearthing racism

So what kind of racism is racial harassment? It is strange how a question like this seems completely out of step with traditional analyses, but it is crucial. A useful point of departure for the approach we have in mind has been formulated by Cohen (1988:155), it is close to invoking what we describe later as 'contextuality':

> The first and largest problem is how to devise a framework, whether analytical or organizational, which both distinguishes clearly between different types of racism and recognizes the historical individuality of those subjected to them.

It is important to decide whose experiences we are trying to analyze, rather than dredge up yet another vague, omnipresent general theory. Furthermore 'placing' these experiences historically *and geographically* contextualizes the focus of our analysis. This is the scope of the task involved in trying to understand the variable social experience of British racism encountered by Asian and Black people since the 1950s. Although the subsequent turbulent politics of immigration, settlement and public justice are by now well known (see Solomos, op. cit.; Ramdin, 1987), it is possible to use these insights to re-think an analytical, *retrospective*, characterization of the period. The regional/national construction of post-war Britain seems to have incorporated a social 'logic' driven through contingent, quasi-sequential, uneven repertoires of racisms. Or more figuratively, a 'three-geared white racism'. In 'first gear' the sociality or racism generated various levels of white opposition to segments of the population caricatured as 'non-white', as 'coloured *immigrants*' who were different. Where difference was marked with the stamp of inferiority, a symbol of subordinate status, which in turn attracted an intrusive 'logic' of *regulation* (e.g. police intimidation, scandalous news coverage). The move into a 'second gear' quickly emerged and was always likely wherever Asian and Black people variously challenged their treatment or at least refused to subscribe to its basic tenets. In this gear the momentum of racism reinforced or extended a baggage of practices which precipitated in an additional, individual and institutional 'logic' of *social exclusion* from employment, housing, civil rights, public respect and so on. At other times or in other places, depending on the political exigencies of 'local' crises or 'national' social panics, racism shifted into a third gear, shoring up a *territorial logic* to re-draw the contours of the law, state, economy and nation against the 'non-white' presence, pressing the case for expulsion. Like wild fire, wherever it took hold, the heat generated by this racism produced the type of smoke-screen which made the politics of white territoriality look both outrageous *and* respectable. Especially when senior politicians publicly empathized with so-called white 'fears' about 'having a nigger for a neighbour' or being 'swamped' by 'alien cultures'. It is perhaps this *territorial logic* of racism which is most telling and yet mostly unexplored. Over the last forty years, through each racial gear manouvere and change, back and forth, racism has been entrenched in the territorial relationship particular categories of white identity and dimensions of institutional formations have with the idea of 'Britain' and the 'British'. The racial exclusivity of this white proprietorial fixation is not universally perceived as ordained however, it has been continually under challenge. Racial harassment and the resistance to it has been the spatial outgrowth of these social roots. Whether the ownership claim to territory (e.g. the land, the citizenship, the language) is justified in terms of blood, culture or commonsense, it aspires to deliver the deeds of identity and nationhood to a 'white past, present and future'. Defending this configuration against ethnicized incursion or change in the British 'geographical' memory and the British 'historical' population is where the territorial logic of racism is at 'work', apparently unnoticed, underground. It is in this way that racial harassment, embroiled as it is in recurrent abuse, violence, damage to property, and the periodic deaths of 'non-whites', expresses the desire to expunge these ethnicized 'others' from the white terrain. Racial harassment is thus nurtured, sustained and preserved as the locus of a threatened white identity (see also Chapter 5). Only with ignorance can we fail to see how the present re-configuration of Europe, drags in the wake of the '1992 Single Market' *family resemblances* between racial harassment in Britain, France, Germany, Italy and elsewhere on the continent. It is politically stimulated where 'race' has been 'culturalized' as a strategy of deceit, to facilitate social investment in (white) European interests and social disinvestment in the (non-white) non-European presence. This territorial logic has its roots in the 'white racism' which underpins racial harassment, it lies beneath the surface of the celebrated or contested 'multi-cultural community'. It speaks behind the protestations 'we are in Britain', 'we are British'! It refuses to allow citizenship and community to incorporate in practice more than a white cultural identity.

## Contextuality and cartography

These are the issues which form the theoretical and political backdrop to this book. It is however rare for racial harassment to be considered from more than one perspective in a single text. In order to highlight our remedy of this deficiency, this book is clearly structured in two parts. The first part presents an analysis of the contextuality of racial harassment. In other words we attempt to convey a substantive understanding of its specificity through its situatedness in Waltham Forest at the end of the 1980s. Through our contextual approach in each of the related Chapters, we excavate the policy and analytical implications of racial harassment. Chapter 1 broadly chronicles aspects of the Asian and Black communities racial territorial experiences during the 1980s. It tries to establish a sense of the racial harassment legacy bequeathed to the Borough at the close of the decade. In Chapter 2 we focus on the most significant public agency in this context, the police. This Chapter examines the policy role of the Metropolitan police generally and in the Borough over the same period. In particular it questions whether police action/inaction actually reinforces or dismantles the local context of racial harassment. A similar approach to analysis is undertaken in Chapter 3 where the local Council is the focus. Here we also illustrate how and why the Council failed even to achieve the level of theoretical coherence in policy exhibited by the police. Over-all this first part attempts to codify the elements to *focus* analysis.

As a compliment to this the second part is more concerned to develop a model for the *framework* of analysis. Our understanding of cartography as a method here is primarily metaphorical. It utilizes distinct analytic approaches to 'map' the boundaries of knowledge concerning racial harassment. But it is also used as a basis to theorize its terrain by emphasizing the importance of 'spatiality' in any diagnosis of its 'objective' incidence and 'subjective' impact. Chapter 4 introduces this section with a secondary analysis of local racial harassment statistics. This is used to demonstrate the potential of a spatial analytic approach. In Chapter 5 we argue for the importance of examining the impact of racial harassment on its victims and explore this through an experiential analysis which is anchored in a sense of social geography and victims rights. Finally in the Conclusion to Part 2 (and the book) we use our theorization of racial harassment to tie together the significant threads of policy analysis which have implications for local policy developments. In addition we conjecture on whether the nature of racial harassment, as a crime against specific persons, raises, in common with other similarly 'personalized dehumanizations', a public policy requirement to think towards a theory of safety. Certainly if we can no longer afford to neglect the specificity of racial harassment, we can no longer afford to specify it in isolation from the specificity of other forms of social dehumanization.

# Notes

1. By this we mean geographical areas which are defined in terms of local government administration.

2. We maintain the use of this term throughout because the category 'harassment' enables us to emphasize the processual nature involved.

3. We refer throughout to 'Asian' and 'Black' communities not only to highlight the distinctive self-consciousness of these communities but through the conjunction 'and' to stress similar (albeit varied) experiences of 'white racism'. Where we have quoted other texts whose usage does not follow ours, we have hopefully incorporated that style (e.g. 'black' meaning African-Caribbean and Asian) without causing too much confusion.

4. Our understanding of Anti-racism here is quite simple: Any public initiative (civil or institutional) which attempts to discredit or eliminate racism as a rationale for maintaining a 'social' order. The extent to which public initiatives are effectively designed in these terms is of course another matter.

5. The perspectives we outline here are not based upon party-political distinctions, they cut across such distinctions and can probably be found in each distinction.

6. This concept was initially formulated by the French philosopher Jacques Derrida.

7. It is worth noting that many local authorities (including Waltham Forest as from 1990) specify in their tenancy clause the prohibition of harassment based on 'national, gender, sexual orientation or religious' grounds as well as racial. It is not the case necessarily that 'race' is specified in isolation.

8. By social crime we are referring to instances of personal dehumanization (or environmental spoilation) which are perpetrated recurrently and violate particular categories of the population and/or their conditions of existence.

# Part 1
# Contextuality

# 1 Racial harassment and 1980s Waltham Forest

*Barnor Hesse and Christine Bennett*

> Life for racial minorities in Waltham Forest is becoming a bitter experience. All too frequently it is a shameful catalogue of harassment, attack and degradation. All the signs are that racism is on the increase in many parts of the Borough yet the police and council seem powerless to stop it.
>
> (*Waltham Forest Guardian*, 4 December 1981)

> The brutal murder of Mrs Khan and her children, burnt alive in their Walthamstow home by racist arson attackers in July 1981, has been rejected as a case for investigation by Leyton police. The tragic slaughter of his family was eventually to take the life of Mr Yunus Khan who died of 'a broken heart', meanwhile the number of racist arson attacks in Waltham Forest continues to escalate.
>
> (*Asian Times,* 12 April 1985)

> Following a spate of attacks on Asian homes (unsolved by the police) and a sharp rise in racial harassment during the early 1980s, the Pakistan Welfare Society set up vigilante Groups in the Waltham Forest area.
>
> (*Pakistan Welfare Society,* letter to the Independent, 3 February 1989)

The 1980s may appear to be an arbitrary time period for the focus of this study, but it is the case that the issue of racial harassment was debated nationally more throughout those ten years than at any other period and correspondingly more

3

local information became available. Having said this, it is also the case that the end of a decade presents us with as convenient a point as any, to reflect on some of the experiences a particular Borough has *lived* through. In this chapter we will discuss the persistence of racial harassment as reflected in local newspaper coverage during the 1980s in Waltham Forest. With this we attempt to prepare the basis for a subsequent discussion of how recent local history and various regions in the Borough sustain and shape the spread of racial harassment and recurrent experiences of victimization.

Within the limited scope of this study it was not possible to research comprehensively ten years local experience of racial harassment (we cover broadly the period 1981-1989). We chose to focus on two distinct years during the decade which seem to us to mark the highest points of public concern and activities around a growing (visible) incidence of extremely brutal and sadistic racial attacks and violence. We feature the years 1981 and 1985, not to suggest they are necessarily characteristic of the whole period but because they seem to encapsulate what has been and continues to be possible in Waltham Forest where *no effective challenges have been made against the persistence of* racial harassment. In our characterization of the 1980s we also comment briefly on other years and point to the value of our historical commentary for an understanding of the geography of racial harassment in the Borough.

## 1981: The year of belated recognition

National public attention was focused on the horror of racial attacks within the first few weeks of the new year. In January 1981 thirteen young Black people were burned to death in Deptford, South London, following a fire-bomb attack on a party they were attending (Ramdin, 1987). By this time the 'ground' for similar events taking place in Waltham Forest appears to have already been in place. Between 1979 and 1981 there were at least 'seventeen fire bomb attacks on ethnic minorities' in the Borough (*Waltham Forest Guardian,* 20 November 1981). The activities of fascist groups in Waltham Forest were also becoming visible. In March 1981 the *West Indian World* reported:

> Police in Leyton, East London, have this week intensified their area surveillance in light of some very disturbing evidence that has been brought to light by this

4

newspaper that many black householders have been
National Front targets with a number of injuries to people
and property.

The investigations of the *West Indian World* revealed that the property of a
'Trinidadian nurse' had been attacked and threats made to her life. While a 'few
streets away' a Black family had been placed under 24 hour police protection
because of repeated attacks on their home. In the same month William Morris
School, Walthamstow, became the object of racist/fascist abuse and criminal
damage. This was reported by the local newspaper:

> Pupils and staff at William Morris School were disgusted
> and furious when they started lessons on Tuesday - for
> racist vandals had smeared 5ft high swastikas and
> National Front daubings all over a courtyard.
>
> *(Waltham Forest Guardian,* 13 March 1981)

The daubings included National Front and British Movement symbols,
swastikas, racist comments and the letters of the Ku Klux Klan. Also in March,
Zafar and Sayqa Tanveer were attacked by skinheads in Hoe Street,
Walthamstow, and left in a pool of blood. They criticized the police who
apparently just smiled on arrival and showed no interest in the Tanveers'
injuries or their assailants (Waltham Forest Police Monitoring Group, 1983).
In May the premises of Waltham Forest Community Relations Council[1] were
damaged in an arson attack when a fire-bomb was thrown through a ground
floor window. In June the local Fire Brigade Union announced plans to launch
their own investigation into a number of arson attacks in the Borough which
they felt the police had dismissed. Also in June, Bostan Khan and his family
were forced to flee from their home in Wigram Square, Walthamstow,
following unrelenting harassment. The police were criticized again for not
responding (Waltham Forest Police Monitoring Group, op. cit.). By July,
particularly in the aftermath of the Khan family murders (see below), anxieties
about racial attacks appeared to be reaching acute levels as perpetrators became
quite brazen in their activities. One bizarre example was reported by the
*Waltham Forest Guardian* (7 August 1981) under the heading 'Wedding group
in race attack':

5

Rocks, stones, a bottle and racialist insults were hurled at an immigrant family wedding party by young skinheads. A 14 year old girl shouted insults at the family as they left Mornington Hall, Chingford. She then hurled an empty whisky bottle in the family's direction, but it did not hit anyone. Other members of the group shouted anti-Pakistani taunts - *not realising that the family were Cypriots.*

(emphasis added)

Episodes like these not only pointed to the nature of some of the experiences of racial harassment in the Borough, but also to the importance of the Asian and Black community and local press in exposing these activities. Usually racial harassment is not publicized in the mainstream media unless there are fatalities or serious injuries involved, or it becomes the focus of a major public investigation. Waltham Forest became known nationally in each of these terms during 1981. Nationally the year was both momentous and unsavoury in fusing together in the public imagination the distinct victimization concerns of Asian and Black people in Britain. For example, the political debate about racial attacks reached new heights with the release of the Home Office report, 'Racial Attacks'. In addition, the policing of Black communities was thrust into the full glare of public questioning following the disturbances in Brixton, Southall (London); Toxteth (Liverpool); Moss Side (Manchester) and many other regions of Britain ( Ramdin, op. cit.; Benyon and Solomos, 1987).

What has become known as the 'July riots' elevated policing in the 'inner-cities' to the platform of major social policy concerns where 'race' was the issue. On this basis there were two levels of complaint and criticism which, curiously, were not always seen as related. At one level the police were accused of 'under-policing' racial harassment, not treating it seriously and 'playing it down'; the Asian communities were particularly forceful in these criticisms. Over-shadowing this at the time were criticisms that the police routinely engaged in the 'over-policing' or 'heavy policing' of the Black communities, through the excessive use of stop and search powers and physical force. In their respective ways both of these arguably oppressive experiences were indicative of the extremes of victimization inscribed in the experiences of racial harassment.

July 1981 was also the setting for both of these victimization experiences in their most acute and tragic forms in Waltham Forest. The deaths of Parveen Khan and her three children during a fire-bomb attack on their home in Walthamstow (see below); and also that of Winston Rose, as a result of a

6

heavy-handed arrest by Leyton police officers (see below), occurred within a few weeks of each other. The circumstances of these deaths not only created national headlines but signalled the identification of the Borough as a compass of locations where extremely disturbing experiences of racial harassment took place. Throughout the rest of the year the memory of the Khan family murders in particular continued to exert its presence in the Borough as a horrific reminder of the persistence of racial harassment. In October an Asian owned off-licence in Wood Street, Walthamstow, was petrol bombed, six people were almost killed *(City Limits,* 30 October 1981). Once again the police were accused of not being interested in tracking down the perpetrators. During the same month the Council held its first serious attempt to discuss its own response to racial harassment in the Borough. Despite an agreement to pursue appropriate policy initiatives, as suggested by the Commission for Racial Equality, discussions among Councillors suggested that not all of them were convinced of the seriousness or scope of racial harassment. Indeed one Councillor questioned how could Asian women be offended by racist graffiti if they could not read English! *(Waltham Forest Guardian,* 6 October 1981).

By the end of 1981 the *Waltham Forest Guardian* (4 December 1981) had conducted a quite exceptional investigation into a Borough-wide problem. This sterling work was due mainly to the commitment of two local reporters, Martin Howell and Simon Oldfield. In a major expose, entitled 'This shameful catalogue of crime', they described several alarming examples of the 'human suffering behind race attacks'. In some detail the report focused on one housing estate in particular. It observed:

> Threats, intimidation and physical attacks are an everyday event for Asians on the Priory Court estate in Walthamstow.

One of the cases described the experience of a middle-aged Asian man (Mr Malik) with heart trouble who had lived with his wife and two children on the estate for the previous two years. He had his window broken during the middle of the night, his car damaged, had been continually spat at by young white people on the estate and his children were attacked whenever they went out. Mr Malik told the reporters:

> I know who the people are who do this to me, I told the police but they told me 'If we charge them, you will get more trouble'.

7

Other incidents described on the Priory Court estate included families regularly intimidated by groups of 'skinheads', gas cylinders left outside doors and plastic crates set alight and homes constantly stoned. But there were other estates mentioned. The paper described the experience of a young Black woman, Jacqueline Byfields and her four daughters who 'Because of their colour (....) live semi-imprisoned on Highams Park's Selwyn Avenue estate'. This family had endured racist insults daubed on their door, random knocking on the door and according to the report on one occasion:

> A blazing rag posted through the front door set the hall
> ablaze. No one heard the family's terrified screams from
> the bedroom window, but luckily, five months pregnant
> Jacqueline was able to call firemen.

This case was listed on the fire service's arson file. While on the Beaumont Road estate in Leyton the report highlighted the predicament of the Quershi family who were the target for 'racist youths who threw stones, torch batteries and other missiles'. Their windows were continually being broken and they faced 'racist taunts and abuse from the thugs'. In general the report observed that 'telephone threats are a disturbingly common feature of racial harassment in the Borough'.

The *Waltham Forest Guardian* also made several telling references to the position of the Council and the police. It observed that despite a Council report on racial harassment on housing estates which had been discussed in October and apart from 'various utterances by councillors there seems to have been little effect on the people who face the problems'. Equally important the newspaper made a cogent observation which seems as true today as it was then :

> in every case both the police and the Council seem
> impotent. Frequently when harassment is reported to
> either authority, it is passed on to the other. There is still
> some confusion about the Council's policy.

It needs to be said of course that observations like these touched only the surface imagery of a protracted and widely dispersed experience. Nevertheless the quality of the attention devoted to these crimes by the *Waltham Forest Guardian* was quite remarkable when compared with its approach in later years.

At the end of 1981 the Pakistan Welfare Society announced plans to set up unarmed vigilante patrols in the areas where harassment and violence had been prominent. The very idea of these indicated immense dissatisfaction with the

8

role of the police in protecting people from racial attacks. Dr Zafar Malik, President of the Pakistan Welfare Society told the *Waltham Forest Guardian* (11 December 1981):

> If the police do something about racial attacks we will not need our patrols. We want to help the police and we want to do everything according to the law.

Earlier that month Superintendent Graham Bridges had expressed the contrary local police view when he told the same newspaper:

> We try to find the perpetrators. We pay more attention to racist attacks than we would to an ordinary one. Harassment is a difficult thing to stamp out, when we are there it does not occur, when we go we hear of it again (.....). We would be wrong to classify every attack against a coloured (sic) person as a racist attack.

> *(Waltham Forest Guardian,* 4 December 1981)

Profound differences in the viewpoints of the Asian community and the police continued throughout the 1980s, but they found their greatest and perhaps single most furious expression in the circumstances surrounding the deaths of Mrs Parveen Khan and her three children.

## The Khan Family massacre

At 3am on 2 July 1981 the home of Yunus (41) and Parveen Khan (28), and their three children Karam (10), Aqsa (9) and Imran (2) was set ablaze in a horrific arson attack. It appears that a washing-up liquid bottle containing petrol was positioned in the letter box and squeezed; the spray went six feet into the hall. Once lit the fire swept quickly up the stairs, engulfed the back bedroom in an intense blaze and stretched to the front of the house in Belgrave Road, Walthamstow where flames as high as eight feet emerged from the first floor window. Mrs Khan and the children were asleep in the back bedroom where the fire was greatest. Mr Khan was in the front bedroom. Mr Khan tried to get through to his family but was prevented by the flames and sustained facial burns. He eventually managed to escape the inferno by jumping through an upstairs bedroom window. As a consequence he injured his arm, fractured his

9

spine and subsequently spent five weeks at the Billericay Burns Unit, St. Andrews Hospital, where he underwent a series of skin grafts. There was no escape for Parveen Khan and her three children, all of whom perished. According to the inquest, held six months later, the deaths of Parveen, Karam, Aqsa and Imran Khan resulted from the inhalation of carbon monoxide fumes produced by the fire prior to their being burned. The inquest verdict of 'unlawful killing' confirmed that four murders had taken place but failed to address various concerns in the Asian community that this had been a racist arson attack. The police in particular seemed singularly unwilling to place any credence on this interpretation of the events. Their response to the Khan family murders appears from the start to have been dogged by an almost complete inability to comprehend the reality of racial attacks.

Thirty six hours after the Khan murders Scotland Yard initially refused to accept that there were any suspicious circumstances, they seemed to believe the fire started in the front bedroom and was caused by an electrical fault. It was this view which was subsequently conveyed to the press. Although witnesses at the scene of the fire and the Fire officers who attended held the view that the fire started in the front passage following the ignition of petrol poured through the letter box, the police were comparatively slow in reaching this conclusion. Moreover the concern expressed by many in the Asian community and others, that the murders were racist in motivation, was not particularly favoured by the police as a means of explanation once they had announced that a murder investigation was in progress. For example, shortly after a special incidents room had been set up at Leytonstone police station and 40 police officers drafted into the investigation, the head of the investigation, Detective Superintendent Colin Ashdown told the *Waltham Forest Guardian* (14 August 1981):

> We've not established a motive yet (...) We are not ruling out the possibility of it being a racial attack (...) We are looking at everyone and everybody (...) We haven't come up with anything that suggests it is racial (...) The family seems to have integrated into the community very well. We haven't heard a bad word against him in our enquiries, which makes it more of a puzzle.

The police were apparently puzzled by the murders, even though the deaths had occurred in a year when a number of equally 'puzzling' attacks, including arson attempts, had tormented Asian and Black families (see above). Yet the one thing which made 'sense' of the Khan murders and the other attacks throughout 1981 that is, racial harassment, did not 'suggest' itself to the police. This serious anomaly illustrated some characteristics of the police's simplistic view of racial harassment. They assumed mistakenly that attacks were primarily directed at those who were not integrated into the community or who had made particular enemies. As a consequence the police investigation was demonstrably incapable of considering the racist motivations the Asian community were highlighting. This police attitude not only exacerbated the grief felt by Yunus Khan and the wide-spread outrage in the Asian community, it also remained a consistent point of contention between the Asian community and the police.

The outrage in the local community produced episodes of vigorous public activity and campaigning which perhaps would not have been so concentrated or vociferous, except for the fact that the spread of racial harassment in the Borough left tangible traces in many people's recent experiences. In the immediate aftermath of the murders the 'Khan Massacre Action Committee' (KMAC) was set up, with Shahbaz Khan as its chair. Its aim was to express public condemnation at the Khan atrocities and to pressure the police to investigate the deaths as a racist attack. Its origins lay in the activities of the Waltham Forest Youth Congress, whose earlier attempt to persuade Waltham Forest CRC to organize a community response to the deaths had failed. A decision by the KMAC to hold a march and rally in the morning prior to the funeral was opposed by the CRC and the police who applied to the Home Secretary, Mr William Whitelaw, to ban the march. This was granted as part of a three month blanket ban on all marches and demonstrations in London. On the scheduled day, 1500 police (including 80 on horse back) were mobilized in order to enforce the ban. Prior to the scheduled time of the march the anxieties of many were increased when the police began to advise shop keepers to board up their shops. It also emerged that a National Front demonstration against the march was being mobilized. The Borough seemed on the verge of witnessing uncontrollable, sporadic clashes.

The funeral of the Khans took place at 1.30pm on the 11 July. It was therefore the first occasion for a demonstration of mass public concern and anger and was attended by over 4,000 people. It is worth noting that the *Waltham Forest Guardian* (10 July 1981) a day previously had found itself caught up in a fast moving frenzy of events. It provided the following alarmist comments in its editorial:

In the meantime, when nightly our T.V. screens bring us pictures of strife and bloodshed elsewhere, we cannot escape the stark fact that an emotional spark could bring a parallel to our own doorstep.

But only if we let it. Only if we allow ourselves to be egged on and manipulated by the lunatic fringe of racists, political extremists and rent-a-mob rowdies who feed on and make capital out of tragedies like Belgrave Road.

These comments symbolized the fact that a range of intense local feelings had been generated by the murders. But its understandable, though obsessive references to the 'riots' occurring elsewhere in London and the rest of the country, tended to obscure the impact of racial harassment in the Borough. While its fear of public rowdiness failed to place local community concerns in the context of bitter dissatisfaction with the police response. It was undeniable that the police's investigation added to the growth of anxieties in the Asian community.

It is important to recognize that protests emerging in the Asian community had a distinct rationale. This had two objectives, the first concerned the 'public establishment of the true circumstances' in which the atrocities occurred, while the second was concerned with gaining 'official acknowledgement or acceptance of that truth' (Roach Family Support Committee, 1989:7). These sentiments were perhaps best captured by the *City Limits* magazine (30 October 1981) where it observed:

What has angered many local people is a suspicion that the police have not seriously entertained the likelihood of the Khan case being a racialist massacre. Despite a visible fascist presence centred around well known haunts the police haven't probed local fascist groups because : 'We haven't got any files.' *Instead, as in the case of the Deptford fire earlier in the Spring they have apparently centred their attention on the Khan family's immediate circle.*

(emphasis added)

Over a period of four years the police's investigation took a number of twists and turns, each one bizarre and abortive; while there was no sign either that racial harassment in the Borough had diminished or the corresponding police response had improved.

## Going nowhere: the police investigation

In the last week of July a meeting was arranged by Leyton Labour Party and Leyton MP Bryan Magee with the police (in particular Chief Superintendent Southern) and various interested persons in the Asian community. It was pointed out to the police that many Asian people were afraid to go out at night because of racist harassment and that the police were unwilling to investigate these cases. In addition the police's investigation of the Khan murders was questioned closely. The police however rejected any criticism and in turn criticized Asian people for being reluctant to report racial attacks (*Waltham Forest Guardian*, 7 August 1981). This was indicative of the gulf between the views of many sections of local community opinion, particularly the Asian community and the police during this period. The police appeared remarkably insensitive to local sensibilities in the face of recurring racial harassment.

A year after the murders, it was revealed that the police had established three lines of inquiry in their investigations. The first two were the responsiblity of the Special Branch, these concerned 'extremist groups' *and* 'rivalry within the Asian community'. The other line of inquiry revolved around Mr Khan himself, ostensibly his family and work background, at one point even Mr Khan came under police suspicion. The *Waltham Forest Guardian* (2 July 1982) reported that 'Murder squad detectives have also re-opened the files on all racial attacks and arson attacks' in the Borough during the previous year. But it was apparent that the police did not consider this a viable line of inquiry. The comments of the police's press officer David Rangecroft at the time exemplified this:

> While we ourselves accept that racial hatred is a possible motive, we are bound by facts and not by speculation and anyone who has knowledge which can lead to the arrest of the culprits should tell us what factual information they have.

If the police considered it speculative to link the deaths of the Khans with racist motivations, how could they possibly comprehend acts of racial harassment which did not result in fatalities, where the public pressure for a thorough investigation was not so great? This was an obvious question to pose given the various cases sprinkled throughout 1981. Other aspects of the police investigation were revealed at the inquest in January 1982. It appears that Yunus Khan underwent hypnosis, the police had hoped he might be able to remember something more about the fire. This revelation did little to discredit the idea that the police suspected him of possible involvement in starting the fire. At the inquest Detective Superintendent Ashdown repeated the police's puzzlement at the murders. He observed that none of the Khan family had a history of harassment, the house was not obviously Asian and Yunus Khan had no involvement in politics, but nevertheless stated: 'it was not a random racial attack'.

By 1984 police investigations had still not established what the attack was, let alone who was responsible. During this period the KMAC organized several deputations, regarding the Khan murders and subsequent arson attacks, to MP Roy Hattersley in 1982, GLC Councillor Paul Boateng in February 1983, local MPs in July 1983, MP Gerald Kaufman in March 1984, and local MPs again in November 1984. These and other activities kept the issues on the local public agenda. In November 1984 Yunus Khan died following a heart attack. It was remarked by his doctor that he died of a broken heart and since the death of his family he had been in a state of mental torture. A condolence meeting for Yunus Khan was organized by the Waltham Forest Police Monitoring Group on 24 November. At that meeting MPs Eric Deakins and Harry Cohen made extensive criticisms of the police investigation, in particular questioning the police's decision to reduce the number of detectives involved in the investigation after only six weeks and their resistance to treating the murders as racist. The observations of the *Waltham Forest Guardian* (November 1984) following the meeting provided a reasonable summary of the issues that had been debated and contested for three years:

> The case has provoked considerable controversy. Apart from it making many Asian families live in fear, the way the police conducted their investigation has created much hostility. Local MPs have several times met with North East London police commander John Allain, but there has been no progress.

By the begining of the following year, just two months after Yunus Khan's death, the police announced they were closing down their investigations. Despite local protests Commander John Allain justified his decision publicly in an interview with the *Waltham Forest Guardian* (1 February 1985):

> the investigation had engaged up to twenty five police officers from the start. A fresh team of six officers, one of them Asian, were later appointed and they made many off-shoot inquiries. Although the incident happened at

14

about two or three in the morning and there were no known witnesses, 1,400 people have been interviewed and 450 written statements have been taken. Inquiries were made throughout the Home Counties as well as the Indian sub-continent, and prisoners were questioned in fifteen different jails. The dockets of the case stand a foot high on my desk.

Commander Allain clearly provided one perspective on a protracted, ultimately ineffective, four year murder investigation. A rather different perspective was supplied by MP Harry Cohen:

> The whole police investigation into the disgusting and tragic massacre has been a complete failure. The investigation is a blot on the history of local policing; it has strained to the limit police relations with the local ethnic minority communities and shaken any confidence that people might have had that the police would deal with such cases in a thoroughly competent and conscientious manner. It will be recalled for example that for a long while the police refused to acknowledge even the possibilty of a racial motive in the attack.

(Waltham Forest Police Monitoring Group, 1985)

The public debate of the Khan murders investigation symbolized in excess many of the elements that characterize the *racial victimization scenarios* described by us in Chapter 5. These include: the personal tragedies arising from the occurrence of the atrocity; the extreme difficulties entailed in gaining official (i.e. police) recognition that the atrocity was racist, and finally getting something effective done about it, in this instance the apprehension and prosecution of the murderers. In four years the tragedy of the Khan murders became compounded by the farce of the police's response. This left an indelible memory of anger and disillusionment which again found expression in 1985 (see below). In 1986 the Council linked a new housing development with the name of Yunus Khan. Situated off Queens Road, Walthamstow, the establishment of 'Yunus Khan Close E17' was part of the Council's contribution to the International Year of Peace. At the opening, Councillor Amarjit Devgun reflected on its significance:

15

This is a message of peace to the whole community. Keeping Mr Khan's name alive in this way spells out our determination to build on his example and to bring fellowship and mutual respect between all residents of Waltham Forest.

(*Waltham Forest Guardian,* 14 November 1986)

On a couple of occasions after its installation the street sign was stolen and had to be replaced, on other occasions it was defaced. These were perhaps reminders that not everyone in the Borough was consoled by the message of peace.


## A day in the death of Winston Rose

Where racist stereotypes, *unreasonable suspicions* and forceful policing are combined consistently against members of a particular community, the outcome is invariably a form of state racial harassment. But the police's involvement in the *instigation* of racial harassment is often discounted (although as we demonstrate later in this study not by those in the African-Caribbean communities).

The death of 27 years old Winston Rose, a Black man, at the hands of Leyton police officers on the 13 July 1981, is to some extent explained by this context. For example every year since 1980, at least two Black people have died as a result of a controversial juxtaposition of circumstances involving the police. In London alone, during that decade there were 17 police-related deaths of Black people (Hesse and Hill, 1989). Winston Rose was one of these. Yet the immediate background to his death is also integral to its understanding.

Winston Rose was married, he had a family and had suffered a schizophrenic breakdown in early 1981. By the beginning of July his wife Thora had expended considerable time and effort trying to get adequate professional help for him without much success. Moreover, Winston was extremely agitated by the prospect of going to seek help. On the morning of 13 July Thora Rose had arranged for a meeting of professionals to take place at her house to discuss what should be done about Winston's condition. In an interview she described the events leading up to his death:

When Winston saw all of us coming in, he asked what we were doing, it was explained that we wanted to talk. He said that he didn't want to talk to anyone, and insisted that everyone left the house.

16

Finally I told him that unless he talked to the doctor, I would be forced to take the kids and go and stay somewhere else for the night.

One of the professionals said to me, 'Look, we need to get Winston to the hospital, we can't call an ambulance, we have to call the police because they are the ones that are trained to restrain people'. *I just agreed. I thought that if that was what was needed to get him treatment, then it had to be done.*

Winston stood in the room saying 'Get out, get out, I don't want you lot in here'. *I suppose I thought that they all knew what they were doing, they were all trained, I could sit back and let them cope with it.*

(Walker, 1990; emphasis added)

The police were called not because Winston was acting violently, or a crime had been committed, but because he was in a state of heightened anxiety. When the police arrived Thora asked them not to use force or handcuffs on Winston as she recalled that in 1979 when Winston had been 'sectioned' under the Mental Health Act (1959), he had been handcuffed so tightly that for a time he lost use of his hands and had to have physiotherapy.

According to Mrs Rose,

As soon as Winston saw the police, he ran into the back garden. I was in the front of the house with the two police and the social workers and doctors, his mum and his sister. I went out to the back of the house, there were police everywhere and I just freaked out because everything was happening so fast. The police told me to go back to my friends house and they would come and get me when they had taken Winston to hospital. So I went back to my friends house.

(Walker, op. cit.)

The wider policing context of the times is a relevant consideration here. By the middle of July radically divergent views of policing and Black communities were the momentary staple diet of headlines and commentaries in the print and broadcasting media. In debates and issues that vied for national attention an undeniable leitmotiv was the police's racist reaction to the presence of Black

17

people and their accompanying excessive use of force, *particularly where young Black men were concerned.* The Leyton police officers who confronted Winston Rose as he ran from his refuge in the garden shed added an appalling local dimension to a national scandal. One officer charged at him with a metal dustbin lid striking Winston on the chest. Four of the other officers then ran at him, Winston was thrown to the ground and grabbed around his chest and legs. Once on the ground, a police officer got Winston's head in a 'headlock' and attempted to apply a 'filterum' hold to his nose and throat. While Winston was held in this manner, in order to further restrain him, the other officers delivered blows and pressure to his body. Having restrained Winston like this the police handcuffed his hands behind his back and carried him through his neighbour's house, into the street where he was thrown face down into the back of a police van. In the van Winston began to vomit and choke. None of the police officers present had the key to the handcuffs. By the time an attempt was made to release him, Winston Rose had died.

Although over-shadowed by the Khan family murders that had taken place eleven days earlier (see previous section) this tragic death did initially attract public concern and ignite activities of protest. The issues were raised briefly by the Khan Family Massacre Action Committee and became the focus of a relatively short-lived Winston Rose Defence Group. In October 1981 the inquest into Winston Rose's death returned a verdict of 'unlawful killing'. Despite this the Director of Public Prosecutions who examined the case, subsequently failed to find any grounds for a criminal prosecution to be brought against any of the police officers involved; none of the officers were even disciplined.

*Obscured but not ignored*

Eighteen months after Winston's death, his wife Thora Rose emerged from the overwhelming burden of grief and depression to engage solicitors to initiate a civil court action for damages against the Metropolitan police in respect of Winston's death. Given the public lack of confidence and obloquy which coincides with even the idea of a police complaints system where (then as now) the police are seen to investigate themselves, the settling of matters in the civil courts has for several years represented the only forum where a limited form of public justice is possible. Civil actions however, take a considerably long time to get to court. In November 1989, two and a half months prior to the commencement of proceedings in the High Court, the Metropolitan police 'accepted liability' for Winston's death but expressed no 'word of apology to the family' *(Caribbean Times,* 13 February 1990). The police opted to offer an 'out-of-court settlement' of £130,000 to Thora Rose to cover costs and damages. This was eventually accepted by her in February 1990. In an interview with the *Caribbean Times* (op. cit.) she reflected,

> These eight and a half years have been the worst of my life. My two children Natalie, now aged 12 and Sebastian, now aged 10 - have grown up with little if any memory of the wonderful man their father was. I have lost the pleasure of living the rest of my life with the one I loved.
>
> These losses are impossible to convert into pounds. The figure which the police were eventually forced to offer myself and my children as compensation only adds insult to my injury.

The uncertainties of the legal system obliged Thora Rose to accept the police's offer because, inter-alia, a protracted court hearing may well have resulted in exorbitant costs for her, and also the likelihood of a judge, sitting without a jury, awarding a greater sum was minimal. While the sum hardly counted for compensation it did not add up to much justice either considering three of the principal officers involved, although no longer attached to Leyton police division, remain as serving officers of the Metropolitan police.

## 1982-1984: An uncertain interim

Although the issues connected with the Khan family murders continued as a local *cause celebre* during this period, local media coverage of other racial harassment experiences was relatively sparse, all of which presents difficulties in trying to characterize the period. It is tempting, in a superfical sense, to think that during these three years racial harassment declined in significance as a Borough-wide problem. What little evidence is available suggests however, that specific local Asian concerns had not been reduced. In addition, reports of police harassment of Black people were increasingly evident.

At the end of 1981 vigilante patrols were being discussed in various quarters of the Borough. By February 1982 these discussions were being condemned by the local CRC who felt that the proper focus for redress should rest on the exisiting institutions. The Chair of the organization, Shaukat Khan, declared:

> We are part of the society in which we live. We must also
> be part of the political processes and achieve the action
> we require through the proper channels.

(*Waltham Forest Guardian,* 5 February 1982)

There was no easy co-existence of perspectives on these issues; although a common thread was the regular occurrence of incidents that attracted public alarm and criticism. In April 1982 a Black youth, Emile Foulkes and his mother, Esme Baker were assaulted by police officers from Leyton division. Emile was sitting on a wall near his home on Priory Court estate, Walthamstow, when police officers from an Instant Response Unit arrived, accused him of taunting white youths and called him a 'black nigger'. When Emile's mother tried to intervene she was grabbed and both of them were forced into the police van. They were charged with threatening behaviour and assaulting the police, but were subsequently acquitted.[2] In August 1982 the Sadiq family eventually left their home in Lawrence Road, Walthamstow, after several arson attempts. The police however did not accept these were racial attacks. Three months later in November Mr Hussein's home in Walthamstow was burgled. He called the police, but when they arrived ninety minutes later, they took no interest in the crime, preferring instead to search his brief case and examine his family's passports. In the same month, a Black youth, Phillip King (15) was on his way home when a white youth racially abused him. He chased the white youth, plain clothes police officers in the vicinity however, confronted Philip in Hoe Street, Walthamstow and assaulted him. He was taken to Chingford police station, his parents were not informed, no doctor was called and he was subsequently charged with burglary. He was later acquitted (Waltham Forest Police Monitoring Group, May, op. cit.).

Also in November, as Shekhar Bhatia, a freelance journalist was driving home, he came across a police operation outside the *Coach and Horses* in Leyton High Road. Young Black people were being taken out of the pub by the police. When he began to take photographs he was assaulted by police officers, the film in his camera was confiscated and he was charged with obstruction. The operation he had stumbled upon was a drugs raid. There were no eventual charges of drugs possession arising from the raid and Shekhar himself was acquitted (Waltham Forest Police Monitoring Group, ibid.). Incidents like this and those described above simply point to some of the dimensions of policing in the Borough in 1982 which were experienced as racial harassment and highlighted for public attention.

We are not able to say much about the years 1983 and 1984 as our information was quite limited. The *Waltham Forest Guardian* (March 1985)

20

in a catalogue of racist attacks over four years did identify two cases of arson in 1983. In February an Asian sweet shop in Chingford was gutted by fire and later in December four youths were sentenced for racist arson attacks on Asian property. By the end of 1984 it was apparent that the debate about racial harassment in the Borough had not abated and the views of the police and concerned members of the Asian community were mostly incommensurable. An audience at a community relations seminar in the Asian Centre, Walthamstow, in November were startled to hear Police 'J' Division Commander, John Allain declare:

> From my knowledge (....) racial harassment does not
> happen very much in Waltham Forest.

> (*Waltham Forest Guardian,* 23 November 1984)

This observation was extraordinary, particularly in the light of the controversy surrounding the police's investigation of the Khan murders. Commander Allain seems to have accepted that his knowledge was possibly inadequate, but suggested the reasons for this was the reluctance of the victims to come forward with complaints, be prepared to make statements and go to court. A rejoinder to this was supplied by Ali Mahmood, president of the Pakistani Welfare Association who said during the meeting's vote of thanks:

> We do report every incident - but we end up under
> suspicion ourselves.

> (*Waltham Forest Guardian,* ibid.)

The meeting was also attended by MPs Eric Deakins (Walthamstow) and Harry Cohen (Leyton), and the Joint Councils of Asian and Afro-Caribbean organizations. The discussions raised some important issues, these were summarized by the *Waltham Forest Guardian* and included complaints about: the police abusing their 'stop and search' powers against Black people; families on council estates hounded by 'racialist thugs'; users of the Asian Centre in Walthamstow, Mosques and other community centres, taunted and intimidated as they come and go; victims of racial attacks being mistreated by the police. What these observations pointed to was the persistence of racial harassment and the concerns associated with it during 1981-1984. Although it is not possible to say whether there was a rise or decline in the actual experiences of racial victimization, it seems clear that more precautions and support activities were being urged throughout this period because of the inadequacy of existing

21

provisions. In September 1984 it was announced by the Pakistani Welfare Society (PWS) that a 'Racial Violence Support Group' was to be launched. The rationale was explained by PWS president Dr Zafar Malik:

> We hope to give immediate relief to the worst cases of
> attacks, something that is not available elsewhere.
>
> (*Yellow Advertiser*, 7 September 1984)

By the end of 1984 the Waltham Forest Police Monitoring Group[3] (a voluntary sector organization) was claiming that many Asian people were living in fear, a spokesperson informed the *Waltham Forest Guardian* (7 December 1984):

> Most seal their letterboxes so that petrol, excrement and
> matches are not pushed through the door. Women are
> afraid to go shopping, will not open their door and live
> in a siege 'mentality'.

That events had reached this stage said as much about the ineptitude of local statutory agencies as it did about the spread of racial harassment itself. The following year was to demonstrate that the Monitoring Group's observations were symptomatic of recurrent, unrelenting scenarios of racial victimization, the seriousness of which continued to be underestimated.


## 1985: The burning of the houses

No one died in the Borough as a result of racial attacks during 1985 but the number of attempted murders that year through arson attacks was so great, that it probably ranks as the zenith of local public debates over racial harassment during the decade. Yet a view like this is only based on levels of local awareness and concern expressed about cases that become *cause celebres,* raise wider issues and animate sustained community activity. Much depends on whether these are reported in the local press and on occasions the national media. Arguably, the media only finds itself covering particular cases once it is able to feature the more dramatic incidents of racial victimization. Only then do less sensationalized and more mundane incidents manage to gain exposure. Once the reporting of racial harassment becomes fashionable, it becomes frequent. This is what happened in 1981 and was taken to unprecedented heights in 1985.

At the January meeting of the local Police Liaison Consultative Group,[4] Commander John Allain announced that only 'three confirmed' 'racial incidents' took place in the Borough during 1984 out of 21 reports of possibly 'racially motivated offences'. The police had made 13 arrests, and furthermore Commander Allain claimed:

> The figure of 21 is probably not the true figure in Waltham Forest but the police can only act on things reported to them. It is absolutely vital that people receiving racial harassment and abuse do come and report it.
>
> *Waltham Forest Guardian,* 1 February 1985)

A contrasting perspective on the local experience was supplied by Councillor Amarjit Devgun , who argued:

> The common view among victims is that their lives are made a lot worse if police cannot quickly go ahead with legal proceedings.
>
> (ibid.)

Both these view points highlighted the dual and contradictory way in which racial harassment was perceived. On the one hand emphasizing the responsibility of the victims in reporting and how the police are really trying; on the other re-iterating the responsibility of the police and how people were continually being harassed. At the beginning of 1985, these were not the only terms of debate. In addition, a persistent background theme questioned what racial harassment was, the extent of its incidence, and what should be done. It was in this context that the Council revived its stumbling policy interventions. For example, in February Trevor Jex, the Director of Housing, revealed the Council had no formal policy on dealing with tenants who perpetrate racial harassment. Furthermore, the Council position of transferring persecuted families, rather than taking action against the aggressors, was still a debating point (*Waltham Forest Guardian,* 1 February 1985). This over simplified what was more disturbing about the Council's approach. In other words, in almost four years since the deaths of the Khan family in 1981, the Council still did not treat racial harassment as a serious priority for policy development. It had still not decided what constituted effective Council action. If it is harsh to say that it had abdicated its responsibility, it is certainly not unreasonable to say its intermittent deliberations between 1981-1985, looked remarkably like posturing.

Whatever the quality of the debate in the Borough, racial harassment continued, exhibiting the all too familiar characteristics. In February, Talib Hussein, a young Asian man, was attacked by a gang of white 'skinhead youths' and left unconscious after being wounded with a broken milk bottle. The attack took place in Wellesley Road, Walthamstow. A passerby contacted an ambulance. Mr Hussein was rushed to hospital with 'deep gouges near his eye', whilst there he had 'fifteen stiches - six to his face, the rest on his hand'. He was 'scarred for life'. The police however, felt unable to define this as a racial attack (*Waltham Forest Guardian*, 1 March 1985). The police were heavily criticized by the Pakistani Welfare Society (PWS). According to the *Waltham Forest Guardian:*

> Pakistanis have given police two weeks to catch the skinheads they say beat up young Talib Hussein at the end of February. If justice is not seen to be done by them, says the Pakistan Welfare Society, it will arrange a picket at Leyton Police Station.

The urgency of this declaration, although directed at a single case, cannot be really appreciated without considering other racially motivated crimes elsewhere in the Borough. Also in February, an elderly white woman was rescued from her home in Leyspring Road, Leytonstone, after arsonists had poured inflammable liquid through her letter box (*Waltham Forest Guardian*, op. cit.). What was particularly significant about this attack, was its *apparent miscalculation*. Following an investigation, the *Asian Times* (12 April 1985) found Leyspring Road to be highly populated with Asian people, and therefore conjectured:

> Racist arsonists took advantage of the high density of Asians in the road and set alight to one of the houses; the attempt to murder an Asian family however went pathetically wrong - *the arsonists chose a house at random which turned out to belong to a white woman who has now been forced to move her accommodation.*

> (emphasis added)

The plausibility of this observation rests on the extent to which it explains the *randomness* of racist attacks on Asian peoples homes. In other words, it underlines that these attacks may miss their target. Less than two weeks later,

24

a Greek family in Liverpool Road, Leyton, narrowly escaped death when flames engulfed their home after inflammable liquid was also poured through their letter box. In early March, Khadim Hussein, his wife, and their two children, were awakened by flames in their home in Lindley Road, Leyton. When Mr Hussein opened the bedroom door, the hall was engulfed by fire and dense smoke. Fortunately, he was able to lead his family to safety, before tackling the fire himself. Although Mr Hussein felt it was a racial attack, according to Inspector John Chapman of Leyton Police, only the *possibility* of arson, was being looked into (*Waltham Forest Guardian,* ibid.). Also in March, Aslam Malik and his brother were targeted for a 'murderous attack' (*Asian Times*, op. cit.). They were watching television in their flat in Alexandra Road, Walthamstow, when after hearing a noise at the front door, they found burning paper had been stuffed through the letter box, setting the front door curtain alight. Having extinguished the fire, they informed the police, but according to the *Asian Times*, 'The CID visited the Maliks two days after the incident; since then they have not heard from the police'. The *Asian Times* who visited the homes of three recent victims and spoke to people in the vicinity, provided a timely and instructive reminder of the nature of these attacks:

> Peculiar to the murderous attacks are the evil tactics of
> their perpetrators - the fires are usually started in the
> middle of the night by pouring petrol or putting burning
> material through the letter box and the response from the
> police is minimal if not one of total apathy.

This attempt to construct a pattern out of apparently random events was, and is, a very important task. It presented however, only a dimension of one part of the picture. It is also worth noting that at least two of the reported arson attempts in February/March, and the assault of Talib Hussein, took place within a three quarter mile radius of the site of the fatal arson attack on the Khan family in 1981. It is important to recognize 'experiential' facts like these are not lost on the communities subject to racial victimization, invariably, people form *mental maps* of the locales of racial harassment in the vicinity.[5]

An announcement of community patrols by the Pakistan Welfare Society in March, was perceived by the police in negative terms. While it was understandable that Superintendent Jack Brough of Leyton Police should proclaim, 'We can't have people taking the law into their own hands to get things done' (*Waltham Forest Guardian,* 1 March 1985), this failed to appreciate the strains and stresses under which the initiative was taken.   For example, the implications of the police's refusal to treat the attack on Talib

Hussein as racially motivated, was at least recognized by the *Waltham Forest Guradian* (ibid.), who reported, 'if no one is prosecuted they fear it will encourge more attacks similar (to the Khans)'. With regard to the accusations of vigilantism, Dr Zafar Malik of the PWS replied,

> I don't think we are over reacting. Four of our people have died in a racist attack and we're determined to make sure the same thing doesn't happen again. We don't trust the police to be on the side of black people in these attacks, otherwise they would take it more seriously. The police will have to reassure the community that they are not here to protect one section of the community and exclude the other. Until that happens, we will go ahead with our patrols.
>
> (ibid.)

Towards the end of March, the PWS organized a picket of Leyton Police Station in protest against the police's 'mis-handling of racial crimes'. Over eighty people attended, criticisms were made that the police ignored racial attacks and there were demands that special squads should be established to deal with them. In particular, the protest made historical links between the recent case of Talib Hussein and the Khan family murders. The picket underlined a strong local conviction in one sense that a *geographical fact* had emerged, suggesting that 'many Pakistanis and Asians living in Walthamstow and Leyton are singled out for attack because of their race' (*Waltham Forest Guardian,* 29 March 1985). The public response of the police was provided by the Community Liaison Officer, Inspector Terry Page, who was concerned to emphasize that every crime was investigated in the same way and that:

> Mr. Hussein's claims are still being fully investigated, and any allegations that they are not are foundless.
>
> (ibid.)

This of course, missed the entire point of the demonstration. In the words of Dr Zafar Malik, the point was:

> The solving of racial crimes in this area is abysmally low. We want equal protection and we want it now. Our

community is fed up with these attacks and we hope this
picket will draw attention to the fact.

(ibid.)

Clearly the opposing terms of the 'debate' had not shifted since 1981. That the
police in Waltham Forest perceived the incidence of racial harassment and local
assessments of their response to it, in a less concerned way, was quite
extraordinary, but certainly not unpredictable. By June, Leyton police felt able
to claim, 'a closer watch on incidents involving ethnic minorities is kept in the
Leyton Division than anywhere else in the Metropolitian police area' (*Waltham
Forest Guardian,* 21 June 1985). The irreconcilability of this bold statement
with the criticisms and protests articulated in the earlier part of the year, was
further confirmation that the police and victims of racial harassment, although
located within the same geographical boundaries, nevertheless experienced
completely different levels of concern.

While the brunt of the criticism was directed against the police, the Council
was perhaps even more negligent in formulating and implementing an effective
response. In July, it eventually arranged a special meeting of its Housing
Committee to discuss racial harassment on Council housing estates. By virtue
of the range of decisions agreed, many reflecting similar decisions agreed in
1981, it was clear that the Council had initiated an astoundingly ineffectual
response since the deaths of the Khans. Many of its recommended initiatives
had not been implemented or developed. Moreover, it failed to recognize, as
had also been the case in 1981, that there was a specific problem of racist arson
attacks in the owner occupied sector. Remarkably, none of the recent arson
attempts appeared to have come to the attention of the Housing Department.
By the middle of 1985, the Council and the police differed widely in their
respective styles of uncertainty, inconsistency and ultimate ineffectiveness,
where tackling racial harassment was being pressed as an issue. Both however,
were remarkably similar in the enormity of their shared ignorance vis a vis the
enormity of a shared problem.

*The long hot harassment*

The summer of 1985 was an intense period of violent racial harassment in East
London generally. Arson attacks seemed to escalate and proliferate like a
running riot that variously sputters, flickers and suddenly bursts into activity
over a period of weeks and then months. The eyes of the national media began
to open and focus. For example, Ian Walker, a reporter for the *Sunday Observer
Magazine* (22 September 1985) spent some time investigating the predicament

of Asian victims of racial harassment. After interviewing many of the families in Waltham Forest who had experienced arson attacks during the year, he concluded:

> For several years, and especially throughout this summer, Asian families in north and east London have been the victims of arson attacks on their homes. They are afraid, they are frustrated and they are angry. They claim that the police are not doing enough, often not even acknowledging that fire-raisers have racist motives.

One incident in July particularly incensed and outraged many people in the Asian community and elsewhere. This was the petrol-fire attack which resulted in the deaths of Shamira Kassam and her three sons aged six and five years and fourteen months at their home in Seven Kings, Ilford. Significantly the geography of that fatal arson attack bordered on Waltham Forest and was part of the same Metropolitan police jurisdiction, 'J' District. Only 'three weeks before that fatal fire, petrol had been poured through the front door of the Kassams house, setting fire to the carpet' (Walker, 1985). Once again the police were severely criticized for failing to acknowledge that the attack was racially motivated. Indeed the police apparently went so far as to suggest the fire might have happened because the house was previously occupied by an Indian doctor and that the attack may well have been directed against him and not the murdered victim (ibid.).

At the end of July the Pakistan Welfare Society held a national press conference, to launch a 'new political party for immigrants' and to campaign for a 'police anti-racist squad' similar to the 'drug and fraud squads' (*Waltham Forest Guardian*, 2 August 1985). The launch followed a series of publicly expressed criticisms of the police's handling of the racist murders in Ilford; the similarities with the Khan murders in 1981 were unmistakable. According to Dr Malik, president of the Pakistan Welfare Society, who spoke at the launch:

> Attempts by the police to play down a racial motive and create ambiguity are exactly the same as they were then. We know racial crimes are being played down. The situation is so bad that even our school children are at the receiving end of this racial violence. Mentally our children are getting very disturbed, which is not good for the future of this society.

> (ibid.)

During August as public awareness of racist attacks in East London broadened, even the *sunsational* national newspaper *The Sun* (14 August 1985) was tempered into a responsible commentary in one of its editorials:

> The spate of arson attacks on the homes and properties of Asians in London is highly alarming. The police have an open mind on the motives and other sickening attacks. But the Asians are convinced they are the victims of a hate campaign by extremists. They deserve the sympathy and support of all decent people.

Three weeks (10 August) after the Kassam murders, an arson attempt took place on an Asian family in Shortlands Road, Leyton. The house which contained fifteen Asian people at the time was set alight in the early hours of the morning. Although everyone escaped there were several minor injuries, and the landlord of the house Mahmood Kayani required '21 stitches for a deep cut to the arm after he broke a window to enable the occupants to escape' (*Asian Times,* 16 August 1985). The *Waltham Forest Guardian* (23 August 1985) described the immediate local reaction to the Shortlands fire in the following terms: 'Angry and scared Asians have been told by church and community leaders to stay calm but alert'. Waltham Forest CRC in particular appealed to people not to let things get out of hand, warned that the community was losing confidence in the police and called upon the police to 'set up arson squads, give priority to investigate racial attacks and stop harassing victims' (ibid.). At the same time the *Waltham Forest Guardian* itself took a highly partisan editorial stand. It was at pains to point out that 'these tragic situations' could be manipulated by 'those anti-authority groups who love to create controversy'. It rejected criticisms of the police, urging that the 'community MUST continue to support the police', and was emphatic in asserting:

> We remain unconvinced that a special police arson unit should be established. We very much doubt if it could do any more than existing local officers, who have been in touch with their counterparts elsewhere in East London.
>
> (ibid.)

In other words the suggestion here was that the police could do no more than they had done. As we have seen, this was only one side of the argument. While it supported the claims of the police, it failed *to also* support the demands of the victims.

By the end of August there were immense differences of view between the police and prominent sections of the Asian community. An increasing welter of public activity around the issues constantly raised the profile of racial harassment in the Borough. MPs Harry Cohen and Eric Deakins arranged for the Labour Party's Shadow Home Office Minister, Alf Dubbs to meet local Councillors and community leaders and to 'tour the sites of recent racist incidents' (*Waltham Forest Guardian,* 30 August 1985). The experiences in the Borough persuaded MP Harry Cohen to introduce in the House of Commons, a Racial Harassment Bill. Discussions took place between Sir Kenneth Newman, the Metropolitan Police Commissioner and the Commission for Racial Equality (CRE). With regard to the arson attacks on Asian families in East London, Newman told the CRE that racial attacks were a police priority and he was 'taking a close personal interest in developments' (ibid.). In the last week of August a public meeting was arranged at Walthamstow Town Hall to discuss racist attacks in East London:

> At the end of the long meeting decisions had been made to urge greater police co-operation, to march on Waltham Forest Council, and to demand an emergency full Council meeting to discuss measures to protect Asians living in Waltham Forest.
>
> (*Waltham Forest Guardian,* 6 September 1985)

In the midst of this it was announced that Pakistan's Ambassador was scheduled to meet the Home Secretary as a result of racial arson attacks in Leyton (*Waltham Forest Guardian,* 23 August 1985). The Leyton police came under renewed criticism in September. In a 'tough protest letter' about the rise in racial harassment, the Pakistan Welfare Society,

> accused the police of turning a blind eye to racial attacks in the Borough and vowed to fight back. But a senior police officer (....) rejected the criticism and stressed that new initiatives have been taken to stamp out harassment.
>
> (*Yellow Advertiser,* 12 September 1985)

It is also worth noting that Chief Superintendent Bishop supported this view by claiming 'the ethnic communities have more confidence in the police' (ibid.). Whatever the relative degrees of truth in either perspective, what could not be denied was that the incidence of racial harassment was causing tremendous alarm and had not been resolved.

## The temperature rises

During the same month Councillor Amarjit Devgun, N.D. Mahmood, Fazal-ur-Rehman, Shahbaz Khan, Tariq Azim and Mehmood Ahmed formed a delegation to meet MP Neil Kinnock, the Labour Party leader of the Opposition. The subject under discussion was 'racially motivated arson attacks in East London'. Following the meeting it was announced that Neil Kinnock would visit Waltham Forest to examine things for himself. In a press statement Mr Kinnock indicated that 'racial bullying' must be condemned and that he would be 'discussing with police at the highest level the creation of a special unit'. At the same time it was reported that a meeting was planned with Dr David Owen leader of the Social Democratic Party (SDP) and moves were also being made to meet with the Home Secretary (*Waltham Forest Guardian*, 20 September 1985).

A public meeting on 15 September at Ross Wyld Hall in Walthamstow, was called to press for wider support for measures against perpetrators of racial harassment. Over a hundred people attended. In addition to calls for the Council and community to respond to racism, there was a specific demand for 'an advisory telephone service to be set up offering help to victims of racial harassment' (ibid.). The meeting attracted a great deal of publicity; racial harassment in Waltham Forest was even projected to an international audience, as the *Waltham Forest Guardian* observed:

> Millions of Americans tuned into Waltham Forest's racial arson attacks problems (.....) when an NBC filmed report was broadcast on the main television programmes in all 51 states.

Shortly after this a meeting took place between SDP leader Dr David Owen and members of the Asian Community. Subsequently Dr Owen announced:

> Motivation is needed on the part of those whose duty it is to enforce the law whether they be police or government funded agencies such as the Commission for Racial Equality.

> (*Yellow Advertiser*, 4 October 1985)

31

In the last week of September, three senior Asian diplomats raised similar issues with the Home Secretary Douglas Hurd, they also stressed that racial attacks in East London 'were causing great anxiety in the Asian communities' *(New Life,* 4 October 1985). This coincided with a report in the *Waltham Forest Guardian* (4 October 1985) of an Asian family who over a period of five years had 'been forced to live like prisoners in their Walthamstow home' because gangs of white youths regularly threw bricks and stones at their home. After the latest attack in the last week of September, the police were called and chased the gang away. The family however, were critical of the police's reluctance to treat it as a racial attack. The explanation for this was provided by a police spokesperson who said:

> Sometimes they pick on Asians, sometimes on other people. It is difficult to say whether this was a racist incident.

> (ibid.)

Yet again the victims version of events was discounted in a spirit that seemed to run counter to the police's putative victim-centered definition of a racial incident. A week later an Asian family's home in Leytonstone was the focus of an arson attempt. This failed only because they noticed flames coming from the front door. It appears the 'villains pushed lighted paper through the letter box and hung lighted material on the washing line' *(Waltham Forest Guardian,* 11 October 1985). Less than a week later during the early hours of the morning, another racist arson attack took place on the home of Mohammed Salin in Maynard Road, Walthamstow. His family and friends were saved simply because it started behind the front door and short-circuited the door bell, which rang and woke everyone inside. According to Fire officers who attended the scene, an inflammable liquid was poured through the letter box *(Yellow Advertiser,* 17 October 1985). Around the same time it was reported that a petrol bomb had been thrown at the house of an Asian family in Colville Road, Leyton *(New Life,* 18 October 1985). It is significant that the bottle containing inflammatory liquid was thrown through the window because the 'letter box was already sealed as the family feared attack'. Against this unrelenting background it was announced :

> Police, councillors and community leaders are to form a new racial incidents panel. Designed to tackle individual

problems like arson attack or riots, it will meet at short notice.

(*Waltham Forest Guardian*, 17 October 1985)

This was a police initiative, engineered through the local police consultative group. However, since it was scheduled for establishment in January 1986, the initiative was less than a little peripheral to the prevailing experiences of racial victimization in the Borough, which concurrently fuelled the passions surrounding local civil protest and public anxieties.

## A little ventured, nothing gained

Throughout this whole period, nearly ten months in all, clear and decisive public interventions from the Council were scarcely in evidence. It played a rather subordinate role to the activities of individuals and organizations in the Asian community and also to that of the MPs for Walthamstow and Leyton. In October however, this general picture was altered, but only slightly. During the first week Council leader Gerald King called for sections of the community in the Borough to support the police in their efforts to combat racial incidents. While the Liberal leader Simon Banks said, 'The police response to racial attacks is often uncertain. Some members of the ethnic community have been rudely treated and it is up to the police to earn the trust of the community' (*Waltham Forest Guardian*, 18 October 1985). On 17 October a special full Council meeting was called to discuss the burgeoning problem of racial harassment in the Borough. The emergency meeting was requested by the Council's Labour group. Councillors Amarjit Devgun and Neil Gerrard put forward proposals for changes in the way the police and the Council dealt with incidents. The *Waltham Forest Guardian* opined that the objective of the meeting was to 'highlight the lack of confidence the Asian community is alleged to have in the local police force' (ibid.). Included in the proposals were suggestions for the establishment of a special mobile police unit, a 24 hour telephone hot line funded by the Council to offer legal advice and assistance and for Council tenants to be informed that racial harassment would not be tolerated on estates and that steps would be taken to evict perpetrators. The meeting itself appeared to espouse clear lines of convergence and divergence in the political shades of Council opinion. The *Waltham Forest Guardian* (25 October 1985) observed that:

33

Labour and Liberal councillors are demanding a major clampdown on racism in Waltham Forest (.....). The time has come for actions - words are no longer enough, councillors said. But Tory Council Leader Gerald King was scornful. 'Meetings like this achieve nothing but to heighten tensions' he said.

This was a reference to a 'march against racial attacks' scheduled two days later (19 October). This too, prior to its commencement, became a bitterly contested affair. In theory the march was officially organized by the newly formed 'Community Action Against Racism', in practice however, as disagreements flared concerning the value and viability of the demonstration, Shahbaz Khan emerged as its principal co-ordinator. According to Mr Khan, the march was intended to put pressure on the police and the Government 'to make crimes against the Black community a top priority' (*Waltham Forest Guardian,* 18 October 1985). But not everyone agreed with this approach. For example, the Joint Council of Asian Organizations was particularly critical of the march, its Secretary Dr Mumtaz Zafar explained:

> We have decided to disassociate ourselves with the extremist outsiders organising the march. We appeal to all the Asians living in Waltham Forest not to co-operate with the political activists and to boycott the show down in the streets of Waltham Forest against the police.

> (ibid.)

Leaving aside the merits of the dispute, there remained the incontrovertible fact that racist arson attacks showed no sign of subsiding. In the early hours of Saturday, 19 October, only several hours before the march, the home of Sohail and Shaheen Ghani and their three day old daughter was set ablaze. The house in St Mary's Road, Walthamstow, also contained other relatives. The Ghanis were alerted to the fire by the cries of their daughter. Yet again the police were unconvinced of any racial motivation. According to Detective Inspector Graham Taylor 'there were no signs of forced entry and as yet we have no idea how it started' (*Yellow Advertiser,* 25 October 1985). Indeed the police investigation soon turned to Mr Ghani himself.[6]

The march against racial attacks attracted over five hundred people. It was led by prominent victims, these included Mahmood Kayani, Kassam Mirza and Safdar Bokhari (*West Indian World,* 30 October 1985). Also on the march and at the rally that followed were MPs Harry Cohen and Eric Deakins, and GLC

Councillors Paul Boateng (Walthamstow) and Peter Dawe (Leyton). Among the main points to emerge from the rally were: the police must be accountable to local communities; MP Harry Cohen's Racial Harassment Bill must become an Act; the police must give a higher priority to racist crimes; and the police must stop criminalizing and harassing the victims. These points represented a despairing commentary on the experiences of racial victimization during the previous ten months in the Borough. Moreover there had been no respite.

The police's investigation into the Shortlands house fire, which occurred in August (see above), took a strange twist. The police announced that they were questioning an Asian man about the attack and were considering charges. Meanwhile one of the victims, Mr Kayani, complained about his treatment by Chingford police and argued:

> This was definitely a racist attack. I can see no other reason why somebody would try to burn my house down. We have lived peacefully in this country for a long time and we had no enemies. There have been many fires in Asian homes and we are just the latest victims of these racists.

> (*London Standard,* 21 October 1985)

Under a headline 'Arsonists On The Rampage' the *Yellow Advertiser* (1 November 1985) reported an arson attack on the Patel family in Langthorne Road, Leyton, during the last week of October. It was pointed out by the newspaper that this was the fourth fire attack in two weeks the Patels had endured. Three of these had been definitely confirmed as arson. Almost inevitably the police distanced themselves from considering these as racial attacks. According to Commander Allain, to link all the attacks in this way would be to:

> accept a premise that is quite wrong. There have been arson attacks on many premises, more at those owned by whites than Asians, although there are more white owned premises in the area.

> (*Yellow Advertiser,* op. cit.)

Given the experience of East London during the year this was an extraordinarily naive and insensitive view point. It prompted a lengthy criticism by the *Yellow*

*Advertiser* in an editorial which attempted to summarize the implications of failing to recognize the spread of racial harassment in the Borough. It is worth quoting in its entirety:

> To the ordinary man (sic) in the street there would *appear* to be a connection between the recent fires. For a start, two were letter box attacks and the third was similar. But according to the police 'there is no evidence of any link'. Is it any wonder that a poll by I.T.V's London Programme showed that only six per cent of Asians had confidence in the ability of the police to protect them. The police ought to seriously take note of results like this and ask themselves why confidence among Asians is so low. If they fail to take heed then we could see an ugly backlash. For besides having their homes set alight Asians are also attacked on the street. One in four Asians have been attacked, and one in ten seriously, according to the T.V. poll. And the evidence is that, like it or not - and we don't support people taking the law into their own hands - vigilante squads will be set up by Asians. The poll showed 52 per cent in favour of the idea. *Our message to the police is: Give the Asian community confidence. For too long they've thought - rightly or wrongly - that police haven't taken their attacks seriously*.

> (ibid.; emphasis added)

It was remarkable how many different strands of argument could be woven into the debate about racial harassment in Waltham Forest without actually advancing a practical, credible resolution of the problem. As sides were taken and perspectives re-iterated, the first-order problem, racial victimization and the second-order problem, the policing of racial harassment, eluded serious examination. For example, the Metropolitan Police Commissioner, Sir Kenneth Newman described himself as 'disturbed about the lack of trust in the police at Walthamstow'. Those remarks were conveyed in a letter to the SDP leader Dr David Owen. The difficulties facing the police were outlined by the Commissioner. These included lack of evidence, and foreknowledge of the unlikelihood of obtaining a conviction since in that instance taking someone to court would not be a 'proper use of police powers'. In addition he pointed out,

The incidents reported to the police do not always amount to criminal offences for which police can take action, and language barriers sometimes make this difficult to explain.

(*Waltham Forest Guardian,* 1 November 1985)

The relationship between this apparently reasonable explanation and the events in the Borough was vague to say the least. It bore no relation to the various public pronouncements of the local police throughout the year. Furthermore it appeared to ignore unprecedented concern about the almost exclusive development of *racial attacks as arson attacks* and these did amount to serious criminal offences.

The Borough was still on the national public agenda. During the first week of November MP Neil Kinnock, Leader of the Opposition visited Waltham Forest at the invitation of Councillor Amarjit Devgun to attend a series of meetings to discuss racial harassment. This included a special conference with Asian and Afro-Caribbean community leaders on 7 November at Walthamstow Town Hall. According to the *Waltham Forest Guardian* (8 November 1985):

> The Labour leader, Mr Neil Kinnock yesterday called for the setting up of a special police squad to tackle the problem of racist attacks on Asians said to be running at the rate of one a month since the beginning of the year.

Neil Kinnock also visited victims of racial harassment and heard from people who experienced their daily lives like 'living in a prison' and how 'young children can't even play in the back garden anymore, it's too dangerous'*(Waltham Forest Guardian,* 15 November 1985).

Towards the end of the year some of the focus returned to the deliberations of the Council. It was announced that the Council would be prepared as a last resort to evict Council tenants who have perpetrated racial harassment and except in special circumstances would not re-house the tenant. This was qualified and put into context by Conservative Councillor Michael Saille, Vice-Chairman of the Housing Committee:

37

It is always difficult to identify clear cases of racial
harassment and deal with them, but we are seeking
advice from other Boroughs effective in it so we can
instruct our housing staff and estate officers.

(*Yellow Advertiser,* 15 November 1985)

The intention was that the Council's proposals would be explained in a letter
to be sent to all Council tenants in March 1986 highlighting that the 'Council
was clamping down on racism' *(Waltham Forest Guardian,* op. cit.). It seemed
as if a consensus was emerging in at least one public domain of the Borough.
For example, Conservative Councillor Derek Arnold declared:

I welcome this report. It would make it clear to people
that this Council means business and will not tolerate
acts of racial harassment.

(ibid.)

But a significantly contrasting viewpoint was supplied by the Secretary of Low
Hall Association, one of the Borough's many tenants associations:

It is up to me whether or not I choose to like people from
ethnic minorities because this is a free country.
Sometimes these cases are too one-sided in favour of
these minorities.

(*Yellow Advertiser,* op. cit.)

At least two things were clear at the end of 1985. First, racial harassment was
endemic in the Borough and the police and Council had been largely
ineffective; and secondly, while public agencies' knowledge of the incidence
of racial harassment had increased, this had not been paralleled by a respective
increase in the depth of the perceptions regarding its entrenchment and
dispersion.

## 1986-1989: A glimmer of hope?

Throughout these years there seems to have been a considerable decline in the
extent and intensity of community activity around the issues of racial
harassment. Local news coverage was increasingly ephemeral, it was as if racial

harassment no longer seemed newsworthy. Perhaps one way to make sense of this might be to argue that there was a reduction in the actual incidence of racial attacks during this period. However there is no evidence to suggest such a reduction. If anything, the level of cases of racial victimization recorded by agencies like the police and the Council's Housing department remained reasonably constant. What appears to us more plausible an explanation is that with the disappearance of the rampant arson attacks of 1985, the development of new policy initiatives by both the police and the Council shifted local media attention and public interest away from an exclusive concern with the occurrence of racial harassment, towards an increasing focus on the nature of statutory agencies responses. Certainly the mood appears to have been conveyed that the Borough's problems were being tackled and matters were improving.

In the first week of January 1986, at a meeting of the Police Liaison Consultative Group, Commander John Allain took the opportunity to comment on recent policy discussions in the Council and to air a familiar police perspective:

> We support the Council's wholehearted opposition to racial harassment and attacks. But we dispute the view that the Asian community lacks confidence in us.
>
> *(Waltham Forest Guardian,* 10 January 1986)

Commander Allain also reported that the police had 'considerable success' in 1985 and out of 71 incidents, 29 people had been charged.[7] Neglected for comment in all of this was the perennial dispute of what constituted a racial attack. Some of these issues came to light in a relevant crown court case:

> Two young men who started a fire which caused a young Pakistani couple and their baby to flee their Walthamstow home, were each sentenced to 160 hours community service at the Old Bailey,.....*Judge Robert Lymberry Q.C. said the police were 'fully satisfied' that this was not a racially motivated offence, so it was quite irresponsible for one of the country's leading Sunday newspapers to label it a racial attack.*
>
> (ibid.; emphasis added)

This was a significant case because it was one of the few occasions where the Borough's racial harassment problem was raised as an issue in open court and was reported. But more than this, the outcome of the case and the manner of its local reporting reinforced ideas, disseminated by the police repeatedly, that racial harassment was increasingly wrongly asserted. In this particular case the attackers on their way from a pub disco took a rubbish bin off a lamp post, set it alight and put it next to the wooden fence by the home of Mohammed and Arshad Aslam in Maynard Road (April 1985). According to their defence counsel 'there was no evidence that they knew the property,....., was occupied'. The fire was sufficiently serious to cause £12,000 worth of damage. What was described by the judge as a 'disgraceful piece of reckless hooliganism' however is not so easily unstitched from the fabric of the spread of racial harassment. Firstly, both the attackers themselves lived in Maynard Road and so may well have been familiar with the pattern of residential occupation in that vicinity. And secondly, as we have seen, five months later in October there was a second arson attack on an Asian family's home in Maynard Road.

The first meeting of the police inspired Racial Incidents Panel (RIP) also took place in January 1986. From the outset it appeared to promote a perspective which had more to do with the need for the police's role to be understood rather than a concerted attempt to analyze and respond to the local spread of racial harassment. Although ostensibly guided by the victim's version of events, the RIP seemed to confirm the development of an attitude in the police where in the first instance it was not readily accepted that an act of racial harassment had occurred. It is easy to see how this could contribute to an atmosphere which cast doubt on the knowledge and reliability of victims. In the words of Commander Allain:

> The purpose of the panel is to reduce the gap in perception of what is regarded as a racial incident by a member of an ethnic minority and how the police see it.

> (ibid.)

By February the Council's proposals to establish a telephone hotline advice service for victims were emerging as the focus of discussion in the local community. It was revealed that the Racial Harassment Advice Service would initially be a pilot project, to be revised after six months. A full time co-ordinator was to be employed to run the project and legal and other advice would be available through a network of volunteers. While there was general enthusiasm for the initiative, there was one notable exception. The Borough's Victim Support Scheme was extremely critical of the developments. It felt it could do the job itself and that the hotline would 'cause some unrest in the community and therefore, possibly segregate the community into different sections which could have repercussions' *(Waltham Forest Guardian,* 7 February 1986). The basis of the Victim Support Scheme's view was opposition to what it perceived as:

> Making special provision for (.....) one section of the community (.....). Indeed it reckons there's just as much harassment of 'whites' by 'blacks' as vice-versa.
>
> *(Waltham Forest Guardian*, 21 February 1986)

The Victim Support Scheme's stance was doubly ironic and should not pass without comment. Firstly it had never dealt with racial harassment and therefore its own response to victims of crime was also sectional. And secondly, it suggested rather glibly that the Borough was also characterized by racial harassment of white people when there was absolutely *no evidence of a historical pattern of attacks, abuse and violations of white communities.* Furthermore there was no particular region of the Borough which could be identified as a locale where racial harassment of people *because they are white* regularly took place. There was nothing to compare for example, with the campaign of 'racist attacks' and harassment which had driven an Asian family of six from their flat in Hollydown Way, Leytonstone. This culminated in an arson attack in September 1987. Fortunately the Sadiq's (including their children aged 4, 6, 10 and 12) were out at the time of the explosion. The Leyton CID confirmed the attack 'appeared to be racially motivated' *(Waltham Forest Guardian,* 11 September 1987).

The last few months of 1987 also witnessed some curious discussions of the Council's policy on racial harassment. It seems to us that for at least six years the Council's approach had been shrouded in mystery. It was unclear what if anything had been implemented and what the actual practices were. However the general media perception appeared to be that the Council had clear policies on racial harassment. Yet this was not and had never been the case. A completely distorted picture was being disseminated. Astonishingly, even Councillors and Council officers were not exempt from the confusion. This perhaps explains the background to the following headline in the *Waltham Forest Express* (26 September 1987):

> Waltham Forest Council has been given a pat on the back
> - *from its own Race Relations Unit.* Just days after the
> Commission for Racial Equality criticised local
> Councils for not doing enough to stop the rising tide of
> racial harassment, *Waltham Forest has got the thumbs
> up for the steps it has taken.*

> (ibid.; emphasis added)

A similar report was carried in the *Waltham Forest Guardian* (2 October 1987), in addition it was announced that new measures were being introduced to protect the 'Borough's black, Asian and other racial minority groups from physical and verbal abuse'. Moreover it perpetuated what can only be described as a myth that the Council had:

> already implemented a policy whereby Council tenants
> found guilty of racially intimidating their neighbours can
> be evicted. It will not be the responsibility of the Council
> to rehouse them as they would have made themselves
> intentionally homeless.

> (ibid.)

This misrepresentation of reality suggested the only policy question left was implementation; matters however were a lot more complex than this (see Chapter 5).

The other publicly recognized dimension of the Council's approach was the 24 hour telephone advice service. It had been permanently established in April 1987, but by November there were criticisms of its prospective closure. A protest meeting organized by the Victim Aid Action Group held at the Asian Centre was covered by the *Waltham Forest Guardian* (6 November 1987):

> Asian women would be 'terrified' if the planned closure
> of the council-run racial harassment service went ahead
> in Waltham Forest.

In the prevailing atmosphere of Council discussions concerning reductions in its budget expenditure the Racial Harassment Advice Service had been included in a list of potential cut-backs. According to the *Daily Jang* (29 October 1987), since its establishment the Advice Service had dealt with 98 crisis interventions, including twelve night time interventions. However, the Council felt the project needed to be reviewed 'because it has failed to come up to expectations' *(Yellow Advertiser,* 6 November 1987). Whatever the expectations held of the Advice Service, or the quality of its work, it did 'plug a gap' in peoples' sense of security. This may also have extended to a perception that:

> Since its introduction the number of incidents has dropped and organisers fear if it is reduced or scrapped, a fresh increase in race abuse incidents will follow.

> (ibid.)

There is no evidence that the number of incidents declined as a result of the Advice Service's existence, certainly the outrageous arson attacks of 1985 had subsided, but it would be naive to link the two. If anything the numbers of *incidents recorded by agencies over-all* increased during 1985-1987. Nevertheless the telephone hotline's impact in alleviating the fears *following a racial attack* should not be discounted, equally it should not be over-estimated.

During 1988 a steady stream of racial harassment incidents were reported to the police, the Council's Housing department and the Racial Harassment Advice Service. This seemed to confirm the propensity of victims to complain about their experiences, despite the inability of these agencies to focus on the causes of recurring racial victimization. This perhaps pointed to a continuing glimmer of hope in the wider array of agencies that could respond rather than any indication of confidence in that response. But perhaps also it said something about reactions to the cumulative impact of racial harassment in the social environment where the dangers often escalated. In February 1988 the *Caribbean Times* (26 February 1988) reported:

> Arsonists in East London struck for the second time this year at the Leytonstone home of Webster Thomas (.....) only one day after he left hospital to recover from a serious cancer operation.

The victim a 23 year old African-Caribbean, lived alone on the Juniper Court estate in Morris Road. He suffered from lymph cancer, was virtually bed-ridden and had to be helped out of his home by relatives who had been present on the night of the attack. This appeared to be the denouement of a lengthy scenario of victimization; according to the *Caribbean Times:*

> The attack was the climax to years of racist abuse from
> a neighbour (.....) who was known to hurl racist abuse at
> Mr Thomas whenever she saw him. On one occasion she
> gathered a gang with sticks and stones to chase him
> through Leytonstone.
>
> (ibid.)

Mr Thomas felt 'his life has been hell' as a result of these experiences. These views were conveyed to the *Caribbean Times,* they were also made known to the Council. Mr Thomas desperately wanted a transfer to alternative accommodation and was apparently willing to accept almost anything in any area because he feared so much for his safety. The records of the Housing department revealed this as the fourth arson attempt he had experienced. The case also seems to have been reported to the police, their investigations however, produced no effective outcome. According to *The Voice* (26 February 1988), they were keeping an 'open mind about the arsonist'. Mr Thomas was accepted by the Housing department as a candidate for a transfer and moves were underway to re-locate him outside the Borough, but soon after these were accomplished Mr Thomas' health deteriorated rapidly and he died. What is particularly disturbing about this case is the revelation that people with disabilities or serious medical conditions can have their grasp on coping with life briskly destroyed by ruthless racial victimization.

The issue of over-policing emerged once again in May. *The Voice* (10 May 1988) reported that Tony Wallace, a 23 year old Black man in Leyton was:

> Kicked and bodily dragged through his front wall by
> police officers. He suffered from internal injuries as well
> as severe bruising to his arms and face.

Mr Wallace claimed he was locked up in a cell for seven hours, denied the use of his inhaler for his asthmatic condition, questioned in the absence of a lawyer and subsequently released without charge. Mr Wallace complained to the Police Complaints Authority and also employed the services of solicitors to institute a civil action claim for damages against the police.[8]

The end of 1988 coincided with a local press observation that racial harassment in the Borough had 'risen steadily in the past four years' *(Waltham Forest Guardian,* 2 December 1988). This observation was based on figures drawn from three sources, the police, the Council's Racial Harassment Advice Service and the Housing department. In particular it was reported that the Racial

Harassment Advice Service had received 131 reports of racial victimization during the period April 1987 to May 1988. By 1989 it could be argued, as we have already suggested, that more reports were being recorded over-all, because there were more agencies to record them. What this concealed however was an increase in the range of ineffective responses by statutory agencies.

## Looking for a provisional pattern

Our sketch of Waltham Forest's experience of racial harassment during the 1980s is no more than that. If only a relatively small number of racial harassment incidents are ever reported to statutory agencies, then it is apparent that only a minute proportion of these are reported in the press or the rest of the media. What our limited historical commentary outlines are the *headlines* and *sound-bites* which occasionally portray racial harassment prominently on the surface of experiences in the Borough. The real significance of this *history* however lies in how it alerts us to the persistence of a problem, *which can only be understood if we look beyond the prevalence of so-called random incidents of racial harassment.*

In our review of the 1980s there are elements of a pattern which raise two important questions. Firstly, while it might be plausible to think of racial harassment as random or unpredictable over a period of a month or even a year. After a period of nine years, what at first appears random definitely coalesces into a pattern where any one *from particular communities,* repeatedly faces the prospect of racial victimization. In the Borough this has principally meant the Asian and Black communities. Secondly, this may well raise questions about whether an association had developed between racial harassment and particular regions in the Borough. For example, despite the obvious limitations of our commentary, it is quite surprising what is revealed when we consider the reported locations of incidents over the decade. The remarkable thing is that approximately two thirds of these reports occurred within a geographical area of little more than three square miles. This marked out the Walthamstow region of the Borough, from the Priory Court estate in its northern-most section, to Alexandra Road in its southern-most section, and from Palmerston Road in its western-most section to Maynard and Cheltenham Roads in its eastern-most section.( This whole area can be easily seen by examining these co-ordinates on one page of a standard London A-Z.)

At least tentatively there are a number of observations that can be drawn from our review. Unlike any other crime or combination of crimes, racial harassment seems to have a history which exerts a continuous influence over the lives, families and experiences of the communities which are its principal focus. Its persistence over time creates insecurities in various locations and institutes the most brutal and hideous forms of racial victimization as a potential any day, night, week or month of every year. This suggests that any analysis of racial harassment's entrenchment over time, that is its history, must be complemented by its usually less visible dimension, the *dispersion of racial harassment* across various locations that is, its geography. As we shall see in later Chapters it is precisely the *cartographic* implications of this analysis which will enable us to uproot the 'patterns' planted beneath the surface of racial harassment incidents (see Chapters 4 and 5). But before this, in the Chapters which immediately follow, we extend our contexual treatment of Waltham Forest to include an analysis of how and why public agencies like the local police and local authority failed to respond effectively during the 1980s.

## Notes

1. Herein after we refer to this organization by its initials CRC.

2. In 1988 Esme Baker failed in her attempt to sue the police for damages.

3. Waltham Forest Police Monitoring Group was a project funded by the Greater London Council during the early 1980s as part of its London-wide strategy for 'watching over' the police and taking up public issues. The Group folded in 1986.

4. Following recommendations from Lord Scarman's inquiry into the 'Brixton disorders' of April 1981, the Home Office promoted the idea of consultative arrangements between the 'Police and the Community'. Usually this meant the local authority, voluntary sector organizations and the police. This initiative was eventually enshrined as section 106 of the 1984 Police and Criminal Evidence Act which in London placed a duty on the Metropolitan police Commissioner to ensure that Consultative Groups existed in each London Borough.

5. See Chapters 4 and 5.

6. The police subsequently charged Mr Ghani with starting the fire. When the case eventually reached court in 1986, it was thrown out. Following this Mr Ghani began a civil court action against the Metropolitan police for wrongful arrest and malicious prosecution. In June 1990 shortly before the case was due to be heard, the police made an 'out of court' payment to him to settle the matter.

7. The difficulties of assessing statistics like these are discussed in Chapter 2.

8. A civil action was being prepared when Mr Wallace died following an asthmatic attack in 1989. A Police Complaints Authority investigation into the conduct of one of the officers was concluded in 1990. The Crown Prosecution Service advised that the public interest did not require the institution of criminal proceedings against the officer. The Assistant Commissioner of Police was of the opinion that a disciplinary charge of unnecessary violence should be preferred in accordance with Section 8 (b) of the police disciplinary code. The officer concerned left the police force before this action was instituted.

# 2 Policy analysis : The local police

*Barnor Hesse and Paul McGilchrist*

> The Metropolitan police have made considerable efforts in recent years to produce a better service for victims and potential victims of racial harassment.
>
> (Evidence to the Inquiry, 1989)

> As a Solicitor I have been consulted by people who have been attacked. The main complaint is that police officers do not wish to know if they have been attacked.
>
> (Evidence to the Inquiry, 1989)

> For heavens sake, we don't want women and kids burned to death while we do nothing about it, but there are a lot of factors within the Asian community that make it convenient for them to allege racial motivation when its simply caste or money at the root of the problem. We could find the real racist much more quickly if we were told the truth every time.
>
> (Police Review, November 1985)

In terms of policing racial harassment the 1980s inherited a dismal record of public criticism. Many of the key criticisms of the police's response to racial harassment were summarized comprehensively by the Institute of Race Relations (IRR) in its submission to the Royal Commission on Criminal Procedure in 1979. The IRR presented documented evidence which showed that: the police did not protect the Asian and Black communities from racial attacks; the police were reluctant to recognize the racial dimension in attacks on Asian and Black people; the police often were considerably delayed in reaching the scene; the police were unwilling to investigate or initiate prosecutions; the police gave misleading advice to victims and were hostile towards them; and the police often treated the victim as the aggressor. As we can see the criticisms of the police were quite far reaching, and touched many connected aspects of their policy and practice.

While it is true to say that during the 1980s the Metropolitan police made some significant improvements in their policy towards racial harassment, it is equally true that there have been no corresponding changes in the type of criticisms traditionally levelled at the police. This ironic situation is the product of a decade of police policy making which addressed only the superficial aspects of the problem. Racial harassment continued to be one of the Force's most obdurate crime problems because it was viewed *essentially* as indecipherable, discrete events rather than connected crimes with discernable social and spatial contours. The police perception of a sporadic, random occurrence resulted in a policy analytic approach imprisoned by narrow considerations of its incidence; and an operational approach characterized by vigilance rather than action.

Consequently, tracing the development of specific police initiatives against racial harassment during the period reveals at least two recurrent paradoxes. Firstly, although patterning crime is a fundamental aspect of police investigative procedure, the policing of racial harassment was distinguished by the gradual abandonment of this approach throughout the 1980s. Secondly, the main focus in police strategies correspondingly shifted from the perpetrator to the victim. This had the effect of associating the 'problem' of racial harassment in policing terms with the consequences of victimization rather than the activities of violation. At the beginning of the 1990s the views of the police themselves and of those who have experienced racial harassment or provided assistance to the victims could not be more polarized. With the exception of the evidence submitted to the Inquiry by the police, the overwhelming indications are that the policing of racial harassment in Waltham Forest has been experienced as acutely ineffective. The purpose of this Chapter is threefold: to provide a review of the developments in the Metropolitan police's approach to dealing with racial harassment; to assess the status of particular problems with the police response in Waltham Forest; and to consider the policy implications which arise from this.

## Incremental or incoherent policy making?

Although Sir David McNee in the Metropolitan police Commissioner's 1981 annual report made no specific references to racial attacks and harassment, by

1982 the police had introduced what the in-coming Commissioner (Sir Kenneth Newman) described as a 'new system to record all allegations of incidents which included an element of racial motivation' (Metropolitan police Commissioner, 1983). The objective of the system was for the Community Relations Branch at New Scotland Yard to collate the details and to identify 'trends in each type of offence and their frequency'. The assumption behind this initiative was that by distinguishing 'racially motivated incidents' (the definition of which was vague) and ensuring they were reported to the police this would facilitate a 'proactive strategy and appropriate action'. There was little consideration of whether the police would necessarily record reports of racial harassment, or whether without training they were capable of identifying 'racial motivation', or even if racial harassment could be addressed effectively by police practices and procedures which remained essentially unchanged. The supervison and monitoring of these initiatives was never in question. In 1982, 1,516 'racial incidents' were recorded by the Metropolitan police. No clear strategies emerged.

Quite surprisingly by 1983 the Metropolitan police appeared to have grown in confidence despite unrelenting criticisms of their attitude to racial harassment. In his annual report for that year the Commissioner Sir Kenneth Newman declared somewhat boldly:

> there was a time when the Metropolitan police failed to fully appreciate the growing incidence of attacks on members of minorities by indigenous whites. That time has now passed.

> (Metropolitan police Commissioner, 1984)

It is not clear on what basis this view was constructed. It was not drawn from an evaluation of the police's effectiveness in this area since there were no relevant studies undertaken by the police. Rather it seemed merely to point, with some satsifaction, to the latest additions to police policy. This involved two main developments which taken together appeared to strengthen the 1982 initiative to collate 'racial incidents' centrally at Scotland Yard. The first concerned the police's definition of a racial incident. Up until 1982 at least, the definition employed by the police referred to 'incidents which included an element of racial motivation'. By 1983 a more robust definition was in place, it now referred to:

> any incident whether concerning crime or not which is
> alleged by any person to include an element of racial
> motivation or which appears to the reporting or
> investigating officer to include such an element.
>
> (Metropolitan police Commissioner, ibid.)

The significance of this lay in the emphasis it gave to the victim's perception of racial harassment. What tarnished it however was its *unqualified* 'inter-racial' quality, the implication that racial harassment can happen to 'any person'. While true in theory, the problem with this was that it failed to acknowledge that Asian and Black people were the *principal victims of racial harassment.* That is, it neglected the *contextuality* of racial harassment which gives the experience of these crimes their specificity and meaning (this neglect is still a major policy deficiency in this area).

The second development in Metropolitan police policy in 1983 was the introduction of a police *divisional* strategy for responding to reports of racial harassment. According to the Commissioner's report of that year:

> Following all necessary action taken by the reporting
> officer at the scene, details of the incident are reported
> to the local community liaison officer, the Chief
> Superintendent of the division on which the incident took
> place and the Community Relations Branch at New
> Scotland Yard.
>
> (Metropolitan police Commissioner, ibid.)

As part of this strategy the local Home Beat officer was required to visit the victim. The main purpose was to establish an accurate picture of racial harassment locally and to communicate to the victims that the police were treating the issue seriously. But there was no explicit discussion of action against perpetrators. In 1983 the number of racial incidents recorded by the Metropolitan police stood at 1,277. By 1984 this figure had grown to 1,515 and was described by the Commissioner as *'worryingly large'* (Metropolitan police Commissioner, 1985). His report for that year set out for the first time a concise rationale in this area. The long-term goal was to reduce the 'number of such attacks and the fear of harassment among minority ethnic populations'. Never before had such a firm commitment been publicly expressed by a Metropolitan police Commissioner. Yet it was still a long way from being proclaimed a central plank in policing strategies for London.

This incremental approach to policy making seemed devoid of direction, moreover it raised questions consistently about how seriously the police were treating racial harassment and precipitated many allegations of sheer public relations. Although the Commissioner eventually included action against racial harassment in his 'Force Goal' (i.e. policy objectives) for 1985, other elements of the Metropolitan police's thinking had a less commendable appearance. For example an internal Metropolitan police strategy document, the 'Force Appraisal of 1986', a policy evaluation report (made public the following year) highlighted a number of considerations governing the attitude of senior police officers to racial attacks. In an analysis of the incorporation of action against racial attacks as part of the 1985 Force Goal, the 'Force Appraisal' stated unreservedly:

> the implications for the Force of failing to be seen to get to grips with the intractable problem are severe. Firstly, the insidious nature of racially motivated misbehaviour and its divisive product are clear. Secondly, perhaps cynically but nonetheless pragmatically, the Force will be without political friends. The votes of Asians - who have consistently been the victims of 68-70% of reported incidents over the last 3 years - could be decisive in many parliamentary seats. Unlike the Black (Afro-Caribbean) or young vote the Asian vote can be mobilised and will respond to leaders within the various Asian communities.

> (Metropolitan police, 1986a)

By 1985 the number of racial incidents recorded by the police had risen to 1,945, (a 28% increase since 1984). The 'Force Appraisal' recognized that the issue was being perceived as damaging to the image of the Metropolitan police as well as presenting a social order problem. The accompanying analysis described 'Indians and Pakistanis' as accounting for 70% of racial harassment victims and suggested this had remained unchanged since 1983. Interestingly it also accepted that the majority of attacks were committed by 'white skinned Europeans'. Also in 1985 the Association of Chief Police Officers (ACPO) of England and Wales issued a statement of guiding principles concerning racial harassment. This incorporated the Metropolitan police's 1983 definition of a racial incident and stressed the significance of the definition as two-fold:first, to ensure that police records became more comprehensive by including all appropriate incidents, and second, to ensure that the victim's perception of the motivation of the offender was included. The ACPO principles described in detail elements of a broadly standardized approach. As guidance it made an important distinction between 'effective monitoring systems' and 'the response of individual officers on the ground *which matters most'* (emphasis added). But it was extremely obscure concerning specific methods of investigation. It placed an equal stress on responding in a 'committed and speedy way' to give the victim confidence in the police response *and also* avoiding 'the impression that when an arrest is not made or if any attack has not been prevented, this is because the police are not sufficiently concerned'. At the very least this implied that the police found the investigation of racial attacks acutely problematic, although they were clearly concerned to be seen to have an impact.

The Metropolitan police issued 'Best Practice Guidelines' in 1986. These endorsed the thrust of ACPO's approach. In addition it was proposed:

> As a general rule, therefore, the presence of a suspected racial motivation should be regarded as a complicating factor justifying a higher level of police response than to other similar but non-racial incidents.
>
> (Metropolitan police, 1986a)

These 'Best Practice Guidelines' divided the Force's policy into two parts. The first stressed improved monitoring and investigation, plus maintaining good relationships with victims; the second emphasized the role of a *multi-agency* approach (see Conclusion). Also included were a number of 'minimum requirements' designed for incorporation into local divisional directives in order to promote a standard response. The key features comprised the following:

> * The Chief Superintendent is responsible for reviewing the investigation and procedures followed in cases.
>
> * Reports of incidents are made to the Community Liaison Officer who informs the Divisional Chief Superintendent and A7 Dept. (at Scotland Yard).
>
> * All investigations are passed to the Chief Superintendent through the Community Liaison Officer.

\* All victims are visited in order to maintain communication.

\* The Community Liaison Officer maintains and monitors local records, identifying trends to the Divisional Chief Superintendent.

On the face of things this represented a concerted attempt by Scotland Yard to introduce an effective system into the police divisions. It was an implicit recognition that much of the policy making in the Metropolitan police neglected to consider practices on the ground (i.e. in the divisions). But policy communication was one thing and practical implementation another. According to the 'Force Appraisal' (1986) when these guidelines were issued in January 1986, six months later they were still unknown to many Chief Superintendents. Moreover, the guidelines were no more than guidelines, *they could not be enforced*. In 1986 the number of racial incidents recorded by the police in London was 1,733 (an 11% drop compared with the previous year). By 1987 Sir Peter Imbert had succeeded Sir Kenneth Newman as Metropolitan police Commissioner. Later that year a Metropolitan police 'Force Order', an instruction to all police officers, was issued on racial harassment. This represented an instruction to all divisional Chief Superintendents to implement the 'minimum requirements' of the 'Best Practice Guidelines'. It also advocated a new approach to prosecuting offenders. This was based on one of the recommendations of the Parliamentary Home Affairs Committee (July 1986). The committee had recommended the police to initiate prosecutions 'where sufficient evidence exists and the victim consents'. Finally the 'Force Order' emphasized the possible use of section 47 of the 1861 Offences against the persons Act in cases of racial assault. In particular it stated:

> Actual bodily harm may be inferred if pain or tenderness or soreness results from the act even if no physical injury is visible. It will be sufficient if the act merely causes psychological injury such as an hysterical or nervous condition.

The substantive shape of Metropolitan police policy on racial harassment up to the end of the decade was determined by this, 1987, ' Force Order'. *So far there has been no public evaluation of its effectiveness.*

Interestingly a Police Order of 23 November 1990, operational on 1 January 1991, apparently revised the recording procedures for incidents of racial harassment. This Order required *all* racial incidents to be recorded whether a crime or not, for any incident involving 'an element of racial motivation' or an 'allegation of racial motivation *made by any person*' (emphasis added), to be regarded as a racial incident; and for all such reports to be included in police statistics. As valuable as these measures appear, they merely echoed the directives of a previous Metropolitan police Commissioner, Sir Kenneth Newman, who (as we have already seen) as long ago as 1984 defined a racial incident to be one 'alleged by *any* person' and exhorted the Force to 'record *all* allegations'. In this light it is questionable whether anything new has been signalled by these particular instructions beyond an attempt to enforce a policy that consistently eluded practical implementation. [1]

*Statistical trends*

During the last three years of the decade the annual number of racial incidents recorded by the police increased successively. In 1987 the figures were 2,179; in 1988, 2,214; and in 1989, 2,697. The year 1989 represented a 39% increase in recorded incidents since 1985 when Sir Peter Imbert's predecessor had described the figures as 'worryingly large'. Table 2.1 below displays the rising trend in the numbers of racial incidents recorded by the Metropolitan police during 1982-1989.

**Table 2.1**

**Recorded racial incidents in the Metropolitan police area, 1982-1989**

| Year | 1982 | 1983 | 1984 | 1985 | 1986 | 1987 | 1988 | 1989 |
|------|------|------|------|------|------|------|------|------|
| Total | 1516 | 1277 | 1515 | 1945 | 1733 | 2179 | 2214 | 2697 |

Source: Metropolitan police Commissioners reports

It should also be noted that although 1989 represented a 22% rise in recorded incidents, a staggering figure, this was not in fact a record annual increase. In his report for 1989, Sir Peter Imbert made the additional observation that 'of real concern was the increase of 161 (nearly 25%) in the number of racially motivated assaults' (Metropolitan police Commissioner, 1990). At the same time the clear up rate had fallen from 33% to 31%.

## Shifting emphases

By 1990 the policing of racial harassment was still a major public policy concern. What was less clear, was the *effectiveness and rationale* of the Metropolitan police's approach. In a memorandum to the House of Commons Home Affairs Committee in November 1989, the Metropolitan police stated that by June 1988, 30% of the divisions had at some stage employed 'targeting procedures' against perpetrators of racial harassment. For example in 1986 a plain clothes 'Organised Racial Incidents Squad' was established in Newham. Elsewhere it appears 'ad hoc targeting procedures' had been employed. According to the police, targeting had not resulted in much success because 'generally speaking there is no 'pattern' to racial assaults'. They suggested that targeting, if it is involved at all, 'must remain an ad hoc tactic'. It is apparent that the police's failure to identify patterns or trends in racial harassment and their inability, consequently, to act strategically in combating it resulted in a *shift in the emphasis of their approach.* For example, they now make rather less public comment on taking action against perpetrators in the first instance.

### Police campaigns against racial harassment

Some clearer indications of where the emphasis has been moved are evident in the components of what the Metropolitan police referred to as their 'campaign against racial harassment'. Towards the end of the 1980s two racial harassment pilot schemes were established by the police, one in Newham and Ealing (1987) and the other in Tower Hamlets and Redbridge (1988). Both involved the distribution of 'Racial Harassment Action Guides' which explained the courses of action available to potential victims. The pilot campaigns in Newham and Ealing for example, lasted for three months and were based on the following three objectives: to give practical advice and reassurance to those most at risk; to explain the role of the police and their response to crime; and to counter ill-informed or misleading criticisms levelled against the police. None of the objectives were principally directed at taking effective action against the perpetrators of racial harassment, moreover, according to the London Borough of Newham, (1987a): 'the "Action Guide" spent a disproportionate amount of space upon what people could do to assist themselves and *very little on what action the police were undertaking to protect the public'* (emphasis added).

Nevertheless the Metropolitan police proclaimed both the pilot projects a success. In concise terms this was reported to the House of Commons Home Affairs Committee in the following way:

In both pilot schemes the levels of awareness in, and reassurance of, the local population were much improved: the reporting of racial incidents in the pilot sites increased during specially designed local campaigns and for 12 weeks after it ended, thus meeting one of the main campaign objectives.

(Metropolitan police, 1989b)

This assessment of 'success' however, was quite misleading in two ways. First it disguised the fact that the police appeared to be defining the *problem* of racial harassment *not in* terms of an *ineffective* police response (the criticism documented increasingly throughout the last decade) *but rather* in terms of the victims failing to report their experiences to the police. Second it promoted the assumption that the current police response was adequate and that this merely needed to be broadly publicized in order to make the police appear more *user friendly*. It is worth noting that the London Borough of Newham in their consideration of the police's evaluation of the campaign in Newham and Ealing were quite critical of the police's criterion of success. According to them the campaign was a failure,

because it was employed as a vehicle for police objectives and not for addressing the needs of local people. Success is premised upon delivering a service to meet the stated needs of local people and not by launching a campaign to 'educate' potential victims or to explain the role of the police.

(London Borough of Newham, 1987a)

On the face of it this is a reasonable criticism. As we discuss below, the evidence to our Inquiry suggested strongly that local awareness of the police as an agency that can and should respond to racial harassment was considerable, but the evidence also suggested that people were extremely frustrated by their experiences of reporting incidents to the police.

In February 1989, it seems the experience gained from the earlier pilot schemes was used by the Metropolitan police to launch a higher profile, wider based campaign. At a cost of £400,000 this campaign ran for one month in 19 London Boroughs divided into primary and secondary targets. In the primary Boroughs there was door to door distribution of publicity material which included the 'Action Guide' (produced in 14 different languages). The secondary Boroughs were supplied with copies of the Action Guide for distribution to public places like Libraries, Town Halls and places of worship. Waltham Forest was not included in the campaign at either level. In evidence to the Inquiry, Deputy Assistant Commissioner Walter Boreham explained:

> The primary Boroughs were chosen on the basis that they were more prone to the problems of racial harassment and therefore in greater need of concentrated effort. The secondary Boroughs were seen to be in need of similar attention but not to the same extent.

The police's basis for deciding which Boroughs were particularly affected by racial harassment was quite elementary: those with the highest numbers of incidents recorded by the police themselves. If we consider the Boroughs, which together with Waltham Forest, form the Metropolitan police Area 1 it is clear for example, why *on this basis* the Borough of Islington was selected as a 'primary target'. Table 2.2 below sets out the numbers of racial incidents recorded by the police in the various Boroughs comprising Area 1 during the period 1986-1989. It is clear that since 1987 the highest numbers of racial incidents have increasingly been recorded by the police in Islington.

**Table 2.2**

**Numbers of recorded racial incidents in Metropolitan police Area No.1 during 1986-1989**

| | Years | | | |
|---|---|---|---|---|
| *Borough* | *1986* | *1987* | *1988* | *1989* |
| Waltham Forest | 66* | 80 | 55 | 71 |
| Epping Forest | - | 8 | 12 | 6 |
| Redbridge | 93 | 76 | 73 | 57 |
| Islington | 79 | 83 | 101 | 162 |
| Haringey | 44 | 40 | 42 | 37 |
| Enfield | 41** | 44 | 68 | 74 |
| Broxbourne | - | 3 | 4 | 4 |
| Welwyn/Hatfield | - | 0 | 1 | 0 |

Source: Metropolitan police: Evidence to the Inquiry (1989) and Metropolitan police statistics (1989)
*Includes Epping Forest*
**Includes Broxbourne and Welwyn*

It is highly questionable whether aggregate numbers of recorded incidents should alone determine the policy perspective regarding racial harassment. An approach like this fails to acknowledge the impact of racial harassment in Waltham Forest, giving the impression that the problem is minimal by comparison with other Boroughs. But the police's 1989 racial harassment campaign also baffled us in a further respect. As we understand it the campaign was generally constructed to raise the public awareness of racial harassment and to encourage potential victims to perceive the police as a responsive agency. It was apparent from their previous pilot projects that the police measured awareness of racial harassment in direct proportion to increases in the levels of incidents recorded. If this is so, it does seem rather curious that the police should have selected the Boroughs with the highest number of incidents for their 1989 campaign. Arguably the 'logic' could also have been pointed in the opposite direction. In other words, could not the Boroughs with comparatively lower levels of incidents *recorded* be seen as more appropriate locations for *increasing levels of awareness?* On this basis for example, Waltham Forest could have been a prime candidate for the focus of a police campaign against racial harassment. The point is not that some Boroughs should have been chosen as opposed to others, but rather, local police statistics in isolation are *poor indicators of the impact of racial harassment over time and across various locations in a particular Borough.* As we argue in Chapter 4, it is the spread of racial harassment, its connected local history and geography, which is the real problem, not the random reporting of incidents.

Another factor, worth mentioning here, was the campaign's exclusive focus on the public. The lack of a corresponding focus on individual police officers themselves was a serious ommission, even when considered in the police's terms. The 1989 campaign ignored the Association of Chief Police Officers 1985 injunction that what mattered most was the response of individual police officers *on the ground.* Police work generally can have a 'low visibility', where it involves a wide range of discretion and is largely unsupervised. It is reasonable to argue that campaigns of this nature have little direct effect *on the police response in the field.* Difficulties like these arise in trying to understand the police's policy not only because of unacknowledged shifts in emphasis or changes of direction, *but also due to the absence of an effective public assessment of their initiatives.* For example, even though the 1989 campaign was severely undermined by the fact that less than half of the Action Guides were distributed throughout each of the 'primary Boroughs', the police informed the Parliamentary Home Affairs Committee they were satisfied that 'encouraging results of increased awareness and reporting of racial incidents has been indicated in four of the primary Boroughs' (Metropolitan police, 1989b). For us this raises serious questions as to what ought properly to be regarded as the objective of these types of campaigns in general and Metropolitan police policy in particular. In this context the observations of the Greater London Action for Race Equality (GLARE) are quite exemplary. Following a detailed assessment of the campaign, they expressed concern at the Metropolitan police's apparent marginalization of issues relative to the improvement of their performance against perpetrators. In particular they wrote:

> This campaign primarily focussed upon the victims of racial harassment to encourage them to report incidents to the police and to enhance their capacity to protect themselves. While we support these aims they must be balanced by action which focuses on perpetrators of racial harassment with the aim of preventing further attacks and catching race attackers. Failure to plan for this will lay the initiative open to criticism that it is primarily a public relations exercise.
>
> (GLARE, 1989)

By the end of the 1980s, the policy approach of the Metropolitan police to racial harassment had swung almost imperceptibly from a proclaimed commitment to identifying patterns and perpetrators to the raising of public awareness and developing a service for victims of racial harassment. That this unacknowledged shift occurred is easier to highlight than explain in a limited study like this. However, it did correspond with broader police concerns, especially in the latter part of the decade, which emphasized the value of public co-operation in preventing crime. Indeed, the role of community co-operation as a crime reducing strategy in itself, was firmly established by 1986, a year which not only saw a steep rise in the number of Neighbourhood Watch Schemes, but also the creation of a Ministerial Group on Crime Prevention. By the end of the decade police enthusiasm for community involvement against a background of escalating crime statistics and growing public fear of crime, appeared to have eclipsed all consideration of the specificity of racial harassment as a crime. Thus, the information contained in the Metropolitan police's Racial Harassment Guides in 1989 for example, focused principally on target hardening, vigilance and increased reporting and was entirely in tandem with this general trend in situational crime prevention strategies.

Whatever the possible explanations for this shift in the police policy approach, however, one consequence suggested by our evidence, appears to be that the views of the police and those of victims of racial harassment on the adequacy of the police response continued to co-exist in a realm where experiences were invariably 'poles apart'.

## Waltham Forest police/community experiences: The evidence

In their written submission to our Inquiry the Metropolitan police gave particular emphasis to the victim support aspects of police policy. It was pointed out that all incidents occurring within Waltham Forest were reported by the local police to the Community Liaison Officer, an Inspector at Woodford police station, and that all victims were visited by an 'appropriate officer independent of any investigation' in order to maintain communication and report on progress. The theme of an improved quality of service for 'victims and potential victims of racial harassment' was developed further by their reference to a survey undertaken by Chingford police division in 1988. According to their submission, of 18 victims surveyed six were very satisfied, eleven were quite satisfied and 'none felt that they had been poorly or very poorly dealt with'. The view of the police locally was that they provided an effective and adequate service; there appeared to be no conception that it could be otherwise. This is best exemplified by one of the observations of Deputy Assistant Commissioner Boreham who wrote in evidence to the Inquiry:

> Inspector Jackson the Divisional Community Liaison
> officer believes that of the victims he has seen to date,
> the vast majority are satisfied with police action.

In the light of other evidence submitted to the Inquiry this view appears to be extraordinarily complacent. We did not find a single, unequivocal example of satisfaction with the role of the local police response to racial harassment. On the contrary, the criticisms of the police in this regard were legion. What we found suggests that despite various innovations and changes in official police policy, public statements and literature, there had been little impact on the level of security for the Borough's Asian, Black and Ethnic Minority populations. The reasons for this appear to be both multiple and inter-related.

Although it was often difficult to separate criticisms of the police from criticisms of the Council, on the various occasions that the police were singled out, painful and disturbing experiences were reported which raised many questions about the credibility of the police's response. Two main areas of criticism emerge from the evidence, these are: the police do not respond effectively and they are often insensitive and racist. Furthermore, these factors in combination appear to sustain an acute lack of confidence in the police and an unwillingness to report cases to them. The evidence also suggested (and the complacency of the police's own submission to the Inquiry confirmed this) that the *police were failing to acknowledge widespread and intense dissatisfaction among Asian and Black people in relation to the service they provide to victims of racial harassment.*

*The police do not respond effectively?*

This experience was fairly widespread and was reported to the Inquiry from a variety of sources, both individuals and groups. A typical example was described to us by the Waltham Forest Family Service Unit. In 1987 a Black family living in Livingstone College Tower was experiencing 'serious racial harassment'. This included attempts to break down their door, eggs pushed through their letter box and constant exposure to racist abuse. As a consequence the 'family were terrified whilst in the flat and afraid to leave it empty due to attacks'. On one occasion the husband in the family caught the attackers, four white youths, in the tower block lift and called the police. Although the police arrived, they 'refused to press charges'. Other organizations had similar experiences to report, together with additional observations. Sikh Sangat London East, singled out the police as the key agency in providing assistance but qualified this by saying the 'police do not deal with cases of racial harassment they just take notes and no action is taken'. In their evidence this view is summarized cogently; the

> Police are insensitive and dismissive in responding to reports of racial harassment. They do not offer any good service.

Many witnesses described details of incidents in which the police were called out and though there was clear identification of the perpetrators this was insufficient to guarantee that any effective action was taken by the police. An elderly African-Caribbean man informed us of an incident where white workmen on a roof-top in Warren Road, Leyton, threw a bucket of rubble at him, it just missed his head. In his evidence he wrote:

> I reported it immediately to Francis Road police station (i.e. Leyton police) and the police sergeant said he would send someone to investigate the matter immediately. I didn't hear nothing else from the police again.

The significant thing about this and other incidents is that the perpetrators were identifiable - yet still the police did not respond by taking effective action. It is not always apparent why this is. Perhaps one indication is provided by an Asian man who catalogued twenty two separate incidents of racial harassment experienced by his family over a period of two years (1984-1986). He described a throughly frustrating experience with both the police and Housing department. In one of these incidents:

> A teenage boy (whose photograph was taken a week later and who also lives in the neighbourhood) injured my wife's head with a stone while she was sitting in the back garden. This was also reported to the Council and the police and photographs of the boy was also presented, but the police did not take any action whatsoever.

The police appear to be especially reluctant to take action against young people or children when they are implicated in perpetrating racial harassment. When we examined the details of the racial incidents reported to Chingford and Leyton divisions in 1987-1988, it was quite clear that where young people are involved, the police, if they respond at all, prefer to resolve matters informally. But there is also something else, this concerns the extent to which racial harassment is accepted by the police. In another incident reported by the same witness (see above) the Waltham Forest Community Relations Council (CRC) complained on his behalf to the police when his 'front door frame was broken by a boy living only three doors away'. In reply to the CRC, Chief Superintendent Bishop of Leyton police wrote in 1985:

> I have looked into this matter and have also tasked the local Home beat officer,......, with paying particular attention to the vicinity of...... Whilst I accept that Mr X has suffered some damage to the premises at the hands of local children, my enquiries tend to indicate these incidents are in no way racially motivated and really result from the situation of the house adjacent to the children's play areas. PC Baker informs me that the previous occupiers of the house, a white family, suffered similar problems.

This illustrates one of the central problems encountered by victims reporting incidents to the police. The victim defines his/her experience as racial harassment and the police adopt and *enforce* the contrary view by not responding accordingly. While it may be argued that the response of the police has changed since 1985 it is remarkable how many similar conclusions can be drawn from more recent experiences. A local Councillor described to us an incident which took place in 1988:

> I spoke to Mr Z manager at a local store. He had recently opened his business and was greeted with broken windows, dog excrement through his letter box and an attempt to set fire to rubbish at the back of his store. He had no description of the perpetrators and the police when called said there was nothing they could do. I doubt whether this incident was recorded as a racial attack by the police (because the complaint was not pursued after the initial rebuff). I quote this as the most recent case of its type reported to me. It is clearly unexceptional in any way.

Another Councillor, who had himself been the victim of racial harassment, provided the following account of the police's unresponsiveness:

> I have, and other victims have reported the matter to the police. I have personally reported to the police on behalf of many people, but the response has been no different than what it has been in my own case. The police response when you mention you are a Councillor is very reassuring but what comes out of the report is nothing. I was once told that I should advise the victim to ring up the police when racial harassment is taking place. What satisfaction is there in this approach of the police?

This was a fairly common experience in Waltham Forest, almost a predictable 'scenario' (see Chapter 5). The police respond to an incident, but in the experience of the victims do nothing to reassure them and compound their anxieties by insisting that nothing can be done unless the police are there when the harassment is actually happening. In most instances this means the harassment happening again. Yet this is precisely what the victims fear since it is the avoidance of repetition which is their chief concern. Arguably, if public knowledge of the police's failure to act pre-emptively is widespread, this may well reinforce the very forms of harassment to which the police declare themselves unable to respond. The Council Housing department's assessment of the police is most striking in this context:

> In general, the police are not perceived to have been
> effective in responding to complaints of racial
> harassment insofar as perpetrators have rarely been
> apprehended and prosecuted.

Given these negative experiences it is entirely understandable why
organizations like the Victim Aid Action Group described the police's response
as 'totally hopeless' or that a local Asian women's organization argued in their
evidence that the 'police should take racial harassment more seriously and there
should be harsh punishments for (the) guilty party'. Our evidence showed
hardly any approval or praise for the service provided by the police to victims
of racial harassment, on the contrary the complaints were overwhelming.

Quite paradoxically however, while victims expressed a great deal of
dissatisfaction with the police, there was still a sustained expectation of support
or assistance from them where racial harassment was concerned. It was
worrying that none of the witnesses perceived the police as having an impact
on racial harassment or as providing an adequate response to victims. In a
minority of instances witnesses indicated that the response of Home Beat
officers was quite good and that victims were sometimes visited. The problem
here however, was that there appeared to be no follow-up. In the words of one
witness 'if a police man is sympathetic with you - you don't see them again'.
Many witnesses similarly described the worthlessness of reporting because the
police were unresponsive. (The Council was similarly indicted for not being
supportive and not responding.) Indeed the whole area of lack of responsiveness
by agencies was symbolized by the manifest failures of the police who were
seen as the 'lead' agency where immediate action was needed. The dire social
consequences of this for Waltham Forest were summed up by the witness who
declared:

> Perpetrators of racial harassment are confident and carry
> out acts of racial harassment in the Borough knowing
> that nothing will happen to them.

The failure by leading agencies, like the police (and the Council), to respond
effectively to racial harassment perpetrators undermines the confidence of
victims in reporting cases. Certainly many witnesses were reluctant to place
any value on reporting cases to the police. At the same time we were also struck
by the irrepressible fact that considerable problems and dilemmas confront

Asian and Black people in the actual manner of the police response when it does occur.

*Police insensitivity and racism?*

We were concerned to identify the extent to which agencies like the police and the Council were perceived as perpetrating racial harassment. Where witnesses felt able to comment substantively, almost without exception the police were mentioned. In addition we were also made aware of how racial harassment *from the police* was felt to be specifically directed against the African-Caribbean community. Generally these experiences were difficult to separate from perceptions that the police were insensitive when dealing with cases of racial harassment. A significant indication of this was provided by Waltham Forest CRC who conducted what they described as an 'anecdotal survey' of 217 Asian and African-Caribbean people as part of their submission to our Inquiry. In relation to the police, they wrote:

> Allegations were made of racist attitudes by police officers including verbal abuse. Of 36 incidents recorded as reported to the police, 26 were considered to have been handled badly or indifferently.

It is interesting to note the suggestion here that in nearly 3 out of 4 cases reported to the police in the CRC's survey, not only were the victims dissatisfied with the police response they were also critical of their racism and insensitivity. Police racism is seen by some as a highly contentious issue, yet it would be irresponsible to ignore it where it is advanced as a debilitating factor in peoples' experiences. Often it compounds the initial traumas induced by the impact of racial harassment itself. An example of this was described to us by Harry Cohen, MP for Leyton:

> In a local case a mother who had suffered on-going harassment from local children on the way to and from school with her own children, was physically assaulted by a fifteen year old white girl. The victim stated that she was then racially abused by the police when they came to her home. They took her to the police station, held her in a cell and questioned her for four hours before her release. They treated her like the culprit not the victim and this approach is not uncommon.

Experiences like these point to how police insensitivity and racism can contribute to the vast under-reporting in the Borough. This was also suggested by Mr Cohen: 'Local people have told me that they have suffered racial harassment but have not bothered to report it because they feel there is "no point"'. Attitudes like this reveal that major difficulties are associated with the experience of reporting racial harassment to the police, even for those who still retain some faith in the prospect of a sensitive and effective response. For example, a local Councillor in his evidence expressed the belief that the police were no longer 'indifferent' but felt that while some people 'have the courage to talk to the police and still hope that something will follow (.......) many have lost confidence through visiting the police a countless number of times and no notice has been taken'. In addition our analysis suggests that the police appear to be oblivious to the nature of these anxieties.

Another, recurrent, theme in the evidence was the treatment of young Black men by the police. This is not often considered as a specific form of racial harassment, but it was highlighted by many witnesses, most noticeably the organizations representing African-Caribbean interests. The Afro-Caribbean Supplementary Education Service wrote the following:

> We are concerned about the relationship between the police and the Afro-Caribbean community. Our experiences suggest that young Afro-Caribbean males suffer an increased risk of being unduly stopped, questioned, searched and, in some cases, assaulted by the police. This harassment is most likely to take place when the youths travel to or from clubs/pubs or whenever groups of youths meet to socialise.

It is important to acknowledge that some sections of the community experience the police as perpetrators of racial harassment. While this view may be discounted by the police, there is surely something wrong where people perceive themselves routinely to be on the *receiving end* of police power and authority and are dissuaded from approaching this agency for help or assistance. At least this is the view of the Joint Council of Afro-Caribbean Organizations (JCACO) who informed us that:

> There is the added problem - that in some cases, it is the statutory agencies themselves that Afro-Caribbeans should seek help from, who perpetuate racial harassment.

This was a direct reference to the police, it exposed further complexity in the nature of reporting cases of racial harassment, the implications of this were clearly underlined by the JCACO:

> In a situation where it is a body such as the police who are accused of racial harassment, there needs to be an independent body who would investigate the incident and would be empowered to punish the individuals involved.

In this context it can be seen that the failure of some African-Caribbean people to report incidents of racial harassment arises because complaints against the police are investigated by the police themselves. This problem is already widely recognized as one which damages the public's confidence in the police generally (see Lustgarten, 1986; Maguire and Corbett, 1991). But where the police are implicated themselves as perpetrators of racial harassment the problem is even more acute because the victims initially have no one to turn to. Local confidence in the police is shaped by the nature and extent of negative experiences and these are a crucial barometer of whether a satisfactory police response is available for victims of racial harassment.

## Lost confidence in the police?

The Metropolitan police's claim at the end of the 1980s to perceive *a lack of awareness* among victims of racial harassment to report matters to the police is entirely inconsistent with our findings. As our Inquiry's evidence demonstrates the experience of reporting racial harassment in Waltham Forest was an uninspiring one and in many instances was deeply frustrating. It is apparent to us that people do recognize the importance of reporting these experiences to the police principally because they have no other means of defending themselves or of seeking redress. But the experience of reporting itself is often an intense disappointment. There is a prominent view among some Asian and Black people that there is no point in bringing their complaints of harassment to the attention of local agencies because nothing will be done *and it is clear that this view is based upon personal experience* (see Chapter 5). The evidence also suggests that when reports of racial harassment are made and are recorded, getting beyond that juncture is another difficulty. Moreover the victims may well find they expose themselves to further abuse from the very agencies who are supposed to help. These experiences tend to catalyze a reduction of confidence in the capacity of local agencies (especially the police) to take effective action. For example the Walthamstow constituency Labour Party, following consultations with Asian people in the Lloyd Park and Higham Hill wards, wrote in evidence to the Inquiry:

> Of those who contacted us, few Asians seem to have any confidence that the police can protect them or seriously investigate complaints of racial harassment made to them.

This raises serious questions concerning the police's own perceptions of their response to racial harassment. How is it possible for the police to express complete satisfaction in their provision of a service to racial harassment victims without even the hint of a qualification? Our evidence suggests that the perception of local agencies generally as providers of an effective response was quite low. The Waltham Forest CRC commenting on the results of its survey wrote in evidence:

> The survey also demonstrates a lack of confidence in both the local authority and the police in providing adequate support and protection againt racial harassment.

As the publicly perceived lead-agency the police undoubtedly attract the roughest edges of criticism, yet it is important to appreciate that these criticisms have evolved out of lengthy experiences, they appear to be firmly linked to 'racial victimization scenarios' (see Chapter 5) which have shaped the recent history of the Borough. We were informed by the Bangalee Women's Welfare Project that they would expect the police to provide support for victims *but also* that they 'don't have trust in the police'. Although they continued to make referrals to the police, they felt the police 'take a long time to come' and that the police 'don't take Asian people seriously'. This view was quite common. In addition the evidence often suggested that where victims developed a lack of confidence in the police's response to racial harassment, this lack of confidence was sometimes extended to other potential areas of police involvement, for example, the reporting of burglary. It needs to be said, it is not the Asian and Black communities awareness of the police as an agency capable of taking action which is questionable, *on the contrary what is in fact questionable is the awareness and responsiveness of the police where racial harassment is reported.* The continuing source of dissatisfaction with the police resides in the disheartening experience of making abortive reports. There is however one further implication here which directly concerns us, this is the status of racial harassment as a crime and its recognition as a legitimate aspect of competent police work.

## The status of racial harassment as a crime

What does it mean when the police fail to respond effectively even when perpetrators are clearly identified by victims of racial harassment? This question almost more than anything else requires that we consider the factors involved in police investigation. For example, in addition to the issues of insensitivity and racism discussed above, is it possible that the legal framework and organizational approach of policing militates against the serious examination of racial harassment? In order to assess this it is worth re-iterating in summary the main criticisms of police investigations which emerged from the evidence. These were:

* The police do not treat racial harassment seriously (i.e. as crime).

* Where the police do respond there is no follow-up.

* The police do not take action against perpetrators.

* The response of the police is not encouraging.

* The police do not provide support.

* The police treat the victims as the problem.

Taken together these criticisms suggest that the police on the ground do not see the tackling of racial harassment as an important part of police work. Before discussing whether there is a legal or organizational basis for this, it is worth examining related findings from recent Home Office research (Seagrave, 1989) which provide an interesting if contradictory picture. According to this national study, 70% of racial incidents reported to the police were dealt with by an immediate visit from a police officer; 85% of victims had a response within a hour of the report being made and 96% within three hours. In each of these instances the common police response was to interview the victims and offer advice. However, in addition to this Seagrave reveals that in only 25% of cases was a suspect questioned while an arrest was made in 17% of cases.

70

Furthermore, two weeks after the incident was reported a suspect had been charged in 16% of cases and 45% of cases produced no leads or suspects. Finally because of 'insufficient or no evidence three out of ten of all cases initially defined as possibly racially motivated were no longer being treated as such' (Seagrave, op. cit.). What these findings suggest is that the police have a high initial response rate to the victims of racial harassment and comparatively, an extremely low rate of effective action against the perpetrators. In other words *the police are not very successful in investigating racial harassment as a crime.* While this is also true of other crimes (e.g. burglary), a fundamental difference is that victims of racial harassment may well know who the perpetrators are (at least by sight), particularly where victimization is sustained.

As we have already pointed out the crimes involved in racial harassment are usually brought to the attention of the police by the victims themselves. Initially therefore it is rarely a question of police officers 'detecting' the existence of a crime. What perhaps is most crucial to understand is that when a police officer does arrive, there are two main points of contention. These are, whether the police officer, even if he/she accepts the victim's description of the events, will recognize racial harassment as a criminal matter; and secondly, assuming it is accepted that a crime has been committed, whether the police officer will recognize it as racial harassment. Prior to either of these situations the police officer must accept wholly or in part the victim's testimony of what has occurred. In common with the public reporting of crime generally there are several intermediate dimensions which determine whether the initial experience of crime is eventually processed as a basis for a prosecution. But where racial harassment is concerned these dimensions seem to be more problematic and circuitous, it is as if they represent hurdles which need to be jumped, at a pace and height set by less than encouraging police officers. It is likely that public foreknowledge of this dissuades many from reporting their experiences to the police. For all victims of racial harassment this first stage has to be overcome. It may be a difficult process of *negotiation* with the police before a case of racial harassment has the chance of being recorded as a crime. Figure 2.1 below describes the dimensions of police/public 'negotiation' where the status of racial harassment as a crime is in question.

| Category | Explanation | Consequence |
| --- | --- | --- |
| (a) Public criticism of the police | Police are perceived not to treat racial harassment seriously | Non-reporting |
| (b) Police blaming the victims | Victims are perceived as fabricating complaints | Non-recording |
| (c) No-criming | Police decide not to treat the complaint as a crime | Non-recording |
| (d) Other-criming | Police decide to treat the complaint as a crime other than racial harassment | Non-recording |
| (e) Crime report | Police agree with the victim's interpretation | Recorded crime statistic |

**Figure 2.1: Dimensions in police/public 'negotiation' in the recording of racial harassment as a crime**

We can see from Figure 2.1 that before a report or public complaint of racial harassment is processed as a crime, there are a number of circumstances which may intervene to prevent this. With the exception of the role of the public in not reporting cases (category a) there are at least three other ways in which the response of the police themselves *may* lead to racial harassment not being recorded as a crime (categories b-d). It is not possible to say what proportion of racial harassment cases are non-recorded in these ways, but it is clear that there is a range of options available in which racial harassment is *not* treated as a crime. It is equally clear from the experience of those reporting incidents to the police in Waltham Forest, that the local police all too readily avail themselves of these options. This potential for non-recording is heightened by the fact that once a case has been reported (category b onwards) the powers of the police may only be invoked at the discretion of the police officer *in situ.* Obviously, a great deal will turn on the police officer's understanding of the issues involved and the extent to which he/she is familiar with or committed to the emphasis placed by the Force and division on tackling racial harassment.

The police, however, appear to be unwilling to acknowledge that the accurate recording of incidents as crimes may be subverted by these alternative ways of dealing with reports. Indeed, there appears to be an assumption that the process of reporting and recording incidents is an essentially unproblematic prospect for victims; and that eventual recording is an inevitable outcome of reporting in these cases (category e). The frustrating dimensions of the 'negotiation' we outline in Figure 2.1 account in part for the public perception that the police do not treat racial harassment seriously and may be a considerable contributory factor in its under reporting. Since the police highlight non-reporting as *the* major problem in attempting to deal with racial harassment, they appear to be caught in the grip of a peculiar irony in which they are unable to appreciate the degree to which they are themselves responsible for a problem they identify as their principal concern.

## Legal-organizational constraints

There are two legal-organizational constraints which set the context for the problems of police ineffectiveness, insensitivity and racism raised by our evidence. These constraints are major paradoxes in the policing of racial harassment and call into question the notion of an effective policy. The first constraint arises because racial harassment per se is not codified as a criminal offence, it is not recognized by existing law (Forbes, 1988). This startling fact requires some comment particularly as racial harassment is generally *experienced* as a crime by its victims and this same nomenclature has been used occasionally throughout this study. Popular references to racial harassment as a crime appear to encapsulate two observations: one recognizes that in civil terms it constitutes various human rights violations, many of which are specified in the European Convention on Human Rights; while the other recognizes that in the instigation of racial harassment a number of criminal law offences are often combined. This creates an obvious tension between the interpretations of those who experience racial victimization, where the sense of human rights violations may be upper most in the mind; and those of the police where strict scrutiny may be applied only to clear infractions of the domestic criminal law as a basis for action. This does not mean however, that the law is completely unhelpful where racial harassment is concerned only that it is relatively vague. According to Forbes (op. cit.) in certain circumstances 'harassment' is a criminal offence under the Protection from Eviction Act (1977) and also a minor offence under the Public Order Act (1986). Although the Public Order Act itself specifies 'incitement to racial hatred' as an offence, this cannot be prosecuted without the consent of the Attorney General. But the important point to note for our purposes is:

73

> Nowhere in the law are the two aspects of racial harassment brought together, *nor is harassment motivated by racism recognized or defined.*

> (Forbes, 1988:1; emphasis added)

This means that the law insofar as racial harassment is concerned does not facilitate effective policing in *law enforcement* terms. In order to overcome this statutory deficiency it is imperative that the police become skilled in recognizing the spread of racial harassment and committed to using the law creatively to tackle its experiential impact (see Chapter 5). As Figure 2.1 suggests this is not a straightforward process. Moreover, the realities of routine police work offer strong disincentives to responding positively to racial harassment. Not only does its recording involve duplicate police paperwork, (prior to the Force Order of 1990) but the serious investigation of a complaint appears to be wholly dependent upon whether successful prosecution is a *more than likely* outcome. A conscientious response to racial harassment then, does not reward officers for whom administration is a bureaucratic anathema and whose prior concern when hearing a complaint is its potential success, rather than its *merit,* as a court case.

It is important to reiterate the point that the absence of a specific criminal offence covering incidents of racial harassment is a *statutory deficiency*, not a reflection of their relative insignificance. Dominant perceptions of what constitutes 'crime' tend to exclude a range of behaviours manifesting various types of social injury or violation *experienced* nonetheless as criminal by its victims. As we have already suggested, the victimization of 'specific persons' is such a category, one which the police find particularly difficult to deal with. Existing law is operable only in terms of specifically identified offences which do not encompass the variegated expressions of these generic offences, therefore responding to racial harassment in the sense we are describing requires special developments in what has been described as 'police competence' (Fielding, 1988). This may be the rationale behind the Metropolitan police's Force Order. It is because the investigation of racial harassment is not a specific legal obligation for the police that specific policy directives have been designed to inform the use of individual police officer's discretion.

There is no suggestion yet, certainly not on the basis of the evidence submitted to us, that the Metropolitan police's policy has been accepted as an integral part of police work where it matters most, on the 'ground'. This is the locus of the second legal-organizational constraint. Grimshaw and Jefferson (1984, 1987) argue that the primary accountability of the police to the law

74

means that even where police policy intervenes to direct police officers attention to particular issues, this does not inevitably over-ride the judgement of individual police officers in particular circumstances. Policy in other words is not necessarily part of the police's legal mandate. Moreover the fact that racial harassment is not a specific crime consequently leaves open a wide range of options for the use of police discretion and hence to the possibilities of 'no-criming' and 'other-criming' (see Figure 2.1 above). The observations of Grimshaw and Jefferson (1987:291) are quite instructive in this context:

> At the level of the constable, the fundamental general feature of the office is the notion of constabulary independence. The crucial implication of this is to ensure that police-work is conducted within a discretionary framework since its meaning is that *particular acts of law enforcement are the responsibility of individual constables exercising their own (independent) judgement as to when the law has been broken.* This requirement to judge, without undue influence, is in constitutional terms, the guarantor of police impartiality.

> (emphasis added)

Understanding the discretionary basis upon which police powers are exercised is extremely important, particularly when matters of police policy or effectiveness are concentrating the mind. The implications this has for contested aspects of police work can be quite profound. This has been argued by Lustgarten (1986:68) who writes:

> Where failure to invoke the law is a matter of grievance, *as for example among victims of racist attacks,* there is a fundamental difficulty in that the legal process has nothing on which to get a grip. *It is very difficult to review a non-decision.*

> (emphasis added)

Lustgarten points to three major problems of accountability with the exercise of police discretion. Each of these is directly relevant to the police's approach to racial harassment incidents. First, it is police officers at the 'lowest level of the hierachy', for example junior constables, who sometimes exercise greatest discretion principally because much of what they do is unseen by their superiors. Their actions are therefore beyond the scope of assessment,

75

particularly where they have decided *not to invoke the law*. Second, because there are no effective limitations on the use of the police discretion, police officers are able to make an almost infinite choice among various possible courses of action or inaction, insofar as these are 'lawful possibilities'. Third, the fact that police officers are accountable to the law, does not invalidate the corresponding fact that often it is their 'value judgements' or social considerations which determine the readiness or effectiveness of their response. The experiences of victims of racial harassment in Waltham Forest are symptomatic of the way in which these problems conspire to produce frustrating and inappropriate police responses to racial harassment.

At least one significant implication which can be deduced from this discussion is that an effective police response to racial harassment is disproportionately dependent on the individual competence and sensitivity of particular police officers. This makes the whole notion of a viable operational policy highly questionable unless it is supported by police officers themselves. It is perhaps reasonable to suggest that some of the unregulated uses of police discretion induced by these legal-organizational constraints would be lessened if racial harassment was made a criminal offence. An unsuccessful attempt to introduce this into legalisation through the auspices of a Private Members Bill was undertaken by Harry Cohen MP in 1985 (see also Chapter 1). He explained the background to this in evidence to our Inquiry:

> It was the death of Yunis Khan's family in an arson attack in Walthamstow which led directly to my attempt to get a Racial Harassment Bill through Parliament. The first and only such Bill ever introduced. The Khan case was never resolved and demonstrated the need to make racial harassment a specific criminal offence. The police initially did not recognise a racial motive for the attack, concentrating their efforts in questioning Mr Khan's associates. The resulting message given out by those investigations was that the victim was somehow to blame. (.....).

> I introduced my Racial Harassment (Housing) Bill on 17th July, 1985, to protect defenceless families living in a state of siege and to entitle them to the right of peace and comfort in their own home. It also gave legislative powers to evict a proven racist, rather than forcing victims to flee for their own safety. My Bill was aimed to:

* Create for the first time, the criminal offence of racial harassment.

* Provide a definition of 'an act of racial harassment' and a schedule delineating such acts.

* Lay duties on the Police to conduct investigations, maintain records and publish their findings.

* Lay duties on all landlords and local authorities to inform their tenants and ratepayers of the offence and its consequences.

* Make it an offence for an officer of a 'body corporate' to connive against or neglect to deal properly with a racial harassment case.

* Enable injunctions to be sought to stop further acts of harassment occurring.

* Enable stiff fines and/or imprisonment on conviction.

* Enable perpetrators of harassment to be evicted in severe cases, including the possibility of a CPO [Criminal Prosecution Order] being instituted against a convicted racist owner-occupier.

My Bill was an important legislative attempt to do something about the issue of racial harassment.

The problems which were the focus of Harry Cohen's abortive Bill still remain. But it would be misleading to consider the assorted difficulties we have described as the mere failure to translate police policy into practice. The issues of police ineffectiveness, insensitivity and racism exacerbates an existing constitutional problem of the *slippage* between the police's legal mandate and their policy directives. In other words the tackling of racial harassment is determined by the responsiveness and competence of individual police officers use of their discretion and also the extent to which they 'own' or support police policy in this area.

## Measuring police performance

It is of course possible within a limited context to discuss the police's performance despite the legal-organizational constraints discussed above. It

77

was clear an emphatic belief prevailed among the police in Waltham Forest that their response to racial harassment was effective. As we have argued this was contradicted by virtually all the other evidence submitted to us. Some of the police's confidence in their approach appeared to be based on a 'statistical perception' of their own performance, as evidenced by local arrest and 'clear-up' figures. These form part of the 'official' picture of police performance in relation to any notifiable offences. It needs to be stressed that in general the major way in which the police become aware of crime is through reports by members of the public, especially those who have been victims (Bottomley and Pease, 1986:34). This is overwhelmingly the case where crimes of racial harassment are concerned. Therefore any arrests which occur or 'clear-ups' which are obtained are more likely to be 'victim-initiated' than 'police-initiated'. Because of the large number of racial harassment incidents which are not reported to or recorded by the police, the figures indexed to police performance represent an extremely limited 'account' of their effectiveness. In addition that 'account' is inherently problematic.

Table 2.3 below presents Chingford and Leyton police's arrest and clear-up figures for racial harassment throughout the years 1987-1989. Before we analyze these there are two comments that need to be made. First, the stated numbers of arrests does not necessarily mean that prosecutions followed or even that charges were made. Second the 'clear-up' rate, although publicized by the popular media almost as a scientific guide to the police's impact on crime is in reality more vague than this. For example, in evidence to our Inquiry, Deputy Assistant Commissioner Boreham provided the following Metropolitan police definition of a 'clear-up' where 'racial incidents' are under consideration:

> Incidents are classified as cleared-up, when the matter is *appropriately resolved*. If the incident were a crime, for instance this will be done when the offenders are charged or summoned. If it were not a matter that could be dealt with in this way, a referral of the parties to the appropriate means of resolution, such as Civil Courts or other statutory agencies (e.g. Local Authority, CRE, etc.) would indicate the matter was 'clear'. Similarly if the allegation was found to the satisfaction of the complainant and the police, to be based on a mistaken assumption, a 'clear-up' would also apply.
>
> (emphasis added)

This definition establishes clearly that not all racial incidents are treated by the police as 'crimes', a point which we discussed in detail above. In addition it highlights the wide range of discretion available to police officers when deciding whether to record an incident as a crime or to resolve it in a different way.

### Table 2.3

### Numbers and percentage of arrests and clear-ups of racial incidents in Chingford and Leyton police divisions, 1987-1989

| | Chingford | | | Leyton | | | Av. % for 1987-1989 in both divisions |
|---|---|---|---|---|---|---|---|
| | 1987 No. % | 1988 No. % | 1989 No. % | 1987 No. % | 1988 No. % | 1989 No. % | No. % |
| *Arrests* | 9(17) | 6(18) | 7(18) | 7(22) | 5(24) | 2 (6) | 6 (17) |
| *Cleared up* | 10(21) | 26(76) | 19(50) | 18(56) | 8(38) | 15 (45) | 16 (48) |
| *No. of incidents* | 48 | 34 | 38 | 32 | 21 | 33 | |

Source:  Metropolitan police evidence to the Inquiry (1989) and Metropolitan police racial incident statistics for 1989

In interpreting these figures we need to recognize that they do not indicate anything about whether the victims were satisfied with the police response or the conduct of any resulting investigation. Their focus is much narrower: they purport to show the extent to which Chingford and Leyton divisions are effective in tackling the incidents *recorded by them.* The obvious suggestion is that the higher the clear-up rate the more effective the police performance. The average arrest and clear-up rate for both divisions is similar to recent national findings (Seagrave op. cit.). But it is when comparisons are made with other crimes that one aspect of the clear-up rate's significance emerges. For example, the clear-up rate for both divisions with regard to *all offences* in 1987 and 1988 varied between 15% - 21%. It can be seen that with the exception of Chingford in 1987, the clear-up rate for racial harassment in each of the years between 1987-89 has been considerably in excess of the rate for all offences. This suggests, falsely, that the police are more successful investigating racial harassment than other crimes. The high clear-up rate however, is more likely to be an indication of the use of police discretion to resolve racial harassment cases in terms other than criminal law enforcement. The figures bear little relation to police action against perpetrators.

On the basis of a divisional comparison there is one significant difference: proportionately more recorded incidents, arrests and clear-ups took place in Chingford division. Taking the Borough as a whole during 1987-1989 the suggestion is that just under half (48%) of all cases reported to the police were cleared-up. Without a more detailed break-down of the figures it is not possible to say what specific proportion of these clear-ups were distributed among the charging/summonsing of offenders (i.e. primary clear-ups), or referrals to other organizations or identification of complaints based on mistaken assumptions (secondary clear-ups). Because of the various dimensions of a clear-up it is difficult to assess precisely the pattern of the police's response to racial harassment in law enforcement terms, although we would imagine this is quite minimal. The clear-up rate is obviously a poor measure of police performance in these matters.

We are aware that the Metropolitan police are increasingly turning to indicators of consumer satisfaction as measurements of effective service delivery. This appears to be a positive development. In the Commissioner's Annual report for 1988, Sir Peter Imbert (1989) wrote:

> any organization should pause from time to time, to examine its purpose and style, it should take stock of the environment in which it is operating and ask its customers - and itself - whether the service it is providing meets expectations.

It is precisely this proposition which needs to be applied to the experiences not only of victims of racial harassment, but also to those communities affected by it. Although we accept that the Chingford police organized a survey of 18 victims in 1988, who for the most part were satisfied with the service they received from the police, the question is of course *how sufficient* is a limited survey of this nature; and equally importantly, how are the radically different experiences conveyed to us during this Inquiry to be accounted for? A close look at divisional policies on racial harassment yields some enlightening if surprising answers to this question. In fact the way in which such policies are formulated suggest that success is almost a presumed outcome in the construction of local police divisional objectives.

80

## An analysis of police divisional policies

Since the latter half of the 1980s the Metropolitan police divisions have produced reports which describe the incidence of crime in the division, any noteworthy initiatives undertaken by the police in that division and also set out a number of objectives (usually four) which are reviewed in the following year's divisional report. In Chapter 1 we saw how 1985 was one of the Borough's most tempestuous years as far as racial harassment was concerned, it is interesting to note therefore the different observations made by the divisions a year later. The 1986 Leyton divisional report emphasized its improved system of recording racial incidents:

> This system identifies at an earlier stage areas of tension. It also provides a visual display of the location and type of racial incident for officers being briefed for duty. Police involvement has increased and many cases although of a relatively minor nature in relation to the actual incidents, are concerned to be of major importance due to their racial connotations. Home Beat Officers have been tasked with following up and ensuring that the victims of these occurrences are reassured and given all assistance possible.

In contrast the 1986 Chingford divisional report highlighted the following:

> This Division has always sought to achieve good relationships with local Ethnic Minorities and generally these have been maintained. However, police are mindful of the destabilising effects of criminal behaviour in which there has been some element of racial motivation. In some cases this racial motivation is self-evident, but in others the evidence is unclear and sometimes definition is made impossible because of insufficient evidence. However, a much more liberal interpretation is now applied to offences which may have racist overtones in order that proper priority may be given to investigations of these serious matters.

What both perspectives have in common however, is a strongly expressed *conviction* of the division's capacity to respond to racial harassment effectively. An analysis of the subsequent yearly divisional reports (1987-1989) reveals the unambiguous image of the police's approach continually being enhanced in a completely uncritical climate. Yet this is clearly at variance with experiences of victimization discussed by us in this study.

In addition it is interesting to note that despite the recent history of the Borough, the Chingford and Leyton police divisions have not always featured racial harassment as an objective that particularly required their attention. During the period 1986-1989 the reports of each division both announced racial harassment as one of the divisional objectives, on two out of a possible four occasions. For the year 1989 neither division specified racial harassment as a divisional objective (see Figures 2.2A and B).

| Year | Objective | Strategy |
|------|-----------|----------|
| 1986 | 'Enhancing the corporate approach to racial incidents' | 'involving all members of society in a concentrated and co-ordinated move towards increasing awareness in relation to racial incidents' |
| 1987 | 'To increase the detection of racial incidents' | 'liaise closely with the Community Relations Council, the Borough Community Officers and Ethnic Minority Groups' |
| 1988 | (N.b. No explicit objective, was recognized as part of the Force Goal) | N/A |
| 1989 | (N.b. As above - in addition: 'We will continue to encourage the victims of racial attacks (...) to have greater confidence in us') | N/A |

**Figure 2.2A: Leyton divisional objectives regarding racial harassment, 1986-1989**
Source: Leyton divisional reports, 1986-1989

| Year | Objective | Strategy |
|------|-----------|----------|
| 1986 | (N.b. Racial harassment did not feature as an objective) | N/A |
| 1987 | 'To improve community involvement in the investigation of racial incidents' | 'The development of such groups as the Racial Incidents Panel will be combined with enlisting the involvement of other groups not formally concerned with the problem. Such groups would include Neighbourhood Watch Schemes, Victim Support Schemes, Tenants and Residents Associations' |
| 1988 | 'To further improve the quality of service provided by the police to victims of racial incidents' | Combination of 'improved level of investigation already established' and 'increased contact with the victims, to support and assist them either directly or by referral to other agencies e.g. Victim Support Schemes' |
| 1989 | (N.b. Not made a specific objective, but included in local priorities) | 'investigation and the support of the victims will remain a high priority without the need to feature as a divisional objective' |

**Figure 2.2B: Chingford divisional objectives regarding racial harassment, 1986-1989**
Source: Chingford divisional reports, 1986-1989

It is ironic that during the same year the Metropolitan police sought to emphasize the importance of tackling racial harassment in a high profile campaign (see earlier sections), the police in Waltham Forest were scaling down the level of their own publicized commitment. Even in mere public relations terms, the demotion of racial harassment from an explicit to an implicit objective carried with it misleading connotations that either the issue was no longer an issue or had been contained and redressed effectively.[2] Even this still managed to leave questions concerning the basis and viability of the initiatives that have been variously proclaimed by the Waltham Forest police over the years.

*Divisional objectives : rational management?*

Divisional police initiatives operate within the wider context of policing by objectives (see Weatheritt, 1986), a supposedly rational approach to developing policy and assessing performance adopted by the Metropolitan police as a whole. The theory however, has been constrained by a less than satisfactory practice which, in Waltham Forest, was distinguished by the inability of the police either to assess thoroughly the identified problem, or to move coherently through a process of developing and evaluating their response. On this basis there are at least four specific problems raised by the issues we have highlighted which we need to examine, *assuming that the divisional objectives are real priorities and not just for public consumption.*

*Choice* The first concerns the basis upon which divisional objectives are chosen. This is important because in effect (if not in theory) the objectives explicity chosen by the police as priorities for their division 'stand out' publicly as matters that warrant their special attention. Although it may be argued by the police that divisional objectives emerge from a process of consultation with the 'local community' (or more precisely the individuals and organizations represented on the Police Liaison Consultative Group); it is not clear why racial harassment was chosen as an objective in some years and not in others *unless these decisions were made solely by the police, or the Police Liaison Consultative Group was distinctly unrepresentative of local Asian, Black and Ethnic Minority opinion.* The police's deletion of racial harassment from the divisional objectives in 1989 represented *a serious error of judgement.* No matter how unintentional, it could have been construed as a signal to the victims *and* perpetrators of racial harassment that this crime was no longer of major significance to the police. Having said this of course much depends on whether it is accepted that the issue of racial harassment, as implied by the police, was a diminished or diminishing problem in the Borough.

*Formulation* Our second concern is with the way in which particular objectives for the division are formulated in relation to a particular issue or crime. The objectives which have focused on racial harassment in both Leyton and Chingford (see Figures 2.2A and B) appear to have no consistent or strategic rationale in terms of racial victimization *as it was actually experienced in the Borough.* For example, one of the common complaints reported to us was that the police fail to take action against perpetrators (the longevity of this complaint should be apparent given the time-period covered by this study). Furthermore it was evident to us that particular locales (e.g. electoral wards, clusters of streets, etc.) and places (e.g. housing estates) had historically become associated with racial victimization. On this basis alone a consistent (i.e. necessarily regular) and strategic (i.e. incorporates relevant local data) objective would require an explicit commitment to identify and respond to the entrenchment and patterns of racial harassment, or what we describe as its *spread* (see Chapter 4). The absence of a clear divisional objective like this throughout the 1980s defies credibility.

*Strategy selection* Thirdly the *strategy* invariably selected by the police to tackle their racial harassment objectives (whatever their particular formulation) had been some form of community involvement or liaison. Although on the face of things these are quite useful and practical ideas, we need to ask *what real relationship do these 'strategies' or methods have to their objectives?* This is an important question. As we have seen there are choices to be made between different formulations of divisional objectives, a similar criterion can be applied to the choice of methods. An example from Chingford division should suffice to illustrate this point. In 1987 Chingford police expressed the view that community involvement in the investigation of racial incidents should be improved and specified, inter-alia, 'groups not formally concerned with the problem', for example Neighbourhood Watch Schemes, Victims Support Schemes, Tenants and Residents Associations. Assuming for the moment that the way the objective is designed is rational, can the same be said about the strategy? The roles of Neighbourhood Watch, the Victim Support Scheme and the majority of tenants/residents associations in the Borough were socially distant from any concerns with the issues of racial harassment. To transform aspects of their established practices in the manner envisaged by the police would require extensive policy developments and community work. Yet none of this was discussed, highlighted or even mentioned by the Chingford police. The prospect of the strategy being successfully implemented, had the appearence of being assumed a fait accompli; and as we discuss below the absence of any proper evaluation of these methods by the police in subsequent divisional reports *reinforced the impression of relevant objectives and strategies being accomplished and implemented almost as a matter of course.* Despite this, the major issue which requires serious examination is what the police mean by 'community involvement in investigation'. Phrases like these are outwardly obscure and correspondingly difficult to define or measure. Does it mean supplying the police with information, if so, what sort of information? Does it mean getting organizations to carry out their own investigations? Does it mean developing strategies for raising public awareness? Or does it mean all of these things? The point is strategies need to be clear in order to enable us all to understand not only what, but how things are being tackled.

*Assessment*   In addition to this however, we need to have some idea of how the performance of the police, in terms of how the relationship between the declared strategy and objective, *is to be measured.* This is the fourth area of the divisional objectives which concerns us. The police divisional reports (1987-1989) commented unfailingly on improvements in their performance. Although this is a necessary component of a *criteria of assessment,* it is not sufficient by itself. A more independent measure is required which bears a real and relevant relationship to the objective and strategy of the division's approach to racial harassment. This would allow for a clear public evaluation of the police's impact. For example, let us suppose, that through some form of *public* discussion, the objectives of either division were being formulated with regard to racial harassment, a specification which could redress the concerns we have expressed so far might look something like Figure 2.3 below.

Objective:

> To identify and respond to the spread of racial harassment in the division.

Strategy:

> (a)   Directed patrolling which covers specified locales (e.g. electoral wards) and places (e.g. streets, housing estates, etc.)
>
> (b)   Ensuring that all police officers are conscious of the divisional objective.
>
> (c)   Ensure that police officers in (a) above are familiar with the latest analysis of crime patterns and trends in racial harassment.
>
> (d)   Involve officers in (a) in developing or contributing to the analysis in (c).
>
> (e)   Where possible initiate charges against perpetrators of racial harassment and publicize successful cases, and disseminate information regarding support provisions.

Performance measure(s):

> *   Evaluation and reports of the impact of directed patrolling [see (a) above].
>
> *   Monitoring of victim's satisfaction with the police response [see (b) above].

* Production of trends, patterns and analyses available in police stations and public information places, together with the names and/or observations of officers engaged in directed patrolling [see (c) and (d) above].

* Publication of cases (e.g. in the press) of successful prosecutions and number of cases recorded [see (e) above].

**Figure 2.3: Model of a police divisional objective in relation to racial harassment and a criteria of assessment**

Admittedly the objective specified in Figure 2.3 is quite detailed. It may be argued that insufficient police resources exist to justify such an approach or that perhaps it could be divided into two objectives and implemented in stages. Clearly there are various ways in which the formulations of the objective, strategy and performance measure could be modified or amended. In addition it would need to be agreed in practical terms what would be the precise format of the strategy and performance measures as well as estimating personnel requirements.

The significance of all this however is that these are issues which could benefit from public discussion and it *is the principle of this criteria of assessment which opens up the possibilities, currently they do not exist.* Examined in this way, the divisional objectives which include racial harassment, would improve our knowledge and understanding of racial victimization in a Borough like Waltham Forest. We should not forget however, that the issues we have discussed at length here are issues of policy and not of law, therefore they will still be subject to the legal-organizational constraints which supply the context of individual police officer's discretionary use of police powers.

*Yet another paradox*

But there is a further problem affecting the approach we have suggested which needs to be rectified. It is unclear what status the divisional report has with police officers who are not senior management or indeed the extent to which it actually does shape the initiatives undertaken by the police. For example it was suggested by Leyton division in 1987 that Home Beat officers are tasked with paying attention to racial harassment on their Beats, but in the subsequent year's reports there was no mention of this. The idea, although in one sense attractive, is in another paradoxical: Home Office research on this form of 'directed patrolling' found that many of the police officers interviewed 'appeared to have little idea of policy at divisional level' (Burrows and Lewis, 1988:39); while an earlier study by Ness in 1985 (see ibid.) found that 83% of officers had no knowledge of force objectives and half did not even know whether their own divisions had any plans. According to Ness,

> If policemen (sic) are to forgo reactive policing in favour of directed patrolling in support of objectives, they will constantly have to be informed of those objectives, above all convinced of their meaning, their importance and the vital part they have to play in pursuit of them - both individually and as a team.

This is particulary important, but can only take place if relevant information and relevant objectives are being developed. *Moreover it is unclear what information on racial harassment is given to police officers on patrol.* In their evidence the Metropolitan police presented no analysis of trends or patterns despite their detailed collation of information; this suggests that the information or instructions provided to police officers are rarely 'derived from systematic analysis of crime patterns or trends' (Burrows and Lewis, op. cit.:41). Nevertheless there may be some *mileage* in the approach we are suggesting, it might go someway perhaps to balancing out the deficiencies. In the absence of a change in the law to make racial harassment a specific criminal offence and an accompanying change in the discretionary basis of the exercise of police powers, only limited adjustments seem possible. But in this heavily circumscribed policy context a positive police divisional strategy may begin to prise open the prevailing log jam.

## Facing the future

Though the 1980s saw racial harassment for the first time being considered as an issue for a serious and committed Metropolitan police response, the decade failed to deliver that response. In Waltham Forest, the police's inability even to begin to make sense of the contexts in which racial harassment presented itself locally, was a failing second only to their disastrous record in handling investigations and initial reports. The evidence analyzed in our research was replete with criticisms of the way in which the police conducted investigations into racial harassment. But as well as being dismissive of these criticisms, it is

88

clear that the police were blind to the way in which their own procedural conduct at the initial point of contact with victims itself discouraged reporting and therefore confounded their attempts to accurately record the incidence of these crimes. Their heavy reliance upon arrest and clear up rates as a measure of their performance served to sustain the illusion that public satisfaction could be presumed as a consequence of favourable statistics rather than experiential 'facts'. This, in part, may be seen as a consequence of managerial directives which attempted to raise police consciousness on issues of effectiveness and efficiency. However the greater emphasis on corporate effectiveness which characterized the organizational thrust of Metropolitan police policy through the 1980s tended, arguably, to make a fetish of 'results' at the expense of more considered, coherent approaches to specific policing problems. Hence the absence of specific performance measures in divisional objectives, allowing these statements of intent to become self-fulfilling prophecies of success.

In terms of stimulating, let alone developing, innovative responses to those occurrences which did not conform to the dominant perception of a 'crime', it may be that the abiding preoccupation with cost effectiveness as an organizational principle has been an abiding obstruction. In terms of conventional crime categories racial harassment seems to have a relatively low statistical incidence. Consequently in an organization driven by narrow statistical concerns, racial harassment commands a low prioritization (notwithstanding divisional or Force objectives) which therefore elicits only a restricted service provision. The irony of this procedural logic is that public recognition of this restricted service provision can in turn provoke a poor reporting rate. Thus a cycle is established and perpetuated by the fixity of police evaluative criteria. The task facing the police requires both a radical shift in perspective and a qualitative change in operations. The police, do not yet appear to be receptive to such an approach, in spite of an ostensible commitment to the rationality of policing by objectives. Further as Weatheritt (1986:122) has argued:

> If rational analysis is to be more than a fig leaf, the police service as a whole will have to begin to understand its discipline more adequately than it seems to do already and begin to take on its habits of thought. This is unlikely to happen readily in a culture deeply devoted to action and its rewards.

It is far too easy for policy, however well intentioned, simply to attach its focus to the surface of the problem. A realistic police response to racial harasssment can only be achieved if policy is assiduously fashioned to fit the distinctive profile it manifests in various localities. If they are to be effective then, the police cannot continue to consider questions of racial harssment in isolation from their own role in reinforcing *and* failing to perceive its contextuality.

## Notes

1. These and other measures were announced in the public document 'Working Together for Racial Harmony' (December, 1990). Although containing some welcome initiatives (e.g. installation of attack alarms; computer marking of previously attacked premises), their status as distinct from the stipulations associated with the 1990 Metropolitan police Order was unclear. Sir Peter Imbert's foreword to the document, which provided a Statement of Intent regarding racial harassment, also revealed that it did not in fact carry a duty for divisions to operate them:

> These intentions have to be translated into action and it
> is very much hoped that the ensuing guidance will assist
> in achieving this objective.

The inauspicious fate of previous guidelines on racial harassment however can hardly inspire confidence for directives whose status is anything less than an imperative. A more fundamental concern perhaps was the conceptual basis from which the document derived its impetus. Its emphasis on reporting; on 'situational' crime prevention as detailed in its Racial Harassment Guides; and on the efficacy of Racial Incidents Panels, suggested that there had been no stringent assessment of inherently problematic conceptions (see below). Moreover, notions of 'racial harmony' and 'community spirit', even when accompanied by what appeared to be a newly determined resolve to be seen to enforcing the law, are at best vague invocations which, even as admirable aims, are sufficiently indeterminate for the problem of racial harassment to continue to be diagnosed as a simple failure to 'bring people of differing social and cultural backgrounds together' or to 'integrate and welcome the visible minorities' (Metropolitan police, 1990a).

2. In the 1990 and 1991 divisional reports there was no discussion of racial harassment.

# 3 Policy analysis : The local Council

*Barnor Hesse and Dhanwant K. Rai with the assistance of Paul McGilchrist and Masood Lone*

> If the Council put its foot down 80% of racial harassment would disappear.
>
> > (Evidence to the Inquiry, 1989)

> The Council doesn't do anything.
>
> > (Evidence to the Inquiry, 1989)

> Much of the work being done by local authorities is to fill a perceived gap in law enforcement left by the failure of the police in some areas to take effective action against those responsible for racial harassment.
>
> > (Forbes, 1988:4)

The local authority is in many respects the institution best placed to develop the most comprehensive strategic impact on racial harassment. This of course also requires that the police as the main 'front-line' agency are responding effectively. Certainly evidence to our Inquiry indicated that the local authority was regarded as an alternative to the police when victims of racial harassment were anxious to report the experience. Moreover, it was clear that Council tenants expected the Housing department to tackle racial harassment on the estates. Yet in order to understand the context of the problems posed by the local council in Waltham Forest, it will be necessary to take a detour through a pathway of issues that perplexed local government generally in the 1980s. Against this background then, the aim of this Chapter will be to identify the route of Waltham Forest Council's failure to respond to the inadequacies of its efforts to tackle racial harassment.

# The local government context

In general terms the initial local government recognition of racial harassment as a policy issue took place in public sector housing. Consequently local authority housing departments increasingly took the lead in the policy field throughout the 1980s. It was only during the latter half of the decade that the needs of racial harassment victims in private sector housing, educational establishments or other areas of Council provision (e.g. Social Services) became the focus of policy discussions. During this whole period a few advice agencies and a great many Asian, Black and Ethnic Minority organizations in the voluntary sector were active as advocates on behalf of racial harassment victims and as pressure groups on the statutory agencies. All of this contributed to a vast but uneven policy debate where the urgency to respond in immediate or practical terms sometimes resulted in local authorities adopting the latest ideas on offer rather than the best available. Moreover, a detailed examination of the spread of racial harassment in the local authority jurisdiction or the experiences of racial victimization hardly figured as an influential basis for the initiatives that eventually became policy. It was quite exceptional for local authorities either to sponsor or commission research into local racial harassment and they were therefore disturbingly reliant on limited data drawn from elsewhere, much of which had not been collected for their specific requirements.

In spatial terms at least, it can be argued that the relevance of the provision of public sector housing is that to an extent it 'manages' the environmental landscape of the social relations of the people housed and 'shapes' the settings for patterns of social inter-action in those locales. Housing location also establishes a social relationship to the immediate geography. For example, patterns of use of local resources such as shopping facilities, parks; patterns of local travel to work or school and so on. The local authority, through its housing allocations policies, can place people in estates according to particular management criteria, (e.g. child density, ethnic composition, family sizes). This in turn may depend on resources available in the estate (e.g. play areas, meeting places, housing sizes). Within this social environment, the problem of racial harassment is experienced *locationally* and therefore needs to be addressed as well as these other social experiences which disperse the potential of racial victimization throughout many areas of every day life. How the local authority tackles this is extremely important, *but first it must be recognized*. The perspectives from which racial harassment is viewed, the policies chosen and the commitment to implementation and evaluation will determine the extent to which the problem is recognized. Once the spread of racial harassment is seriously considered as a spatial phenomenon, the problem of policy should also be recognized as the problem of various agencies responses. There are however a number of problems traditionally associated with local authority responses in this context that require specific mention.

## Some problems associated with Council policy implementation

The trend of Council policies to address racial harassment on local authority estates, has given scant regard to private sector housing or to other contexts of service provison. Even the housing department policies which have ranged from mere statements of intent to detailed guidelines, do not seem to have tackled racial harassment. It would be tempting to conclude summarily that 'the main problems, . . . (are) identified with implementation rather than policies themselves' (London Borough of Camden, 1988). But this ignores all too easily the relevance of how policies are developed. Often they are not based on locally identified patterns of racial harassment and are formulated without the necessary consultation with the relevant staff. This has resulted in policies that are not specifically related to the local experiences of victimization or to the work culture of the organization. These two factors are extremely important in the development of policies which respond to racial harassment over time and across locations in the particular administrative space of the local authority.

Having said this there are of course many reasons why policies on racial harassment are not implemented in local government. Policies that make sweeping statements about their intent, without providing additional procedural guidelines with clearly identified responsibilities will always obscure the relationship between policy and action. It has not always been clear how actions will be carried out and by whom. Racial harassment has been dealt with as a marginal problem, accorded low priority and delegated only to specialist staff. Although it is important that racial harassment has its own clearly defined policy responses, these should be developed with other policies and integrated into the procedural work patterns of the organization, particularly those involving staff who deal directly with public complaints and problems, and those who have a responsibility to ensure these are dealt with.

This leads us to consider another regular omission in some policies on racial harassment, that is, training for staff. Failure to identify training for staff who are assumed to implement the policies, equally fails the staff by not enabling them to be clear what their role is. Training is crucial, it should provide not only information about the policies and how they are to be implemented, but it should also develop the skills of personnel whose responsibility it would be to deal with the different aspects of the policy. It is also vitally important that staff are knowledgeable about the division and/or hierachy of responsibilities involved in implementing aspects of the policy. In addition, the absence of effective communication channels between personnel in the same department and with other departments easily leads to a crisis in the implementation of policy. Similarly, lack of co-operation with other agencies, may lead policies into crisis in other areas. A typical example is, when a policy states that support is available for the victim from other agencies or community groups, without clearly establishing, who would provide it, in what circumstances and for how long. These anomalies not only exacerbate experiences of racial victimization but drag local agencies and community organizations into thorough disrepute.

At the minimum, a carefully considered planned response is required, but what also needs to be developed are *adequate measures of policy performance*. These are the key to an *effective* performance. The rationale behind recording racial harassment, monitoring cases and evaluating outcomes therefore needs to be the focus of detailed discussion. This too requires clearly stated responsibilities allocated to specified personnel. This is a traditional realm of neglect, it has generally resulted in local authorities producing non-systematic evaluations of policies on racial harassment. The production of racial harassment statistics has often been made without an accompanying policy analysis. For example, it is extremely difficult for policies to be evaluated by statistics, which in themselves, have little meaning because they are presented in a manner which is unrelated to specific questions of location. In this sense policies need to be evaluated against the *spread of racial harassment* in order to assess whether objectives are being achieved and to identify gaps or necessary revisions in practices, local agency co-operation, procedures, training, information and so on. As we shall see, throughout the 1980s Waltham Forest Council persistently failed to come to terms with this level and quality of organization.

## Council words evade action

In October 1981, three months after the murder of the Khan family the Council's Housing Committee discussed a report concerned with racial harassment on housing estates. This however was not a direct response to the Borough's experiences during the year (see Chapter 1). It appears to have arisen following the publication of the Commission for Racial Equality's report 'Racial Harassment on Local Authority Housing Estates'. The action, eventually agreed by the full Council, contained a range of initiatives that have formed the basis of its approach ever since:

94

* Racial harassment was recognized as a serious phenomenon separate and distinct from ordinary vandalism.

* Opposition was expressed to acts of racial harassment and to the underlying racist attitude.

* Support was expressed for in-house training for all staff concerning good race relations.

* The importance of tenants associations in combating racism and harassment was recognized.

* Endorsement and publicity was to be given to the role of the estate officer as the first point of contact for victims of racial harassment.

* Responsibility for monitoring and co-ordinating information and statistics was to be included in the duties of a senior officer in the Housing department.

* Endorsement was to be given to the action of the officers Housing Panel in considering transfer requests where racial harassment was proven to the Panel's satisfaction.

* Area based records of racial harassment cases were to be kept.

* Arrangements for repairs and the removal of graffiti were to be carried out quickly in racial harassment cases.

Since 1981 the main focus of the Council's response to racial harassment had been directed at Housing estates. This obscured the fact that many of the serious incidents which resulted in community pressure on the Council did not occur on high density estates, indeed a high proportion of the arson attacks involved properties in the private/owner occupied sector. An obvious example was the murder of the Khan family. Observations like this provide a clue to understanding the sense of the Council's initial attempts to respond to racial harassment; *they do not appear to have been based upon a detailed examination of the problems in the Borough.* Despite the apparent value of the proposed initiatives, it needs to be recognized that they were announced at a time when there was immense public pressure on the Council to be seen to be doing something about a problem that had catapulted the Borough to national media attention. By the end of the year grave doubts were being raised about the implementation or effectiveness of these measures.

In 1982 the Council decided to maintain 'ethnic' records of applications for Council housing, allocations and transfers. The information for the ethnic record was based upon voluntary self-classification. By 1984 the Council had secured Home Office funding for two Community Housing officer posts (in the Estates division), part of whose responsibility was to monitor and respond to racial harassment on Council housing estates. Whatever the status of the Council's commitment to its policies, by 1985 it was coming under renewed public criticism. 1985 was a year of burgeoning racist violence and arson attacks in the Borough amidst a range of inept responses from statutory agencies. In July a special meeting of the Council's Housing Committee was held to discuss 'Racial harassment on housing estates'. Representatives of the Commission for Racial Equality were invited to participate. The issues emphasized (and in some instances re-emphasized) in that meeting illustrated the nature of the criticisms levelled at the Council:

* There was a need for a clearer definition of racial harassment.

* The role of Estates officers and Tenants Liaison officers in dealing with racial harassment needed further development, together with the provision of appropriate 'in-house' training.

* A wider liaison with the community generally on all aspects of harassment needed to be maintained.

* The conditions of tenancy should be considered in terms of all forms of anti-social behaviour as grounds for obtaining possession and not restricted to racial harassment.

* Consideration should be given to the feasibility of maintaining a record of perpetrators of racist offences, including non-Council tenants.

* A previous Council decision associated with publicity material on the issue of harassment in appropriate ethnic minority languages should be pursued.

* The time taken for the Council to respond to complaints should be minimized.

\* Quicker efforts should be made to remove racist graffiti.

\* Tenants associations in the Borough should be reminded of their important role in combating racial harassment.

In many respects the policy initiatives and concerns expressed by the Council in 1985 were a repetition of its reactive responses in 1981. The Council had in effect been challenged on two highly public occasions by local community outrage to take its responsibilities seriously in this context but had failed each time to make any creditable headway. At this point it is worth considering why. For all the detail of the initiatives espoused by the Council, what they lacked was a clear policy framework of administration, implementation and monitoring, with equally clear lines of responsibility. There was in other words no conception of strategy.

Equally important perhaps was the failure to appreciate the extent to which a clear public commitment and *relevant* policy developments (i.e. a strategy) had to be 'worked into' all the organizational cultures of the Council. This was underlined by the Council's blinkered pre-occupation with the public sector housing dimensions of racial harassment, particularly when so many of the arson attacks in 1985 had affected Asian family homes in the private sector. Moreover, the other social implications of racial harassment seemed less than peripheral (e.g. public relations, education, social services) and this had the effect of placing the whole thrust of the Council's potential responses overwhelmingly on the housing dimension of its operations. However, not all these deficiencies can be accounted for simply by indicting the Council for being reactive rather than proactive, it has to be said that during this period (and since) the Council was at best inefficient and at worst ineffective. Nowhere was this more apparent than in the case of the Council's Racial Harassment Advice Service.

*Racial harassment advice service*

Following the increased number of arson attacks in 1985, there were various forms of protest against local agencies and many demands were made on them. One of these demands was the establishment of a 24 hour telephone service that would provide immediate legal advice and assistance to victims of racial harassment in English and Asian languages (see Chapter 1). It was agreed by the Council that a pilot project should be set up for a year employing a co-ordinator who would develop the service and recruit and train volunteers.

Following consultation with the Asian, Black and Ethnic Minority organizations and other groups in the voluntary sector about setting up the service, a debate ensued about whether it should be based in the voluntary sector or in the Council. The arguments for basing the service in the voluntary sector revolved around giving it an 'independent' status. Community organizations argued that this factor would encourage the Council's housing tenants to use the service with confidence. The Council, on the other hand, felt that the service should be based in the Council to demonstrate its commitment to tackling racial harassment. In this debate, the local Victim Support Scheme (VSS) was totally opposed to the existence of the service whether based in the Council or any other organization in the voluntary sector (see Chapter 1). The Council's Race Relations Advisory Committee finally recommended that the Racial harassment advice service (RHAS) should be based in the Town Hall (Walthamstow) in order to ensure *adequate resources and arrangements and demonstrate commitment to engender confidence in its effectiveness.*

The RHAS was set up as a pilot project for a year, and a co-ordinator was appointed to run the service in August 1986. Trained volunteers recruited to cover the 'out of office hours' service, soon became paid sessional workers, who were able to offer a basic advice and interpretation service. The scheme was officially launched in April 1987.

A Council review of the service in September 1987 revealed that while it had not attracted quite as many 'out of office hours' calls as had been anticipated, it had been valuable in terms of highlighting shortcomings in the way in which Council departments and other agencies dealt with cases of racial harassment. It was also revealed that Council departments and other agencies had begun to refer cases to the service, and that many cases were already being dealt with by other organizations.

In a short time the service became a 'dumping ground' for agencies in the Borough. In addition victims of racial harassment contacted the RHAS directly with the expectation that it would use its influence to persuade relevant agencies to deal with their case effectively and speedily. It was soon realized that the service did not have these powers. The Council review led to the decision that the pilot project would end in its present form except for the continuation of the 'telephone hotline' service. As a step towards developing the service more strategically the post of the co-ordinator was re-evaluated. Subsequently a 'Racial Harassment Policy Development Co-ordinator' (RHPDC) was appointed in September 1988. The objective of this new post was to develop effective Borough-wide policies on dealing with racial harassment. The RHPDC was also to deal with calls during office hours.

Although the telephone 'hotline' service provided a point of contact for victims of racial harassment, its effectiveness was always in question.

According to the evidence we received, many people were not even aware of its existence. Those who were, had been dissatisfied with it. For example, an Asian woman who had been suffering racial harassment from neighbours on her estate had received no help from the police or the Council, wrote in her submission to the Inquiry:

> I have attempted to use the hotline several times. It has
> never been answered except once when the phone was
> picked up and then immediately put down again.

The service in its established form was seriously under-developed. The 'out of office hours' service simply functioned as a message point for action to be taken the following day, or as a means of contacting the police on behalf of victims. Provision of appropriate advice and legal assistance was not readily available. Even if it was clear that some form of 'hotline' telephone service needed to remain, it certainly needed to be re-evaluated. Its relevance could be accentuated by consultations with the local Asian, Black and Ethnic Minority organizations. To ensure effectiveness a full back up system of advice, including legal advice would need to be developed. Furthermore any volunteers recruited would need to be properly trained, to deal with the 'emergency' situations effectively and to provide immediate 'crisis' counselling to alleviate the distress of the victims of racial harassment.

## The corporate profile

By the end of the 1980s the lack of policy co-ordination and shared commitment and understanding throughout the Council was undisguisable. In addition there were specific difficulties raised by the practices of some departments, while the relevant role of other departments seemed to be obscure both to their own staff and the general public. In order to understand this we need to consider some of these departments in a little more detail.

As we have seen the strategic burden of developing Council policy had customarily been with the Housing department. This had left other areas of the Council in a position where racial harassment was for the most part considered in negligible or marginal terms prior to the advent of an inter-departmental working party established in 1988. This skewed a necessary corporate Council response into a narrow Housing departmental perspective. It also had sustained elsewhere an almost autonomous departmentalist culture where even the perception of racial harassment implications for service delivery proved insufficient to generate a commitment to 'own' the responsibility for developing appropriate policies and practices. Against this it should be added however, there are real difficulties in attempting to persuade traditional areas of the Council to respond to so-called non-traditional issues, like racial harassment, which cut across several contexts of Council service delivery. Sometimes the failure to intervene is as much a question of ignorance as reluctance or circumspection. This is the framework in which we discuss the significance of four other Council departments.

*The Housing department*

The co-ordinates of the Council's policy and thinking had been shaped almost exclusively by developments in the Housing department. Developments which were far from coherent or systematic. In evidence to the Inquiry the Housing department stated:

> There has been a continuous development of policy since then (1981) as a result of reports to Council Committees and, as a result, *there is no single document which can be regarded as a definitive policy statement.*
>
> (emphasis added)

This suggests that throughout the 1980s the Council in general and the Housing department in particular, produced intermittently, a variety of 'free-floating' ideas and commitments in different policy statements and varying practices which had no coherent *root* in the culture of the organization. For example, it was not until 1988 that the Housing department attempted to codify the practical implementation of its policies through the production of 'Guidance and procedural notes for staff'. These guidance notes provided instructions for Housing officers on: how to respond to victims of racial harassment (e.g. initial and follow-up visits, liaison with other agencies, issuing warnings to perpetrators); the monitoring of incidents (e.g. investigations by Senior Estate Officers, necessary repairs noted and responded to, regular visits to victims); action against perpetrators (e.g. the issuing of oral and written warnings, orders for possession, injunctions); and also the identification of perpetrators (e.g. circular letters to tenants, liaison with tenants associations and community organizations). On paper at least the Housing department appeared to have arrived at the point where it could claim to have developed a responsive policy framework. However evidence to our Inquiry suggested not only that this policy development had been haphazard but its implementation in practical terms ranged from the piecemeal to the non-existent. In addition there were other areas of Housing department policy *which made the consistent implementation of policy initiatives against racial harassment a structurally problematic enterprise.*

*Allocations policy* The thrust of the policy, *varied in theory* between the transfer of racial harassment victims and the eviction of the perpetrators, with a historical emphasis on the former (see below). The rationale of this in practice, however, cannot be understood simply in its own terms. It has to be placed in the context of the *constraints imposed by the department's housing allocations policy,* which, although an independent development, was inextricably related to the ultimate effectiveness of the department's policy response to racial harassment.

In addition to the severe shortage of Council properties, the potential transfer of racial harassment victims appeared to be circumvented by the Council's Housing allocation policy. Since 1981 a 'no trading up principle' had been in operation. This meant that transfers to alternative 'better quality' accommodation were only considered where a 'housing need' could be demonstrated. Applying this principle to victims of racial harassment resulted in offers of accommodation in (and subsequent transfers to) similar estates and locales affected by racial harassment. The difficulties created by this contradiction were at least recognized by the Housing department who observed:

> In terms of perpetuating racial harassment, the current policy is not clear on how to address the clear dilemma of allocations to areas with a history of racial incidents. There is plainly the need to avoid the placement of Black and Ethnic Minority families in areas of previous harassment wherever possible, but without creating 'no-go' areas. There also remain difficulties in achieving moves to similar property elsewhere if all high density estates are perceived as being potential areas of likely attacks.

But the Housing policy response to racial harassment was a lot more problematic than even this candid view suggested. In general the department's policy on the transfer of victims *was subordinate to its policy on housing allocations.* This largely determined in practice when and in what circumstances it became possible to transfer victims of racial harassment. Effective interventions at this level were therefore dependent on the extent to which the Housing allocations policy had accommodated the commitment to tackling racial harassment. This was minimal in the case of Waltham Forest; indeed it appears that the Council extoled a commitment to transferring victims which it simply could not implement consistently or effectively. We illustrate some of these structural difficulties in Figure 3.1. This identifies the context imposed by the Housing allocations policy which constrained the Council's capacity to respond rationally in this area.

| 1. Policy objective | Removal of victims from racial harassment locales. |
| 2. Primary difficulty | Initial allocation of potential victims to those locales. |
| 3. Secondary difficulty | Transfer of victims to similarly affected locales. |
| 4. Statutory obligation | Housing the homeless. |
| 5. Resource problem | Shortage of available properties. |
| 6. Social policy principles | (a) Avoidance of 'no-go' areas<br>(b) Equal opportunity access (i.e. no trading up)<br>(c) Best use of housing stock |
| 7. Practical consequence | Infrequent successful transfer of victims. |

**Figure 3.1: The constraints imposed by the Housing allocations policy on the transfer of racial harassment victims**

Items 2-6 in Figure 3.1 above show the distinctive *inter-related* constraints involved. The objective of transferring the victims (see item 1) was seriously undermined by the failure to address, in policy terms, the social impact of the pervasiveness of racial harassment *and the historical legacy of racism in the operation of housing allocations* (see item 2). Although racially discriminatory criteria like residential requirements, local connections or preferential treatment of white transfer applicants had largely been eliminated, the effects of these previous racist allocation practices continued to exercise an influence in the present: Asian and Black people were predominantly concentrated in the worst sections of the housing stock which were mostly high density estates. Many of these estates which were identified with particularly high rates of racial victimization also appeared to be characterized by high levels of general crime and other anti-social activities.

Figure 3.1 suggests that the prospect of Asian and Black families being allocated or transferred *away from locales of racial harassment* was possible but not likely in any consistent sense (see items 2 and 3). The statutory obligation to house the homeless (item 4) and the shortage of available properties (item 5) were unavoidable constraints which further reduced the policy room for manoeuvre. But the social policy principles (see item 6) which appeared to under-write housing allocations did not assist, and were in many respects a hinderance. In particular the notions of 'avoiding no-go areas' and the 'best use of housing stock' seemed to have developed outside of any direct reference to the Council's commitment to tackle racial harassment or if necessary to transfer victims. It is interesting to note the Housing department's perspective on this:

> It has not however, been felt to be acceptable for the actions of perpetrators to have the effect of changing the equal opportunties housing needs basis for selecting prospective tenants for Council owned accommodation.

What then, in this context, was the status of the Council's commitment to tackling racial harassment? It was certainly not as strong as a policy obligation, it seemed wholly discretionary, at least this expressed the views of the Housing department:

> in general terms, whilst *sensitivity* will be utilised when considering applicants for vacancies, the over-riding basis for selection is housing need and the best use of the housing stock. *This is not seen as conflicting with the Council's commitment to deal firmly with the perpetrators of and provide support to victims of racial harassment.*
>
> (emphasis added)

This was revealing in a number of ways. First, it was clear that the Housing department did not consider the transfer of racial harassment victims to constitute the best use of housing stock. Secondly, as our earlier discussion suggests, the tackling of racial harassment was not really regarded as a social policy principle (that is, it did not have the same importance as the elements in item 6, in Figure 3.1 above), and thirdly, one of the extant principles, the understandable need to avoid 'no go' areas was being maintained *at the expense of minimizing the spread of racial harassment locales* (see Chapter 4), since the latter was not the subject of any development or strategic work. Arguably a reconsideration of the Housing department's social policy principles could have assisted the strategic development of Council policy where racial harassment was concerned.

*Housing transfers* We have discussed in detail the policy constraints which reduced the possibility of victims being transferred. It was doubly ironic then that housing transfer was in practical terms the principle means of victim support. But, even where transfers did occur, matters were not straightforward. The average waiting time for an offer had been around 2 years with some victims being moved after 4-5 years. While it may be argued that transfers were a 'last resort', in Waltham Forest this had often been an illusory last resort. The length of time which victims had to wait for a transfer (and these were the more serious cases), meant that victims had to endure harassment for extremely long periods of time with little support in the intervening periods. Between 1984 - 90 there were 19 offers of transfer to victims of racial harassment, of these 9 resulted in either rehousing or an exchange of accommodation.

According to the Housing department's evidence, in instances where the nature of the harassment or circumstances of the family required urgent removal from their existing environment, a facility existed for emergency measures to be taken. This involved an emergency offer for admission to temporary accommodation (if available) as an interim measure. However, this understanding appeared to extend only to cases where there had been an arson attack or the property became uninhabitable in any other way. *At the time of our research no case of racial harassment had been offered emergency accommodation and no specific provisions existed for such an eventuality.* In general the guidance and procedure notes introduced in 1988 had not been effective, thus a considerable gap existed in the credibility of the Housing department's support for victims.

*Action against perpetrators* There had been little consideration of the Housing department's role in effective action against perpetrators of racial harassment. *The unsystematic and incoherent way in which responses had been implemented was not conducive to the development of policies and consistent practices for the identification of perpetrators, the collection of evidence or the referral of cases to the appropriate Council departments and other agencies.*

According to the Housing department's evidence, in only 2 or 3 of every 10 reported cases was the perpetrator identified. Interestingly though, where perpetrators had been identified it argued: 'in almost all cases a warning combined with the knowledge that a further offence will lead to the Borough Solicitor being asked to start possession proceedings has to our knowledge stopped further harassment'. However the Housing department had no impact whatsoever in taking action against perpetrators of racial harassment *as a rule;* and such exceptions where they had occurred could only be described as negligible. However, an observation like this needs to be balanced against the debacle over the insertion of a clause on racial harassment in the Council's tenancy agreement.

*The tenancy agreement debacle*  Since 1981, considerable misunderstandings and misrepresentations had developed concerning the Council's position on the eviction of tenants who perpetrated racial harassment. This confusion centred on the 'existence' of a clause on racial harassment in the Council's tenancy agreement. Although it was considered by the Council in 1983 and in 1985 (where it was agreed that the clause should be widened to include all forms of anti-social behaviour, e.g. sexual harassment, religious harassment, etc.); by 1990 the decision had not been implemented. As we saw in Chapter 1 this had never been publicly recognized. No consultation ever took place with tenants in 1986 as was predicted in the local press. Instead the impression had been allowed to remain that the Council did indeed have a policy to evict tenants in this context.

There are certainly major problems to be confronted when Council rhetoric greatly exceeds the reality of its practices. The direct implications of this were identified in the evidence of a NALGO union official in the Council's Housing department:

> This would mean that if a situation arose whereby the Council was seeking a Possession Order against perpetrators we would have to use the nuisance and annoyance clause of the tenancy agreement. This would be far from ideal and may not necessarily give an adequate picture of the case.

The issues raised by this observation are significant. It is evident that the Council's capacity to act against perpetrators of racial harassment *had never been developed.* Historically, this dimension of policy appeared to have been shelved unceremoniously. According to the union official's evidence, a Housing working party had failed to deliver any developments on the tenancy clause, this led him to conclude that:

> if nothing else comes out of the Inquiry but a clause on racial harassment in the tenancy agreement, it would have been worthwhile.

It was not surprising therefore that the Council should find itself at the begining of the 1990s with a huge credibility gap where its position against perpetrators of racial harassment was concerned. A clear indication of its seriousness could have been signalled by the inclusion of a tenancy clause on racial harassment at least by 1985. Throughout the 1980s there had been very little publicity from the Council directed at perpetrators of racial harassment, it had maintained no ultimate sanctions in this context and did not codify even a limited series of initiatives (e.g. oral and written warnings) until 1988. All this greatly mythologized the Council's likely response and assisted in leaving the spread of racial harassment largely untouched. Consequently, perpetrators of racial harassment on housing estates for example, confronted very little to dissuade them. Whether by design or default, action against perpetrators was something that the Housing department had traditionally not pursued. [1]

## The Education department

The department's first significant response to racial harassment was made in July 1985 when the Chief Education Officer organized a seminar for Head Teachers to clarify the Council's position on dealing with racist incidents and racist materials in schools. Schools were asked to report to the department and Governing bodies details of racist incidents and to provide an account of the action taken.

In order to develop departmental policy a working party which included representatives of community organiaztions was set up in 1986 to offer advice and support to schools and to devise a form for schools to report incidents to the department. During 1987, consultations were carried out with relevant groups and agencies on a draft document prepared by the working party and a provisional draft report was presented to the Council's Race Relations and Education Committees in early 1988. The draft policy document was piloted in Autumn 1988 in ten schools in order to:

> (a) Assess the value of the document for information and training purposes and to make necessary improvements.
>
> (b) To test out and develop the reporting systems for racist incidents.
>
> (c) To develop support structures for victims of racial harassment.

It was intended that by the end of the Summer term 1988, the amended finished document would be presented in the first instance to relevant Council Committees and then to Governing bodies for adoption and incorporation within each school's 'Code of Conduct'. Concurrently appropriate in-service training was scheduled for provision.

By 1990 there had been little progress since the piloting of the policy document, principally because after two years of its establishment, the working party had not been able to sustain its membership. The working party was essentially a voluntary effort and officers did not have clear lines of responsibility, indeed the additional workload was not recognized as part of the staff work programme. With the demise of the working party, a new group of Council officers within the department (as opposed to the service) constituted themselves as an 'Anti-Racist Action Group'. Officer time spent on work in this area was apparently recognized by the department. A victim support sub-group was also established but this was confined to the staff in the department. It was not possible for us to assess these later developments.

Despite the commitment shown by the department to respond to various dimensions of racial harassment, its efforts were insufficiently developed to have any prospect of a consistent impact on school students and their families. This much, and more, was openly acknowledged by the Education department in their evidence:

> honesty would also recognise that we do not have well-understood working procedures on racial harassment, that we have not provided in the Department the capacity to effectively investigate incidents and to support others in doing so; that we have not effectively addressed the dilemmas in dealing with incidents which are complex, sensitive, open to interpretation in such a way as to be decisive, supportive to the victims but also recognise the right of the alleged perpetrators.

The Education department, perhaps more than any other within the Council potentially confronted multiple layers of complexity in any attempts to develop wide-ranging responses. This perhaps is a testament to the Education department's importance in tackling racial harassment in a range of settings under its jurisdiction. For example this might raise questions concerning the protection of children from racial harassment by other pupils, including when pupils are travelling to and from school. Moreover, as Forbes (1988:147) has argued:

It is within education authorities that long-term policies to prevent racial harassment must be developed. Both the victims and the perpetrators of racial harassment are often children. *Racial harassment committed by children in a locality is quite likely to be mirrored by similar behaviour within school. The same children may be victims both inside and outside school.*

(emphasis added)

While recognizing the value of this policy focus, the Education department emphasized the problems involved in getting schools to report incidents. It suggested that schools may sometimes be deterred from reporting racial harassment because they feared being perceived as undisciplined or badly managed, or simply that they considered it an internal school matter. In this latter instance the fear could take the form that:

unwanted, unhelpful (press) publicity might be attracted;
that the response might be too slow, inadequate, unsupportive or unfair in some way.

This may explain in part the failure of the Chief Education Officer's initiative in 1985 (see above). That is, why no schools took the opportunity to report incidents of racial harassment to the department. To this it must be added, as also pointed out by the Education department:

that existing reporting procedures from schools have not been successful indeed they have rarely been used.

The problem of the context in which racial harassment could be reported is the key concern here. For example given the consistent, recurring inter-actions between school students each day, it was suggested to us that it was not always clear what ought to be reported or what constituted racial harassment in the eyes of each school. This in turn raised further issues concerning conflicting perspectives and the additional administrative burden of reporting, investigating and monitoring incidents of racial harassment. Where cases had been addressed by schools, the outcome had not always been clear. Interestingly the Education department argued in their evidence:

> because incidents do not appear to be systematically
> reported to the office, this by no means should be
> interpreted as that they are not being addressed.

The obvious rejoinder here is that in the absence of clearly defined and disseminated school practices, there was simply no way of knowing this. Furthermore it is equally important to know how these issues were being addressed. What is fundamental to both these perspectives is knowledge of the current scale and nature of the problem. This was the source of a troubling lacuna in the department's thinking. Other evidence to the Inquiry suggested that racial abuse and to a lesser extent racial bullying, however mildly or severely construed, was fairly common place in the Borough's schools.

Having said this we should not underestimate the implications of the 1988 Education Reform Act, particularly in the sense that schools are now placed in a position where greater autonomy from local government control is a real possibility. In the view of the Education department this meant:

> we must seek to persuade them to have policies on racial
> harassment but it would be foolish to assume we could
> control.

Against this background we could do no worse than recognize the extent to which the Home Office and other Central Government departments have defined racial harassment as presenting a 'serious obstacle to equality of opportunites' and that have expressed the view 'it is Government policy that (Local Education Authorities) should attach priority to dealing with it' (Home Office, 1989).

*Social Services department*

In evidence to the Inquiry the Social Services department showed some awareness of racial harassment and seemed willing to engage in discussions relevant to the department. But there were a number of difficulties which put these ostensibly encouraging signs in a rather different perspective. Firstly, although the department stated categorically that complaints of racial harassment were not reported to it, possibly due to the lack of the department's 'sign-posting' in this area, it seemed reluctant to change the public perception of the department to one where complaints of racial harassment could be made. Secondly, the department was unable to comprehend a potential role beyond the practices of individual social workers. It suggested the issue was one of the social worker's courage, sensitivity and capacity to recognize racial harassment rather than the development of an appropriate departmental response. Both these dimensions it argued could require extensive training but this could not take precedence over other prioritized areas of training. Thirdly in terms of specific victim support the department envisaged it was possible in certain circumstances to provide places for people to take refuge during the day; or to provide emotional support through facilitating the involvement of other families; or even develop a form of support service based upon a joint working relationship between social workers and recruited volunteers. But this, it was pointed out to us, could not take the form of an extensive policy commitment.

Each of the three points made above highlight the historical irrelevance of racial harassment to the Social Services department and also how, compared to the Housing department, a perspective was in place where *it was thought its departmental practices could not be transformed to accommodate a policy commitment to tackle racial harassment.* One explanation offered for this was that their statutory obligations precluded them from advocating extra policy commitments. These specified a duty to promote the welfare of children, and to provide facilities for young people, elderly people and people with disabilities. In our view this has only a *prima facie* plausibility, as the Home Office (1989) observed:

> Social Services departments have had some difficulty identifying a role for themselves in respect of racial incidents and they may be unlikely to regard themselves, or be seen, as in the lead in any multi-racial approach in a given locality. But *it would be a mistake to assume that they have no role, or to undervalue the importance of the contribution they can make - sometimes uniquely.*

> (emphasis added)

The key question here of course is whether this role should be considered as proactive (i.e. necessarily available in anticipation of circumstances) or reactive (i.e. discretionarily available once a circumstance has arisen). The Home Office emphasized a proactive role which by definition must be part of a formulated strategy. In a Council corporate approach the significance of this cannot be over-emphasized because:

> One big advantage the (Social Services department) has
> over the housing (department) is that all its powers apply
> whatever the type of housing in which the perpetrator or
> victim live.

> (Forbes, 1988: 133)

From a wider perspective however, if the Social Services department adopted a more strategic focus, it would 'recognize the impact of racial attacks and harassment *on their ability to deliver services to some communities in accordance with their statutory responsibilities'* (Home Office, 1989; emphasis added). The conceptual distance between this level of Central Government thinking and the Social Services department was enormous. The extent of its role in addressing racial harassment in the Borough had been limited to its representation on the Housing panel where transfer applications for victims of racial harassment were considered. Since this was the 'last resort' stage in cases of racial harassment, the input of the department was marginal. This was especially so because reports in the cases were prepared by Housing officers and a Social Services perspective was usually absent. This in turn was exacerbated by the absence of formal liaison between the departments.

## Borough Solicitors department

The Borough Solicitors department's perception of its role in the development of Council policy and practice on racial harassment was vague. This is illustrated by the following comment from their evidence to the Inquiry:

> Like any other solicitor's office, the department
> responds to requests for advice from instructing
> departments. If advice is not sought, there is nothing to
> respond to.

The reactive and uncommitted stance of the Borough Solicitors department may hold the key to the Council's lack of legal action and policy developments against perpetrators of racial harassment. Indeed, we were informed that departments were often reluctant to approach the service because they did not know what the Borough Solicitor could offer and because the department had tended not to 'sell' itself as a resource. Here again we find an extraordinary level of underdevelopment and ignorance where relevant practices are concerned.

111

Arguably a legal dimension is almost invariably present in racial harassment cases, whether in terms of action against perpretrators or advice and assistance to victims. A Borough-wide Council impact undoubtedly requires procedures which involve the Borough Solicitors at the earliest possible opportunity. Arguably, the provision of legal advice and assistance is certainly an area in which the Council could play an important role. However it was suggested to us by the Borough Solicitors department a problem exists in satisfying this demand since Law Society rules did not permit the Council's Solicitors to directly advise the public, voluntary organizations and even members of staff (only the Council directly or indirectly through its departments). This problem, however, is not as difficult as it may seem, since it was possible for Council departments to seek advice on behalf of a client in relation to issues which arose in the course of their work. More specifically for Council departments, the Borough Solicitor could contribute towards the consideration of the range of legal options available to the department in dealing with particular cases. In other words there was a role for the Borough Solicitors department to develop the Council's interest in tackling racial harassment. This was overwhelmingly a policy brief.

In our view this should also include responding in cases where the police do not take action and the Borough Solicitor is satisfied that sufficient grounds exist for action to be taken. The Borough Solicitors department should be prepared to take such cases directly to the Crown Prosecution Service. It was clear that the role of the Borough Solicitors department's advice regarding evidential requirements, interviewing and taking statements in cases of racial harassment had not received detailed attention. But the full potential of the Borough Solicitors department's role, in policy development or in particular cases, can only be appreciated once it has undertaken the task to codify and publicize within the Council a proactive range of legal measures to facilitate effective Council responses. This is a measure of extreme importance.

*Development department*

The Development department was responsible for resourcing the urban and physical landscapes of the Borough. In evidence to the Inquiry it professed to be 'fully committed to eradicating any form of racial harassment in the community and work place'. Yet it was also evident that although 'racial harassment incidents *may come to the attention of* departmental staff in the course of their work' (emphasis added), as there were no clear and specific procedures for reporting and responding to these incidents, that prospect remained distinctly unlikely.

In the Engineering, Architectural and Building Surveying division of this department for example, considerable time was spent on sites supervising contractors. We were told that the staff:

> must take any racial attack or comments very seriously reporting the incident to their superior. There are remedies within the contract for dealing with items which could loosely be described as not proceeding with work diligently and expeditiously. *This may include racial harassment activities.* The action taken against contractors could include the removal of a person from site. *No such cases have arisen to date with regard to racial harassment.*

(emphasis added)

The point is of course that these potential remedies were not directly applicable to cases of racial harassment, there was in other words nothing explicitly written down in this regard to guide the department's response to 'racial harassment activities'. The department failed to consider arrangements that went beyond the discretionary and variable judgements of supervisors on site who were not necessarily aware of a responsibility to uphold and implement departmental policy on racial harassment precisely because one did not exist.

The Property Services division of the department was responsible for the letting of Council properties for commercial uses. (It produced a monthly vacant property register of office and industrial premises.) The department felt that if tenants were suffering from racial harassment, it 'would come to the attention of this division'. Observations like this however, failed to recognize how much depended upon the public perception of the division as a place where these issues could be raised credibly. Even a Development department survey on Black businesses in 1986 only approached the issue through a circumlocutory line of questioning.[2] It may well be, as the department argued, that 'nothing which would have legal effect can be included in a tenancy agreement to impose a penalty on a tenant for the racial harassment activities'. But this need not limit the scope of the department's response, particularly in surveying the nature of these experiences and raising issues for the responses of more appropriate agencies. This requires serious thinking, for example:

Racial attacks and abuse of shopkeepers may also arise in more than one way. They may be deliberate, perhaps pre-planned and racially motivated from the start. On the other hand the racial component may emerge as a by-product of materially motivated crime such as shop theft where an apprehended thief gives vent to racial abuse (.....). It also seems likely that problems faced by minority groups will vary from one locality to another.

(Ekblom, Simon and Birdi, 1988:1)

It is inconceivable how issues like these could be avoided, particularly when one of the department's other divisions (Planning) was 'directly concerned with promoting black businesses'.

The field of planning itself was not immune to the wider spatial implications of racial harassment. The department informed us that 'Racial comments are sometimes contained in responses to consultation exercises on planning or building control applications'. In many cases expressions of racial abuse were conveyed in letters to the department. These were kept on file and it was felt that over a period of ten years this type of abuse had been increasing, almost in parallel with an increase in Asian, Black and Ethnic Minority applications for planning permission. In particular planning applications for the building of mosques seemed to attract the most vehement opposition. This suggests the initiation of safety interventions and considerations against racist harassment in the social environment need to be an integral responsibility for this department.

## The Council fails expectations

An assessment of the Council's deliberations and various departmental interventions tells only one side of the story. The other aspects our Inquiry pointed unreservedly to a profound local sense of dissatisfaction and disillusionment with the content of the Council's response to racial harassment in the Borough. In particular the Housing department was the focus of the major criticisms. This is largely attributable to the fact that it had, through its own developments, become publicly identified with the Council's response. The general charge was that the Council was unresponsive and ineffective. As we have seen in Chapter 2, there were similar views of the police, but the Council was perceived as the main agency for the provision of support for racial harassment victims. In this context the Council was castigated for not doing

114

nearly enough and *ipso facto* reinforcing the problem. One of the main criticisms lay with Council officers' reluctance in believing that racial harassment was experienced by victims, their persistence in wanting evidence in the form of witness corroboration, and their cumbersome and inefficient way of investigating complaints.

## Racial harassment not taken seriously

As well as experiences which provoked suspicion amongst victims that their reports were not believed, the general dismissiveness with which complaints were met, pointed to major problems in the ability or willingness of Council officers to treat racial harassment as a serious issue.

Witnesses complained that the Council refused to take action. This was experienced either as a blatant refusal, or as an inadequate or inefficient investigation of the report. A case was described to us by a family who had been subjected to racial harassment from their neighbours for a year. They made repeated complaints to the Housing department. The family were visited by numerous Council officers who variously concluded that the incident reported was not racially motivated or that the family needed witnesses to support their complaint. The neighbours (i.e. perpetrators) refusals to answer the allegations seemed to be acceptable to the investigating Council officer.

Victims generally considered most investigations to be cursory examinations which only served to demonstrate Council indifference. In such cases the burden of proof placed on the victim was difficult if not impossible to satisfy. Moreover, the perpetrator appeared placed beyond the reach of official sanction, since officers investigating cases seemed satisfied with a superficial examination of the circumstances. A combination of disbelief, dismissiveness and refusal to take action, not only accounted for the conviction among many victims that they were not taken seriously, but also provided a strong disincentive to report incidents of racial harassment.

## The mechanics of Council inaction

While not considering the victim or the reported problem seriously, the Council also appeared *guilty*, simultaneously, of taking no action in cases it was apparently treating seriously. Witnesses described a principal feature of Council inaction as the abdication of responsibility. A tenant in Council housing, for example, told us that she received racially abusive telephone calls and knocks on her door at night. She reported this to the Council everyday, but 'they said they could not do anything and did not do anything'. A community housing officer told us that sometimes when victims reported racial harassment, they were told by Council officers that 'there is no one here who deals with this kind of thing'. Faced with the twin Council traits of impotence and ignorance, victims found themselves with legitimate, if frustrating reasons for taking the complaint elsewhere.

If in some instances Council officers excused themselves from taking action in cases of racial harassment, in others they simply absented themselves, one witness who was told 'paki bastard - go home' by school children in a park, was dismayed at not receiving any support from the park keeper present. That council employees may not recognize individual responsibility for corporate Council policy in this way, may be symptomatic of the low status assigned to racial harassment in the working practices of some Council departments. It may also be a symptom of a more general ignorance of racial harassment *as an issue* with Council wide implications.

A particularly frustrating experience for victims was the reinterpretation of incidents by officers. In cases where the complainant did not speak English 'very well' the account of the incident could be distorted unnecessarily. A community housing officer told us that 'Council officers don't listen, they say "or you mean this...." and confuse people into agreeing with them'. A teacher's experience similarly revealed that:

> despite understanding what you are talking about they still insist in interpreting/repeating what you say, and say things like 'you mean this or that' when they know what you mean.

Though there were a variety of available measures through which the Council could respond, it seems from the victims point of view, they were all essentially forms of evasiveness and inaction.

## *Reinforcing the problem*

The various ways in which victims experienced Council disinterest or inaction had implications which went far beyond a simple lack of confidence in the Council. Many witnesses considered the Council to be actually reinforcing the problem. The Waltham Forest Family Service Unit felt this was demonstrated 'by the fact they do nothing to prevent or combat racial harassment'. Such was the degree of disillusionment with its efforts that little regard emerged for the Council's ostensible commitment to tackling the problem. The Joint Council for Asian Organization gave one of the few submissions to express any faith

116

in the Council. Though even this concession was conditioned by a recognition of its internal shortcomings:

> Council departments over the period of 2 to 3 years have become sensitive, but it (sic) lacks the structures, and proper planning for implementing (sic) for eradication of racist practices are needed to build up the bridges between the community and Council departments.

It was suggested to us that Council investigations which relied *unreasonably* on the production of witnesses in order to substantiate the complaint also allowed perpetrators the freedom to continue their victimization of others with impunity. In the words of one witness:

> Perpetrators of racial harassment are confident and carry out acts of racial harassment in the Borough in the full knowledge that nothing will happen to them.

As with the police, the lack of a direct challenge to the behaviour of individuals by the Council contributed to a general environment in which racial harassment could flourish. Another witness informed us:

> Council departments are often reluctant to thoroughly investigate matters which can have the effect of encouraging the perpetrators to carry out further acts of harassment.

While witnesses complained that Council actions helped to reinforce the problem, they also found the Council, on occasions, to be indirectly assisting their victimization. Victims found for example, the Council willing to take action against *them* as a result of their complaints of racial harassment. One witness told us that following his complaint he received a letter from the Council threatening eviction for allegedly throwing rubbish outside, making excessive noise and causing water to leak into the flat below; even though he told them this was all untrue.

Actions like this by the Council compounded the pain of the original victimization with the indignity of not being believed. The frustration of some witnesses was deeply felt and unequivocally stated:

I am (the) victim of harassment, intimidation and injustice which has been exercised by the Housing department in the past and continues to be exercised to deprive me from my entitlement and rights illegally, i.e. abuse of authority.

## Concerns and anxieties

Accompanying these criticisms of the Council, were observations on the general lack of support it offered to the victims of racial harassment. While the Council was clearly considered a lead agency in terms of victim support, the common complaint of insensitivity was reiterated in the testimony of many organizations. The Joint Council of Afro-Caribbean Organizations, the Family Service Unit, the Bangalee Women's Welfare Project, the Victims Aid Action Group, and the Community Relations Council, all gave similar observations on the poor quality of Council services to victims. For example, an 'anecdotal survey' conducted by the Community Relations Council, emphasized the extent of racial harassment as a problem in the Borough and that the Council appeared alternately ineffective and uncaring:

> The survey details a horrifying record of harassment suffered by Black and Ethnic Minority people in Waltham Forest. From only 186 people surveyed, 226 aspects of racial harassment have been highighted. Irrespective of age or sex, individuals are abused, attacked and threatened because of their race. The survey also demonstrates a lack of confidence in both the local authority and the police in providing adequate support and protection against racial harassment.

Clearly one of the consequences of this lack of confidence in the Council, was the non-reporting of incidents. For one witness, the only effective course left available after five years of victimization appeared to be *'to hold a public inquiry in our whole case of racial harassment'*.

Witnesses did not simply express dissatisfaction with the Council however, they also had clear ideas about the kind of measures they considered would be effective in combating racial harassment. Uppermost among these concerns was that action should be taken against perpetrators. The Joint Council of Afro-Caribbean Organizations stated in their evidence:

> There needs to be more prosecution against perpetrators.
> Also in the case of perpetrators being Council tenants,
> greater/stricter action needs to take place such as: After
> verbal and written warnings, if Council tenants continue
> to racially harass a neighbour they (perpetrator) should
> be evicted from Council property and they should be
> treated as 'intentionally homeless' and not given priority
> in terms of re-housing.

Witnesses indicated the Council should not be merely reactive in dealing with the problem however. Proactive engagement in preventing racial harassment was considered a priority. The Afro-Caribbean Supplementary Education Service offered their own suggestion for a more incisive Council approach:

> We believe that Council tenants who perpetrate racial
> harassment should automatically be evicted. This
> accommodation should then be offered to a family of the
> same ethnic group as the victim. By taking this lead, the
> Council would be seen to be serious about combating
> racial harassment and the added presence of a family of
> the same ethnic group as the victim would help to obviate
> the feelings of insecurity which many victims of racial
> harassment suffer from.

The salient feature of this suggestion is its concern not simply to remove the immediate threat, but to attempt to change a threatening environment. This is also implicit in the views expressed by many other witnesses who were similarly concerned that where the transfer of the victim is considered appropriate *it should not be undertaken as an alternative to action against the perpetrator.*

What may have been a remedy, to transfer the victim, was also problematic due to operational difficulties which, in practice, made it a solution beyond the reach of many. Waltham Forest CRC believed that where transfers operated the Council should:

> Ensure the transfer system is flexible enough to include
> racial harassment as a criterion of moving and
> safeguarding the interest and property of the victim.

As with every other problem experienced by witnesses in their contact with the Council, the problems with transfers were largely the consequence of its reactive approach.

## Current Council policy dilemmas

Evidence to the Inquiry concerning the Council displayed an unrelenting crisis of confidence in its ability and willingness to tackle the problem of racial harassment. Witnesses not only detailed the problems, but suggested solutions to some of them. Furthermore the Council was called on to demonstrate a clear and determined attitude in tackling racial harassment; to develop and implement effective policies; to make such policies clear to the public; and to take disciplinary action against Council officers who failed to carry out their duties under such policies. Taken together these criticisms and injunctions exposed the abortive attempts by the Council to develop anything approaching an effective response during the 1980s.

### Omissions and uneven development

However, while it is beyond contradiction that the Council's over-all record in dealing with racial harassment was extremely poor, it needs restating that many of these deficiencies were not specific to Waltham Forest. The experiences we have reviewed in this Chapter highlight the many *policy absences* that generally crippled Asian and Black peoples' expectations of local government during the same period. These can be classified in at least six categories of omission and uneven development:

(a) The development of effective, inter-departmental procedures and therefore corporate policy.

(b) A concise specification of the objectives and range of policy development.

(c) The identification and development of relevant, practical initiatives.

(d) The establishment of clear procedures for liaison with non-Council agencies (e.g. the police and voluntary sector).

(e) The development of a coherent analysis and understanding of the local manifestation of racial harassment.

(f) A sustained programme of public education regarding the need to tackle racial harassment.

Each of these areas have been pursued by different local authorities at various levels, in different combinations and changing circumstances. But it is perhaps the last two areas which have received the least comprehensive treatment both generally and in the particular case of Waltham Forest. In Chapter 4 we discuss in detail a more focused, spatial analysis of racial harassment, but we need to touch here the vexed question of public relations. It is worth noting that researchers from Brunel University, in a study of Council tenants in six local authority areas, found that 'fewer than one fifth of Council tenants,....., had any knowledge of the policies adopted by the local authorities to tackle racial harassment' (Luthra and Tyler, 1988). The obvious problem here is that lack of knowledge disenfranchises victims seeking direct assistance. What is equally important to consider however, is the apparent *dilemma* which arises when efforts are made to increase public knowledge. This can be described as the fear of the 'white backlash'. Luthra and Tyler argue:

> Herein lies a key dilemma for local authorities, if they are seen to be forthrightly marketing their race equality strategies, they risk a backlash from a small but significant percentage of white tenants as well as vilification by the tabloid press. Alternatively, a low level approach generates the belief among black tenants that their Authority is unwilling or unable to do anything for them; this leads to feelings of hoplessness and nihilism.
>
> (ibid.)

The importance of *publicly enlisting public support* for the development of Council policies on racial harassment cannot be over-stated. If anything this seemed to be the one thing that had not even the slightest opportunity to become the focus of significant policy discussions or detailed consideration in the Borough. It is not possible for us to say whether the 'white backlash' factor influenced the lack of Council responses in Waltham Forest. But any moves by the Council to develop an effective range of policy interventions will need to have a sense of active public relations at its core.

## Towards contextual action

It is important to emphasize that the problem of racial harassment in policy terms is not an extraneous set of considerations that have been suddenly *visited upon* the local authority and can just as easily be *jettisoned away*. It is not a so-called immigration problem, rather it points to the need to demonstrate the local integrity of 'social pluralism'. This means confronting a problem which is dispersed in spatial patterns of social behaviour entrenched by local racism. As the main providers of *direct-access* services, local authorities are overwhelmingly involved in the practical administration of social policy (housing, education and social services are obvious examples). This puts them in the front-line to establish values, principles and criteria, according to which the allocation of resources can take place in the 'public interest'. The question of how tackling racial harassment fits into this context is where local authorities need to start in policy terms in order to develop a coherent approach. Clearly this requires what is generally known as the 'political will' of the elected administration, but although this is necessary it is not sufficient by itself. In addition at least three further levels of commitment are required. The first is a critical and imaginative interpretation of Section 71 of the 1976 Race Relations Act which places a duty upon local authorities to eliminate unlawful discrimination (Forbes, 1988; Home Office, 1989). *It is the relationship between this and tackling racial harassment in policy and practical terms that needs to be argued and demonstrated.* The second requirement, follows from this and emphasizes the need to utilise the: *'potential* of local government, as separately elected authorities exercising legitimate power over a wide range of functions *within a defined geographical area'* (Jones and Stewart, 1983:5; emphasis added). It is against this background that the spread of racial harassment, (see Chapter 4), highlights the spatial range of the policy perspective. In addition, a third requirement in policy terms recognizes that:

> any practical proposals for the design and execution of
> social policy must be sensitive to the political and *social
> environment* in which they are launched *if they are to be
> of value.*
>
> (Hill and Bramley, 1986:1; emphasis added)

In other words where the provision of housing, education or social services for example takes place in a social environment shaped (historically and geographically) by racial harassment, the avoidance of this issue in the formulation of policy and practices renders the provision of those services susceptible to the charge of *social insensitivity*. It has not always been possible for local authorities in practice to develop and present policy ideas in these concise terms. Nevertheless this has always been the nature of the task.

## Notes

1. It is necessary to note that the 'tenants choice' provisions of the 1988 Housing Act, provide for the transfer of housing tenure from local authority control to housing associations or the private sector. The Housing department will therefore need to incorporate these possibilities in its development of strategy.

2. This began with 'To what extent has your business been affected by problems' and was followed up with 'What exactly are the problems your business is experiencing and how do you think they can be resolved'.

# Part 2
# Cartography

# 4 Racial harassment : A spatial analysis

*Barnor Hesse with the assistance of*
*Christine Bennett and Paul McGilchrist*

> It is not possible to give an accurate picture of the extent
> of the problem in particular areas because there are no
> reliable data. One difficulty is that many incidents,
> particularly the less serious ones, are never reported to
> anyone.
>
> (Home Office, 1989)

> Generally speaking, there is no 'pattern' to racial assaults
> and targeting must remain an ad hoc tactic.
>
> (Metropolitan police, 1989b)

> racial harassment is a feature of life in Waltham Forest.
>
> (Evidence to the Inquiry, 1989)

In previous Chapters we have seen how racial harassment established itself as
a social issue in the 1980s which seemed to be taken increasingly seriously by
official bodies and statutory agencies. This itself was the product of previous
decades which had been mainly characterized by the racially harassed
communities themselves, through various community based organizations,
attempting to pressure agencies to respond to or publicize these social crimes.
Throughout this time however these struggles were chronically punctuated by
research, public discussions and various attempts at local policy making. In
addition, public agencies like the police and local authorities were criticized
consistently for failing to respond effectively. Nevertheless despite this there
is still, considerable ignorance both nationally and locally about the nature and
pervasiveness of racial harassment and its impact on the social environment.

127

Where statutory agencies themselves are concerned often this ignorance is accompanied with a reluctance to believe the problem is particulary serious. Although there have been various 'local' or small-scale studies undertaken at different times, using varying research designs or methodologies, there has been no systematic national study of the problem. This serves to remind us that in general the approach taken by many statutory agencies, including Central Government, has been undermined by a failure to conduct thorough-going investigations capable of generating the information which could perhaps provide a comprehensive analysis of racial harassment. Public policy in other words, has not been sufficiently serious in this context. This in part may explain why racial harassment continues to be speculated about, and not responded to effectively by statutory agencies at the local level.

In our view there is still much that needs to be documented and analyzed in order to resolve some of the contradictory claims and perceptions as to its incidence, as well as establishing the appropriateness of particular policy responses. We are aware that the need for more systematic attention devoted to a national appraisal of racial harassment has been brought to the attention of Central Government. In December 1989 the Parliamentary Home Affairs Committee, in one of its recurrent sessions on racial attacks and harassment, recommended to the Home Office that it 'commission a survey, comparable to the British Crime Survey, to examine the occurrence of racial attacks and harassment' (Home Affairs Committee, 1989:vi). Clearly, if implemented this could contribute to establishing a coherent public policy profile of the issues. However for reasons which are discussed elsewhere in this Chapter, it would be equally important to ensure that local variations and differences are not squeezed out of focus in order to arrive at a national picture. By definition a national survey would find this unavoidable. The development of specifically localized analyses of racial harassment is an urgent priority.

### Below the incidence level

Although our study did not start with a blank picture of Waltham Forest, it needs pointing out that much of the information collected locally about racial harassment had not been analyzed effectively. This has left the impression, wrongly, that there is little to be said with certainty about these experiences in the Borough. In our view, it is only possible to understand the issues in more depth once the situational history and available data have been subject to detailed examination. It is in this context that the evidence submitted to our Inquiry has its own particular relevance.

128

Before trawling through our 'secondary analysis'[1] of various racial harassment statistics, it will be useful to offer some preliminary remarks in order to assist in understanding the approach we intend to develop. We will be attempting to answer the policy question which asks: How can racial harassment be patterned? This is an inescapable question, the reasons are worth rehearsing. Despite the deployment of many public resources and various social policy initiatives in the 1980s, the difficulties posed by the incidence of racial harassment (the first order problem) and the policy response (the second order problem) still remain, seemingly intractable. It appears an impasse has been reached concerning how to conceptualize the frequency and distribution of racial harassment - is it entirely random or are there elements of a pattern? In policy terms this constitutes a significant dilemma since adopting either perspective largely determines how racial harassment is perceived and consequently what type of response is possible. To put the matter simply, if racial harassment is seen basically as a random incident this will tend to lead to a reactive policy response; conversely a perception of racial harassment as structured by a pattern allows for a proactive response. It is perhaps not over-stating the case to claim that the prevailing orthodoxy in Britain, exemplified by the 'official' wisdom of the Home Office and the Metropolitan police, has emphasized the *random incident perspective* (Home Office, 1989; Home Affairs Committee, op. cit.). Needless to say, we intend to challenge that perspective (see also the Conclusion).

The purpose of this Chapter then is to highlight briefly some of the pre-existing research which underpins contemporary knowledge about racial harassment and to analyze local data evidence submitted to our Inquiry, in order to see what can be said about its *spread*. This is the concept we will be using to understand the extent, patterns and locations of racial harassment in Waltham Forest. As we shall argue it is particularly important in illuminating the relevance of *dispersion* as well as *entrenchment* in the incidence of racial harassment in various regions of the Borough. The concept aims to encapsulate the cartography of racial harassment, this means recognizing that 'geography increasingly matters as a vantage point of critical insight' (Soja, 1989:62).

*Some previous research findings*

Although racist attacks had been the subject of concern for many years, the Home Office's official recognition of the problem came after a long period of victimization and campaigning among the Asian and Black communities in Britain. The first extensive compilation of evidence was prepared by Bethnal Green and Stepney Trades Council in 1978. But their report *Blood on the Streets* was ignored by both the Government and police. In 1979 the Institute of Race Relations submitted a substantial catalogue of racial attacks and harassment and police ineffectiveness in their evidence to the Royal Commission on Criminal Procedure. It was not until February 1981, when a Parliamentary Joint Committee against Racialism published a report *Racial violence in Britain*, that the Home Secretary was persuaded to intervene. The subsequent Home Office report, *Racial Attacks* (Layton-Henry, 1984:14) provided an initial policy impetus to change in statutory agencies attitudes to racial harassment when it appeared in November of the same year. It revealed as is now perhaps widely known, that Asian people were 50 times more likely to be attacked on racial grounds than white people, and Black people were 36 times more likely to be attacked. In particular the report argued:

> the incidence of racial attacks presents a significant problem. The frequency of such attacks, often of a particularly insidious nature, and the depth of feeling and concern which they generate in the ethnic minority communities, are a matter of fact and not of opinion.

The Home Office study, was structured as a national survey of racially motivated incidents reported to the police. It estimated that in any one year 7,000 incidents would be reported (Gordon and Newham, 1986:32; Seagrave, 1989:5). Subsequent discussions have focused mainly on the size of the problem and the extent of the vulnerability of Asian and Black people compared with the white populations. For example, a year later the Policy Studies Institute (Brown, 1984), conducted a survey of Asian and Black populations. It found that of those who had experienced racial harassment, 60% had not reported these cases to the police. In addition the PSI suggested the incidence of racial harassment was probably 10 times that estimated in the 1981 Home Office survey. Also in 1982 the Greater London Council (GLC) conducted an inquiry into racial harassment in London. It took evidence from ninety nine organizations and individuals. The GLC concluded that 'racial harassment in London is an increasingly serious problem' (GLC, 1984:2).

What these early studies revealed was the high incidence and potential invisibility of many racial harassment experiences. By the middle of the 1980s very little had changed. A poll commissioned by London Weekend Television's *London Programme* in 1985 found that 1 in 4 Asians in the Boroughs of Redbridge, Waltham Forest, Tower Hamlets and Newham had been racially attacked (CRE, 1987b:16). While a survey undertaken by Leeds Community Relations Council during 1985-86 concluded the level of racial harassment was ten times that estimated by the Home Office's 1981 survey. In Glasgow the Scottish Ethnic Minorities Research Unit in 1987 found that 44% of racial incidents were not reported to the police (Home Office, 1989). This particular problem area was further highlighted in the 'Newham Crime Survey'. In 1986 the London Borough of Newham commissioned the Harris Research Centre, to survey crime generally, with particular reference to racial harassment in the Borough. It reported that: 1 in 4 of Newham's Black and Ethnic Minority residents were victims of racial harassment in the 12 months prior to the survey; 2 out of every 3 victims had been victimized on more than one occasion; only 1 in 20 of the 1,550 incidents recorded by the survey were reported to the police; and 80% of Black and Ethnic Minority victims were dissatisfied with the police handling of the case. In 1987 the Home Office carried out its second survey, since 1981, concerning racially motivated incidents reported to the police. It reported further increases in the victimization rates for Asian and Black people:

> The 1987 survey showed this figure to be even greater with the rate for Asians being 141 times that for whites and the rate for Black people 43 times that for whites.

> (Seagrave, op. cit.)

The particular significance of this welter of research was reasonably summarized by the Home Office led inter-government departmental Racial Attacks Group. In 1989 it published a comprehensive report on the role and responsibility of statutory agencies in combating racial attacks. Following a review of many studies in this area it observed:

> whatever the view is taken about the accuracy of any particular set of statistics or the methodology of any particular piece of research, *all the evidence points to a problem that is worryingly large.*

> (Home Office, 1989; emphasis added)

What was also evident about much of this research was how, once the random incident perspective had been conceded, the policy focus narrowed around competing determinations and estimates of the size of the problem. In our view this distorts rather than illuminates the issues involved. Moreover much of this distorted understanding is *perpetuated by agencies who in a sense are placed in a position to know better.* Trying therefore to characterize the problem from

131

the perspective of any one agency is not an easy or exact task, yet there are a number of important observations which we can make and are of *general* application. Central to this approach is the view that the emphasis of previous research on the *size or incidence of the racial harassment problem* has tended to eclipse the experience of its *spread* over time and across locations. This has resulted in policy makers chasing the comparative shadows of rises in numbers of unreported incidents rather than focusing on locally identifiable patterns. Our research suggests that an alternative and complementary approach needs to start from a qualitative premise that victims of racial harassment are knowledgeable about the experiences of victimization. This is also the context for making use of available local statistics.

**The relevance of local statistics**

During the latter half of the 1980s statistics in Waltham Forest were collected separately by the local police and the Council's Housing department with regard to incidents recorded by them. Given the nature of reporting, [variously estimated between 1 in 4 for crime in general (Home Office, 1989:161) and 1 in 10, for racial harassment in particular (Brown, 1984)] caution must be exercised in their interpretation. Nevertheless we intend to argue the figures are essentially symptomatic of entrenched social behaviour in particular places and locales which need to be appropriately *patterned*. Table 4.1 below sets out the number of incidents of racial harassment recorded by the police and Housing department in the Borough during 1986-1989 (the only years for which comparable figures were available).

In this period, broadly similar levels of incidents of racial harassment were recorded separately by the Housing department and the police.[2] Ordinarily it might be expected that many more incidents would be recorded by the police than any other agency. For example, recent Home Office research in this area found of those who had previously experienced racial victimization, 60% stated that they had reported the incident to the police, 9% to the Council and 22% had not reported it to anyone (Seagrave, 1989:25-26). On the basis of this research, the general expected ratio of cases reported to the police compared with the Council might be just over 6:1. A ratio like this of course is an aggregate of many different regions in the country and obviously does not reflect local variations. But it also needs to be recognized that the *reporting* of incidents of racial harassment or any other crime to agencies does *not necessarily reflect the recording* of those complaints. In other words, the statistics compiled *reflect the particular recording practices* of those agencies. If any agency does not record a case of racial harassment reported to it, it will not feature in the statistics of those agencies. This means that incidents not reflected in the statistics will consist of *levels of non-recording as well as non-reporting.*

## Table 4.1

## Number of incidents/cases of racial harassment recorded by the police and Housing department in Waltham Forest, 1986-1989

| | | Agency | |
|---|---|---|---|
| Year | Police | Housing | department |
| 1986 | 66 | 80* | (54)** |
| 1987 | 80 | 50 | (35) |
| 1988 | 55 | 76 | (49) |
| 1989 | 71 | 71 | (46) |
| Total | 272 | 277 | (184) |

Source:  Metropolitan police: evidence to the Inquiry (1989)
Housing department: evidence to the Inquiry (1989) and statistics on racial harassment for 1989
*total including repeated incidents
**figures in brackets indicate number of households

Examining Table 4.1 in terms of the orthodox approach does not yield much useful information. For example it is clear that during 1986-1989 roughly proportional numbers of incidents were recorded by the police and the Housing department. As there are no great fluctuations in the figures for such a short time-band not much more can be said. It may be that the figures are higher or lower in other jurisdictions, but that does not point to anything significant in Waltham Forest. In short, all the statistics point to (notwithstanding the factors of under-reporting/non-recording), is that the level of recorded incidents is consistent. The statistics do not convey anything about the impact of racial harassment in the lives of its victims, or its sedimentation in particular locations. De-contextualized numbers like these oblige us to see racial harassment as a random occurrence rather than a *pervasive condition.*

Initially a more useful way to make sense of the figures is to place them in the context of what we *know* from previous research about the incidence of under-reporting.  For example, further evidence of the status of under-reporting was revealed when we examined some of the findings of a social survey of high rise estates in the Borough, carried out by the Council's Estates Improvement

Team in 1988. On five estates, where Asian, Black and Ethnic Minority people comprised an average of 40% of the tenants on each estate, about 1 in 6 (15%) had experienced some form of racial harassment. Of those who had experienced racial harassment *just over 1 in 10 (11%) had reported it to the Housing department* (figures on reports to the police were not available). This suggested that levels of racial harassment in the Borough, where they were measured by reports to the Housing department, may have been under estimated by a factor as large as 10. It is also worth noting a survey of Afro-Caribbean households carried out by the Council's Social Services department in 1989 found nearly 1 in 4 of its sample claimed to have been subjected to racial harassment and of this group 61% did not report these incidents to *any agency* (Waltham Forest,1990c).

Despite the value of local statistics they are of limited use if they do not also allow us to indicate the pervasiveness of racial victimization in peoples lives or in their relationship to the social environment. In making observations like these we are aware that racial harassment takes many forms and has various gradations of impact on people (all of which may influence decisions to report) and that some aspects of racial harassment may be more likely to be reported than others. But observations like these however, only point to the existence of individual differences in the way racial victimization is experienced and *should not* be taken to suggest that some aspects of racial harassment are more serious than others for the communities affected, indeed they are usually inter-related. The failure to report racial harassment seems to say more about the experience of dissatisfaction with local agencies responses than about the lack of impact of the incident itself. In order to develop an understanding of the problem we need to look beneath the issues raised by the statistics of under-reporting. Quite simply we need to focus on peoples' experiences of their surrounding locations. We need to be particularly sensitive to the fact that the pervasiveness of racial harassment appears to be shaped by its entrenchment in particular places over time and its dispersion across various locations. We need to conceptualize this as a pattern.


## The concept of spread

The pervasiveness of racial harassment, its apparent longevity, its regular inscription in a social environment highlights for us the basis of a discernable pattern. Ironically it is the consistent levels of recorded statistics which point to this. The key problem in conceptualizing a pattern however has been the temporal bias of these statistics, their yearly periodization as aggregates of random incidents. This has obscured the persistent *spatial recurrence* of racial harassment in the lives of the victimized communities. In this sense our examination of Waltham Forest during the 1980s (see Chaper 1) was quite strategic. It not only alerted us to the analytical importance of contextual experiences beyond the statistical, but to the significance of the *cartography of racial harassment* in the lives of victimized communities as they 'lived' its geography and history. The analysis we develop in the rest of this Chapter uses this insight to demonstrate how the pervasiveness of racial harassment can be patterned in terms of its *spread*. There are two dimensions to this: the first refers to 'dispersion' which describes the configuration of racial harassment across various locations; while the second refers to 'entrenchment', this describes its concentration in specific locations over time. Taken together these interactive dimensions can be used analytically to conceptualize the spread of racial harassment as a territorial pattern in what Jackson (1987:14) describes as the 'complex interweaving of social relations and spatial structures'. However, it is with peoples *mental mapping* of the locations of these experiences that we need to begin our analysis. As we shall see this is an important concept in clarifying the apparent randomness of racial harassment incidents as well as illuminating the patterns of victimization which we discuss in more detail in Chapter 5.

*Racial harassment mapping*

In a bounded jurisdiction like a London Borough, where the use of living and working space is recurrent and habitual, it is always possible for people to cognitively survey the distribution of actual and possible victimization experiences in particular settings. In this way domains of relative safety or places to avoid become focal points in 'ways of seeing' (Jackson, 1989) the social landscape. These modes of understanding the nature of the social environment not only vary across race, gender, sexuality, class and so on, they generally construct the basis of the lived relation to the surrounding locations. Clearly where this spatial awareness inscribes itself in the personal or social skills used to improvise strategies to cope with danger or to wrestle with safety considerations (see Stanko, 1990), a distinctive 'mental map' has emerged.

A significant dimension of peoples experience of location then involves the formation or imaging of mental maps of their social environment. In order to establish a credible basis for identifying the spread of racial harassment (i.e. its history and geography) we believe it is important to place this in the context of what victims or observers of racial harassment know or perceive about its location in the urban landscape. In other words, what are their mental maps? As Gould and White (1974:28) have noted:

135

Cities are not always pleasant places to live in, and the
information that goes into building a mental image of a
particular area *may reflect more than just the knowledge
of landmarks and routes.*

(emphasis added)

The basis of our approach to mental mapping was prefigured in Chapter 1 where
it became clear to us that a trend emergent during the 1980s in Waltham Forest,
was the formation of a perception in the Asian community which identified
various regions of the Borough with racial harassment. In other words the
historical incidence of racial harassment (i.e. its entrenchment) had stimulated
a geographical awareness of its various locations (i.e. its dispersion). Clearly
this process not only refers to the direct experience or witnessing of racial
victimization but also to the responses of local community activity, the media
and statutory agencies in developing a public forum where this knowledge was
both disseminated and amplified. It is certainly reasonable to assume that many
people, particularly victims, have formed their own mental maps of the spread
of racial harassment. Spatial experiences contain indicators of the locations and
patterns of racial harassment. When combined with the statistics which arise
from those complaints of racial victimization actually recorded by local
statutory agencies (e.g. police, Housing departments), despite their limitations,
we can begin to develop firmer indications of these spatial patterns.

## Understanding dispersion

In order to develop an understanding of the spread of racial harassment in the
Borough (i.e. its various locations), the evidence submitted to the Inquiry was
examined using 'content analysis'.[3] *This involved codifying the mental
mapping of racial harassment in the Borough.* Where specific places (e.g.
roads, dwellings) were referred to as sites of harassment, these were aggregated
and proportioned as a percentage for each of the Borough's three parliamentary
constituencies [Chingford, Walthamstow, Leyton (see Figure 4.1A below)]. In
a similar manner electoral wards were also identified. Of these, the five wards
with the highest percentages of references to locales of racial harassment are
shown in Figure 4.1B below.

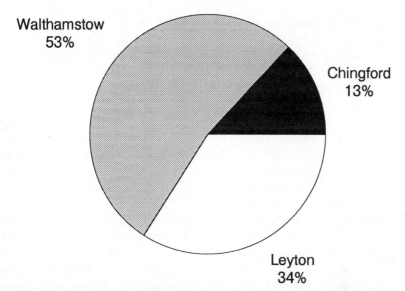

**Figure 4.1A: Spread of incidents of racial harassment in Parliamentary constituencies shown as a proportion of the Borough**
Source : Evidence submitted to the Inquiry (1989)

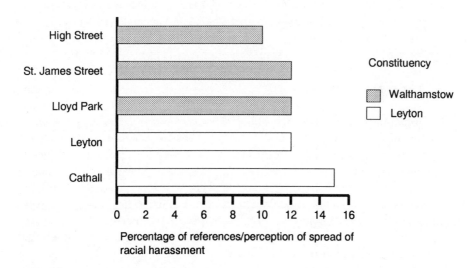

**Figure 4.1B : Spread of incidents of racial harassment in electoral wards shown as a proportion of the Borough**
Source: Evidence submitted to the Inquiry (1989)

Figure 4.1A is based upon incidents perceived to have taken place in specifically defined locations. It clearly identifies Walthamstow as the main problem area. Walthamstow was associated with 53% of the references made; it was mentioned 19% more times than Leyton which was ranked the second most problematic constituency. Both these constituencies it should be noted contain the highest numbers of Asian, Black and Ethnic Minority people in the Borough (see Appendix 1).

Figure 4.1B shows the top five electoral wards in the Borough where racial harassment was perceived to be particularly entrenched. Cathall ward was clearly the worst problem locale, being associated with 15% of the references to places of racial harassment. However the largest concentration of racial harassment was in three wards, all of which are located in Walthamstow. These are Lloyd Park, St. James Street and High Street, together they accounted for 34% of the total of references to locations of racial harassment. These three wards were associated with the same proportion as the whole of the Leyton constituency (see Figure 4.1A above). In all, the top five wards cover nearly two thirds (61%) of references in the evidence to where racial harassment took place in the Borough.

Both Figures 4.1A and 4.1B identify the locations of people's perceptions of racial harassment in the Borough. Although we should not place too much weight on these findings alone, in a provisional way they can be regarded as *estimates* of the proportionate spread of racial harassment across the Borough. What is more interesting however, is that when combined with data drawn from elsewhere (e.g. police statistics, Housing statistics) we can begin to shed some light on the *persistence* of this spread over time.

*Mapping the police statistics*

It is important to recognize the time-space parameters of racial harassment statistics since these greatly determine the value of the sense we can draw from them. For example, we can see from Table 4.2 (below) that since 1986 the spread of recorded racial incidents between the divisions has been fairly evenly distributed. However if 1987 is taken as the base year for comparison then it is apparent that increasingly the Chingford police division has recorded more racial incidents than Leyton division.[4] It is a complex question whether this disparity is due to the greater incidence of racial harassment in Chingford division or a greater propensity for reports to the police in that location of the Borough or a greater willingness of Chingford police to record incidents. The mental mapping approach is helpful here only insofar as it suggests that Walthamstow, which forms part of the Chingford police division, is where racial harassment was most entrenched. This clearly cannot be ignored. A further perspective on this is indicated in the *percentage distribution* between the divisions in terms of the proportions of recorded racial incidents. Again if matters are considered since 1986 the percentage distribution is very close: on average 49% of incidents in the Borough have been recorded in Leyton police division and 51% in Chingford. However, when the figures are considered since 1987 there is a marked difference, the average distribution is Leyton division 41% and Chingford division 59%. Although comparisons over a three year period are insufficient to warrant suggestions of a trend, it is worth noting that in 1987 and 1988 60% and 62% respectively of racial incidents recorded by the police were in Chingford division. Interestingly this mirrors the figures for the proportionate perception of the spread of racial harassment in the Borough constituencies of Chingford and Walthamstow (see Figure 4.1A above). In the terms of our approach 66% of the references to places of racial harassment specified Walthamstow and Chingford [i.e. when the figures are combined (see Figure 4.1A)]. Together these locations as we have already pointed out, correspond very closely to the terrain of Chingford police division.

**Table 4.2**

**Number and percentage distribution of racial incidents recorded in Waltham Forest's Leyton and Chingford police divisions during 1986-1989**

*Year*

| Police division | 1986 No. % | | 1987 No. % | | 1988 No. % | | 1989 No. % | | Total Av. % dist | |
|---|---|---|---|---|---|---|---|---|---|---|
| Leyton | 48 | (73) | 32 | (40) | 21 | (38) | 33 | (46) | 134 | (49) |
| Chingford | 18 | (27) | 48 | (60) | 34 | (62) | 38 | (54) | 138 | (51) |
| Total | 66 | (100) | 80 | (100) | 55 | (100) | 71 | (100) | 272 | (100) |

Source:  Metropolitan police: evidence to the Inquiry (1989) and racial incident statistics 1989

In their submission the Metropolitan police provided details of the racial incidents recorded in both divisions during 1987 and 1988. The details included the *Home Beat* area in which the incident was reported [5] (see Appendix 1). An analysis of these statistics provides further information on the locations of incidents of racial harassment. In 1987 42% of all reports of racial incidents recorded by the police in Chingford division occurred in the Home Beat areas

1B and 2A. It should be noted that Home Beat 1B covers parts of the Higham Hill and Lloyd Park electoral wards; while 2A covers parts of the Higham Hill, Lloyd Park and Chapel End wards. In 1988 the same Home Beats accounted for 51% of racial incidents recorded by the police in the Chingford division. Most of the locales mentioned here are in the Walthamstow constituency. In the Leyton police division in 1987 the concentration of racial incidents covered three Home Beats which accounted for 61% of those recorded by the police. These were Home Beats 4A (covering the Cathall ward), 3D (covering the Leyton ward) and 4B (covering the Leytonstone and Cann Hall wards). In 1988, one Home Beat, 4A, accounted for 33% of racial harassment incidents recorded on Leyton police division.

When the figures drawn from the police Home Beats are compared with our findings of the perceived dispersion of racial harassment incidents in electoral wards (see Figure 4.1B above), it is clear that the wards most identified with racial harassment are Cathall and Leyton (in the Leyton constituency) and Lloyd Park (in the Walthamstow constituency).

*Mapping the Housing department's statistics*

There are some interesting points of comparison with the local police statistics when we consider in detail the Housing department's statistics for the period 1986-1989. The Housing department it will be recalled prepares its statistics on a household rather than incident basis. According to its evidence, about half of the households recorded, experienced repeated incidents of racial harassment. At this level at least, the figures strike an interesting balance between the apparently random and systematic occurrence of racial harassment. The figures also provide another perspective on the spread of racial harassment incidents over time and across locations (e.g. different wards in the Borough). Table 4.3A below shows the relative concentration of racial harassment in the constituencies of the Borough, it differs slightly from what we have considered so far (see Figure 4.1A above). From the perspective of the Housing department, the Leyton constituency appears to be the most problematic region. In keeping with the approach we have taken here Table 4.3B examines the spread of racial harassment across the electoral wards. This supports our earlier findings that the top three wards identifed with racial harassment are Cathall, Leyton and Lloyd Park. It is important to emphasize when interpreting both tables the need to take account *of the persistence over time of recorded incidents across particular locales*. These are necessary indicators of what we have described as the *spread* of racial harassment.

## Table 4.3A

**Number and percentage of recorded households reporting racial harassment to the Housing department in the years 1986-1989, across the Parliamentary constituencies in Waltham Forest**

*Year*

| Constituency | *1986* No. % | | *1987* No. % | | *1988* No. % | | *1989* No. % | | *Total* No. Av.% | |
|---|---|---|---|---|---|---|---|---|---|---|
| *Chingford* | 6 | (11) | 8 | (23) | 6 | (12) | 5 | (11) | 25 | (13) |
| *Walthamstow* | 23 | (43) | 12 | (34) | 18 | (37) | 20 | (43) | 73 | (40) |
| *Leyton* | 25 | (46) | 15 | (43) | 25 | (51) | 21 | (46) | 86 | (47) |
| *Whole Borough* | 54 | (100) | 35 | (100) | 49 | (100) | 46 | (100) | 184 | (100) |

Source: Housing department: evidence to the Inquiry (1989) and statistics on racial harassment for 1989

**Table 4.3B**

**Number and percentage distribution of recorded households reporting racial harassment across electoral wards, over the period 1986-1989**

*Years 1986-1989*

| Electoral ward | No. | Percentage Borough | Percentage constituency | |
|---|---|---|---|---|
| Cathall | 32 | 18% | Leyton | (38%) |
| Leyton | 31 | 17% | Leyton | (37%) |
| Lloyd Park | 30 | 16% | Walthamstow | (41%) |
| Higham Hill | 14 | 8% | Walthamstow | (19%) |
| Wood Street | 10 | 6% | Walthamstow | (14%) |
| Valley | 9 | 5% | Chingford | (36%) |
| Forest | 9 | 5% | Leyton | (11%) |
| Cann Hall | 7 | 4% | Leyton | (8%) |
| Hoe Street | 7 | 4% | Walthamstow | (10%) |
| Hatch Lane | 6 | 3% | Chingford | (24%) |
| High Street | 6 | 3% | Walthamstow | (8%) |
| St. James Street | 6 | 3% | Walthamstow | (8%) |
| Leytonstone | 5 | 3% | Leyton | (6%) |
| Chapel End | 4 | 2% | Chingford | (16%) |
| Endlebury | 2 | 1% | Chingford | (8%) |
| Larkswood | 2 | 1% | Chingford | (8%) |
| Chingford Green | 2 | 1% | Chingford | (8%) |
| Hale End | 0 | 0% | Chingford | (0%) |
| Grove Green | 0 | 0% | Leyton | (0%) |
| Lea Bridge | 0 | 0% | Leyton | (0%) |
| *Total* | 182 | 100% | | |

Source: Housing department: evidence to the Inquiry (1989) and statistics on racial harassment for 1989

Table 4.3A clearly shows the Leyton constituency as containing the largest single proportion of households affected by racial harassment which came to the attention of the Housing department in each year of the period 1986-1989. On average 47% of racial harassment cases were associated with the Leyton constituency for this period, although a substantial amount was also associated

142

with Walthamstow. This contrasts with the data used in our 'mental mapping' method and the police statistics considered earlier, both of which pointed to Walthamstow as the main region of incidents of racial harassment. Of course, given the inestimable levels of non-reporting/non-recording, the apparent size of the problem in various locations measured in numbers of recorded incidents should not be the sole or major concern. What is perhaps more important in this context is the *extent of the spread of households* reporting racial harassment across the Borough. This is the strength of Table 4.3B which illustrates a wide range of household locations in electoral wards. Of the 20 electoral wards in Waltham Forest, 17 have during the period produced circumstances in which reports of racial harassment have been recorded by the Housing department. This highlights the range of dispersion. In the light of this it is instructive to examine the electoral ward spread of recorded incidents *within each constituency* using both the Housing department's statistics and the results from our 'mental mapping' investigation. On this basis we can examine relative levels of entrenchment. It also offers an extremely useful comparison between two differently derived perspectives on the relative locations of racial harassment in the Borough.


## Understanding entrenchment

The observations developed so far in the previous section highlight *the significance of dispersed locations in the incidence of racial harassment*. In our view, this means that racial harassment should not be considered simply as a *general* spatial problem. This level of assessment is too abstract and quite misleading, depending as it does solely on the size or numbers of incidents reported to or recorded by agencies. These after all are an under-estimate of the actual incidence. Racial harassment is more complex than a question of numbers, but it is also more than its various locations. For example, the immediate circumstances of its occurrence may *appear* to be randomly distributed but, irrespective of the putative numbers of reports at any particular time and place, *racial harassment in Waltham Forest seemed to be firmly attached to certain locales, even though it could occur almost anywhere in the Borough.* Local statistics need to be analyzed in this context. This is a *pattern*, it has developed over time and it is this *additional temporal factor* which gives racial harassment part of its characteristic entrenchment in Waltham Forest (see for example Tables 4.3A and 4.3B above). The apparent entrenchment of racial harassment in various electoral wards is where we need to begin in order to demonstrate the relevance of the approach to analysis we have undertaken.

143

There are seven electoral wards in the Leyton constituency. According to the Housing department's figures (see Table 4.3B) racial harassment is spread across five wards, these are: Cathall, Leyton, Forest, Cann Hall and Leytonstone. The greatest concentration of recorded incidents was in the Cathall and Leyton wards which accounted for 75% in the constituency. Our 'mental mapping' approach also specified five wards, these were: Leyton, Cathall, Grove Green, Forest and Lea Bridge. Similarly of these the greatest concentration was perceived in the Cathall and Leyton wards which accounted for 78% of the references to locales in the Leyton constituency.

There are six electoral wards in Walthamstow. The Housing department's statistics suggest that the spread of recorded incidents is across all six wards, these are: Lloyd Park, Higham Hill, Wood Street, Hoe Street, High Street and St James Street. The first two of these wards accounted for 60% of all the recorded incidents; this is where the spread appeared to be most concentrated. Also in the 'mapped' evidence to the Inquiry all the electoral wards in Walthamstow were perceived as locales of racial harassment. The greatest concentration was perceived in High Street, Lloyd Park, Higham Hill and St. James Street which were identified in 80% of the spread.

The Chingford constituency is made up of seven electoral wards. According to the Housing department the spread of racial harassment covers six of these: Valley, Hatch Lane, Chapel End, Endlebury, Larkswood and Chingford Green. The concentration appeared greatest in two wards, Valley and Hatch Lane which accounted for 60% of the recorded incidents. Again, 'mental mapping' identified four wards with racial harassment: Chapel End, Hatch Lane, Chingford Green and Valley. Of these the greatest concentration was perceived in Valley and Chapel End which accounted for 77% of the references made.

Figure 4.2 below displays the wards in each constituency which, according to our 'mapping' overall and the Housing department's statistics in particular, are most associated with the occurrence of racial harassment.In each of the Borough's three constituencies there were at least two wards where racial harassment appeared to be most entrenched. It is important to emphasize here that we are not comparing the wards in one constituency with the wards in another, rather we have highlighted the wards in Figure 4.2 *as locales of their particular constituency where racial harassment is most identified.* (In this way we can also point to the significance of considering the dispersion of racial harassment across different types of location.) This view is drawn from the strong association apparent between the perceptions of victims and observers in their evidence and the statistics from the Housing department for the period 1986-1989. Arguably the experiences of racial harassment, which are associated with these particular wards, have been deeply inscribed in local perceptions and knowledge over time. This can be described as the cartography of racial victimization.

| Electoral ward | Constituency |
|---|---|
| Cathall<br>Leyton | Leyton |
| Lloyd Park<br>Higham Hill | Walthamstow |
| Valley<br>*Chapel  *Hatch<br>End    Lane | Chingford |

**Figure 4.2:  The main electoral ward locations of racial harassment in each Parliamentary constituency in Waltham Forest**

Source:  Evidence to the Inquiry (1989)
Housing department: evidence to the Inquiry (1989) and statistics on racial harassment for 1989
*(*Inquiry evidence and Housing statistics differed as to which ward was jointly significant with the Valley ward)*

## Places of racial harassment

We have so far emphasized the importance of considering locations in the patterns of racial harassment. This can be taken further to encompass more precise locations, that is, particular places where incidents occur. What we need to be aware of is the extent to which different locales (e.g. electoral wards) are 'framed' by places which are used as settings for racial victimization. These may point to 'landmarks' in the social environment which are 'symbols' of 'racially contested space'. In this sense, whatever its general location, racial harassment is always placed. For example, according to Metropolitan police racial incident statistics for 1988 and 1989 the largest proportion of incidents recorded by the police take place in the street. In 1988 and 1989 the street represented 54% of the places of incidents recorded by the police. The second highest category of place in the police's statistics was 'private addresses'. In 1988 this represented 35% of the places recorded, and in 1989 the figure was 34%. The third main category 'businesses', represented 8% of recorded incidents in 1988 and 9% in 1989. (The other categories of place identified by the police are 'religious', 'political' and 'school'.)

A Home Office study of 'racially motivated' incidents reported to the police carried out in 1987, found that over 26% of all racially motivated incidents took place on a local authority estate or in the victim's council house or flat. While 18.5% of incidents took place in the street and just over 11% of incidents took place in shops owned or worked in by victims (Seagrave, 1989). Both this and the Metropolitan police figures point to households and the street as the main places where racial harassment occurs. This finding is supported by evidence to our Inquiry. An analysis of places referred to as sites of racial harassment identified housing estates and the street as equally problematic. The top five places mentioned are set out in Figure 4.3 below.

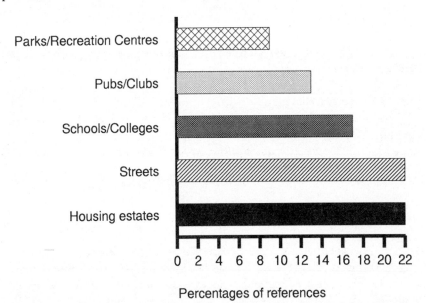

**Figure 4.3: Percentage distribution of places of racial harassment - the top five references**
Source: Evidence to the Inquiry (1989)

Although many other types of places were mentioned, the top five places in Figure 4.3 represented 83% of all the references.

*Housing Estates* Unlike other places of racial harassment in the Borough we are able to comment extensively on particular housing estates because of the greater availability of information. The Housing department in its evidence to the Inquiry provided details of 11 estates with what might be termed a *significant statistical history of racial harassment.* The estates are identified in Table 4.4A below which shows the percentage of incidents recorded by the Housing department for each estate, for each year since 1985. [6]

**Table 4.4A**

**Percentage of incidents of racial harassment on estates recorded by the Housing department, 1985-1988**

| Name of estate | Electoral ward | 1985 | 1986 | 1987 | 1988 | |
|---|---|---|---|---|---|---|
| | | *Year percentage* | | | | |
| Oliver Close | Leyton | - | 6% | 3% | 14% | |
| Leyton Grange | Leyton | 8% | - | 3% | 4% | |
| Beaumont Road (Saints block) | Leyton | - | 5% | - | 4% | |
| Beaumont Road (Court block) | Leyton | - | 6% | 5% | 2% | |
| Cathall Road | Cathall | 17% | 10% | 16% | 6% | |
| Avenue Road | Cathall | - | 5% | 11% | 4% | |
| Downsell Road | Cathall | - | 2% | 3% | 4% | |
| Billet Road | Higham Hill | 8% | 13% | 8% | 10% | |
| Priory Court | Lloyd Park | 25% | 21% | 11% | 12% | |
| Boundary Road | St. James St. | 8% | - | 3% | 2% | |
| Chingford Hall | Valley | - | 2% | 8% | 6% | |
| | | 66% | 70% | 71% | 68% | *Sub total* |
| Others | | 34% | 30% | 29% | 32% | |
| | | 100% | 100% | 100% | 100% | *Total* |

Source: Housing Department: evidence to the Inquiry (1989)

Table 4.4A shows the spread of recorded incidents across 11 areas of the Council's housing stock throughout the period 1985-1988. The ward areas in which these estates are located are also indicated. These estates represented approximately 30% of the Council's total housing stock. During 1985-1988 they accounted for an average of 69% of all incidents recorded by the Housing department. In terms of apparent concentrations of reports of racial harassment

147

throughout this period, there were five estates which emerged more clearly than others. These are ranked in Table 4.4B below.

## Table 4.4B

### Five estates with highest percentage concentration of incidents of racial harassment recorded by the Housing department, 1985-1988

| Rank No. | Name of estate | Electoral ward | Percentage of recorded incidents 1985-1988 |
|----------|----------------|----------------|--------------------------------------------|
| 1. | Priory Court | Lloyd Park | 17% |
| 2. | Cathall Road | Cathall | 12% |
| 3. | Billet Road | Higham Hill | 10% |
| 4. | Oliver Close | Leyton | 7% |
| 5. | Avenue Road | Cathall | 5% |
|  |  |  | 51%   Total |

Source:  Housing Department: evidence to the Inquiry (1989)

It can be seen from Table 4.4B that on average over 51% of incidents recorded by the Housing department were reported from just five estates. Also it is evident that each of the five estates is situated in electoral wards which have featured already in our discussion of the spread of racial harassment. These are of course the Cathall, Leyton and Lloyd Park wards. In particular 39% of recorded incidents arose from three estates alone (i.e. Priory Court, Cathall Road and Billet Road). Quite significantly *the Priory Court estate has by far the worst record of any other single estate in the Borough,* its apparent reputation as a place of racial harassment was already established in the opening years of the 1980s (see Chapter 1). This estate appears to provide the most glaring example of the entrenchment of racial harassment in a particular place, in a particular locale over at least a ten year period.

There are further indications of the spread of racial harassment across some of the estates in the Borough available in the social survey of high rise blocks carried out by the Council's Estate Improvement Team in 1988. Table 4.5 below sets out their findings with regard to the proportions of Asian, Black and Ethnic Minority people on each estate who had experienced racial harassment. The researchers involved in this survey observed that 'racial harassment has been identified as a problem' on Chingford Hall estate and large estates in the south of the Borough 'particularly on Avenue estate which has a 27% Caribbean population' (Waltham Forest, 1988).

## Table 4.5

### Asian, Black and Ethnic Minority experiences of racial harassment on high rise estates in Waltham Forest

| Name of estate | Electoral ward | Percentage Asian, Black and Ethnic Minorities | Percentage experienced racial harassment |
|---|---|---|---|
| Bounday Road | St. James St. | 44.7% | 7.5% |
| Avenue Road | Cathall | 42.6% | 8.1% |
| Cathall Road | Cathall | 34.3% | 6.5% |
| Oliver Close | Leyton | 34.3% | 6.6% |
| Chingford Hall | Valley | 30.7% | 4.2% |
| St. Michaels Tower | St. James St. | 28.6% | - |
| Whitebeam Tower | Lloyd Park | 21.5% | - |
| St. Georges Court | Wood St. | 20.0% | - |
| Northwood Tower | Wood St. | 19.0% | - |
| St. David's Court | Wood St. | 16.7% | - |
| John Drinkwater | Leytonstone | 14.8% | - |

Source: High rise system built housing: past, present and future: Report of Council Estate Improvement Team, Waltham Forest (1988)

It would of course be quite wrong to place undue reliability on the statistics in Tables 4.4A, 4.4B and 4.5 in terms of either indicating the so-called size of the problem in these estates or as saying something definitive about which estates are most entrenched in providing the settings for racial harassment. As a general rule these statistics should always be placed in a locational context. We have already noted that under-reporting is a real concern here: for example it is not possible to say, with any certainty, which of these estates is most affected by it. Moreover, it is also worth re-iterating that the differences in the proportions of incidents assigned to each estate, especially over a period of time, may well reflect differences in the recording practices of various Housing estate officers. An estate officer with greater sensitivity to the problem of racial harassment is likely to record more incidents than an estate officer with less appreciation of the issues involved. What however is significant about these statistics, particularly over a period of time (and when combined with data from other sources) is that they may well be indicative of locations which more frequently than others, produce the circumstances in which reports of racial harassment are generated. With these qualifications in mind what we can say is that in Table 4.4B there *appears to be a consistent historical and geographical association between the occurrence/recurrence of racial harassment and these estates.*

149

## Returning to the incidence of racial harassment

It is convenient but misleading to talk of racial harassment *in general.* This obvious abstraction takes the form of many and various persistent incidents. While there are some difficulties entailed in identifying patterns in the occurrence of racial harassment, these difficulties should not be exaggerated to suggest that there is no pattern involved as the Metropolitan police have done (see Metropolitan police, 1989b). As should be evident from our discussion so far we do not think racial harassment is a sudden 'freakish' event like a flash of lightning. In the experiences conveyed to us by Asian and Black people it seems clear that it can be expected *not only to occur in any location but to recur in particular locations.* It is important to re-state this because there is a great deal of confusion among policy-makers concerning the apparent random and opportunistic nature of racial harassment. Although we have attempted to argue that there is a definite pattern involved (i.e. the spread of racial harassment), we need also to say how that cartography relates specifically to its incidence. It is therefore important to consider how this incidence can be conceptualized especially over time and across locations.

### *Statistical context*

The starting point for an analysis of the incidence of racial harassment is usually the statistics collated by the police. For example in 1988 and 1989, 81% of the racial incidents recorded by the Metropolitan police were concentrated in three main categories. In order of magnitude these were 'Verbal abuse' (36%), 'Assault' (28%) and 'Criminal damage' (17%). These are also the main types of racial harassment which are reported to and subsequently recorded by the police nationally (Seagrave, op. cit.) and by other agencies. In evidence to the Inquiry both the Housing department in its statistics for 1986-1988 and Waltham Forest Community Relations Council in an 'anecdotal survey' of racial victimization identified a similar range of categories (see Figures 4.4 and 4.5 below). In addition these categories are characteristic of the evidence overall submitted to the Inquiry (see Figure 4.5 below).

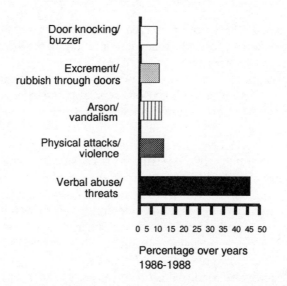

Percentage over years
1986-1988

**Figure 4.4: Main categories of racial harassment incidents recorded by the Housing department, 1986-1988**
Source : Housing department: Evidence to the Inquiry (1989)

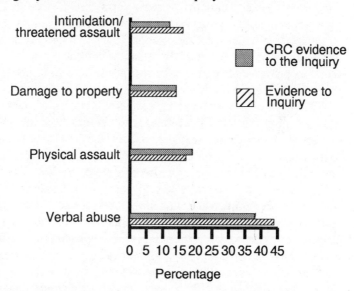

Percentage

**Figure 4.5: Main categories of racial harassment arising from the CRC's anecdotal survey, compared with overall evidence to the Inquiry**
Source: Evidence to the Inquiry (1989)

151

Figures 4.4 and 4.5 have been presented in percentage terms only in order to emphasize the similarities in the relative proportions of the different incidents which, in various combinations, shape the experiences of racial victimization in Waltham Forest. There are however, two important observations which need to be made in relation to these and other racial harassment statistics. First, although useful, figures like these need to be understood in terms of a spatial context. In isolation they provide no indication as to why, or in what circumstances, the incidents displayed *sustain the same relative proportions over time.* For example, what does it mean to say that verbal abuse is the largest single category of racial harassment in Waltham Forest or indeed other parts of London? Furthermore, the evidence to the Inquiry suggests that although verbal abuse was the most commonly referenced form of victimization, it was not mentioned in isolation from other forms of harassment or related activities. In particular the evidence suggests that racial abuse *is also the most common precursor of other forms of racial victimization.*

One pattern which underlies this finding appears to be that persistent verbal abuse can subsequently escalate to assault and that in the absence of the victim(s) retaliating, damage may be done to their property. The time-period between different aspects of racial victimization emerging in this 'scenario' can vary from weeks to months or even years (see Chapter 5). Moreover, the evidence to the Inquiry suggested that this pattern of harassment is sufficiently recognized by Asian and Black people to instill fear and anxiety even where verbal abuse is not followed by assault. Current racial harassment figures therefore provide only partial information, *they say little about the relationship between these incidents in the experience of the victims.*

Our second observation concerns types of racial harassment incidents which are converted into statistical categories. When these are transformed into aggregates or proportions (e.g. percentages) they tend to be presented unrelated to their places of occurrence and locations (e.g. a housing estate or street in a particular locale of the Borough). In other words statistics like those presented in Figures 4.4 and 4.5 provide no suggestion of the locale of particular types of incidents. For example where and in what places racial assaults happen and the relative proportions of connected incidents is as important as how many racial assaults have occurred. It is important to re-emphasize that racial victimization cannot easily be separated into different categories of experience; it certainly does not offer choices. Rather it seems to be part of a 'scenario' or connected set of events over time with its own dynamics which in turn are characteristic of particular places and locations. An Asian household on an estate may report many different types of incident, for example lighted materials through their letter box, racial abuse shouted at them when members of the family venture out, incidents of assault and so on throughout several weeks, months or years.

These incidents are not separable in the experience of the victims; although they may be recorded by statutory agencies as part of this or that statistical category, it is nevertheless important to understand that they may be indicators of a *racial victimization scenario* .

All this clearly has implications not only for the way in which information and statistics are collected but equally importantly how they are presented. One example of a useful presentation which relates proportions of racial harassment incidents to particular places is provided in Table 4.6 below taken from recent Home Office research.

**Table 4.6**

**The most frequently reported racially motivated incidents to the police nationally and the places of their occurrence**

| Location | Offence/incident | | | Total |
| --- | --- | --- | --- | --- |
| | *Personal violence* | *Criminal damage* | *Racial abuse/ harassment* | |
| Victim's shop | 8 | 20 | 8 | 36 |
| Local authority housing/estates | 23 | 33 | 52 | 108 |
| Private housing | 4 | 14 | 29 | 47 |
| Street | 47 | 10 | 16 | 73 |
| *Total* | 82 | 77 | 105 | 264 |

Source: Home Office research, 'Racially motivated incidents reported to the police', Seagrave (1989)

Not only do we see in Table 4.6 the main categories of racial harassment already discussed, but also the varying preponderance of specific incidents in different places. For example it is noticeable that just over half of the incidents of personal violence take place in the street and that just over a quarter take place in local authority housing or estates. This provides some indication at least as to the significance of particular places *used as settings for certain types and combinations of racial victimization*, although, of course all types tend to occur in all places.

The Home Office's research (see Table 4.6 above) identifies Council housing provision in the majority of settings for the greater proportions of different types of racial harassment incidents. On the basis of the evidence submitted to our Inquiry it is unclear to what extent this is indicative of Waltham Forest. But as we have already noted the Housing department, in its evidence, revealed that on average 50% of incidents reported to them had been reported previously. In addition, the Housing department observed there was a 'systematic campaign underway against families on many estates'. Many racial harassment incidents on housing estates in the Borough are premeditated and sustained through calculation. This not only questions the orthodox perspective of the random non-recurring incident, it suggests that at least one aspect of the spread (i.e. dispersal) of different types of racial harassment throughout various locations is also an important aspect of establishing a basis for the pattern of these incidents. Unfortunately figures are not usually collated and presented in this way. Perhaps the nearest example of what we are thinking of is provided in Table 4.7 which is constructed from the Metropolitan police's evidence to the Inquiry. It displays the different numbers (and proportions) of types of racial harassment recorded by the police in the Chingford and Leyton divisions of Waltham Forest.

We should bear in mind of course that the statistics in Table 4.7 are subject to all the distortions arising from under-reporting and non-recording that we have stressed throughout this Chapter. Nevertheless the table does suggest a number of ideas worthy of further consideration. For example, during 1987 and 1988 it appears that the majority of racist arson crimes were recorded in the Leyton division (this includes Leytonstone) and that compared with Chingford (this includes Walthamstow) they formed a more substantial proportion of the incidents recorded by Leyton police (e.g. 10% in 1987 and 19% in 1988). Indeed in 1988 arson was the second highest category recorded by the Leyton police. In both years the greater proportion of serious assaults and criminal damage were recorded by the Chingford police. Whether differences like these point to differences in the nature of the racial victimization scenarios in the divisions or differences in the police response or a combination of both is virtually impossible for us to say. In a limited study of this kind we can only highlight them for attention. It seems clear however that additional insights would be gained if the geographical areas presented in Table 4.7 were smaller and more focused and if the time span was wider. This would improve our knowledge of the local entrenchment of racial victimization across locations and over time.

154

## Table 4.7

## Number and percentage distribution of types of racial harassment in Chingford and Leyton police divisions in Waltham Forest during 1987 and 1988

| | Chingford | | | | Leyton | | | | Total | |
|---|---|---|---|---|---|---|---|---|---|---|
| Type/offence | 1987 | | 1988 | | 1987 | | 1988 | | | |
| | No. | % | No. | % | No. | % | No. | % | No. | % |
| Serious assaults | 7 | (15) | 5 | (15) | 1 | (3) | 3 | (14) | 16 | (12) |
| Minor assaults | 7 | (15) | 3 | (9) | 10 | (30) | 2 | (10) | 22 | (16) |
| Criminal damage | 11 | (23) | 7 | (20) | 4 | (13) | 3 | (14) | 25 | (18) |
| Leafletting | - | - | - | - | - | - | - | - | - | - |
| Treating/abusive/ insulting words/ behaviour | 16 | (33) | 17 | (50) | 14 | (44) | 6 | (28) | 53 | (39) |
| Slogan writing | 2 | (4) | - | - | - | - | 2 | (10) | 4 | (3) |
| Racial discrimination | 1 | (2) | - | - | - | - | - | - | 1 | (1) |
| Disputes | 1 | (2) | - | - | - | - | - | - | 1 | (1) |
| Arson | 2 | (4) | - | - | 3 | (10) | 4 | (19) | 9 | (7) |
| Other | 1 | (2) | 2 | (6) | - | - | 1 | (5) | 4 | (3) |
| Total | 48(100) | | 34(100) | | 32(100) | | 21(100) | | 135(100) | |

Source:  Metropolitan police: evidence to the Inquiry (1989)

## Racial harassment and spatial analysis

At this point it may be useful to reflect briefly on the scope and implications of the analysis introduced in this Chapter. It is usual for observations about racial harassment incidents to be considered by policy makers in terms of amounts and numbers. That much sought after statistic, the so called 'size of the problem' has generally eluded policy makers principally because of the persistent nature of under-reporting  and perhaps the absence of a national survey. While it is generally accepted that the statistics currently available are various levels of under-estimate, this particular approach to 'quantifying' the incidence of racial harassment tends to obscure the significance of other ways of analyzing the issues.

We have argued that an additional approach needs to be undertaken in the analysis of racial harassment. This requires that we move beyond placing the whole emphasis on its incidence (measured in number of reports recorded) in order to evaluate the *dispersion of racial harassment* across various places and locations in a bounded jurisdiction. This should also be combined with an understanding of the time period during which locations of racial harassment have developed. This can provide indications of the extent of its *entrenchment* in particular locales (e.g. the Lloyd Park ward of Waltham Forest). It is this which marks out the spread of racial harassment. In these spatial terms we are in a position to recognize that so called random incidents of racial harassment occur more in particular locations than others, consistently over a period of time. This provides the basis for describing racial harassment as a social experience of location (see also Chapter 5).

With the advantage of this analysis, we can begin to improve our ideas of the patterning of racial harassment incidents. Although racial harassment is often seen as an opportunistic crime which is random and therefore unpredictable, this perspective neglects to consider that racial harassment incidents rarely happen in isolation, are always 'placed' somewhere, and are usually persistent over time. This means we have to think differently about the patterning of racial harassment if effective policies are to be developed. There are at least two stages involved. Firstly where racial harassment occurs, an identifiable pattern is one which relates the proportions of particular types of incident to particular places, in particular locations. We have treated this aspect almost exclusively in this Chapter. As a compliment to this, a second stage of analysis should also consider the circumstances through which racial harassment becomes a connected set of events in the lives of its victims. This is what we describe in the following Chapter as a 'racial victimization scenario'; these have a dynamic pattern or configuration which is inscribed in the victim's experience. The overall rationale and significance of this analytic approach means not only taking the victim's experience of racial harassment seriously *but also the place and location in which it has occurred over time.* Moreover as we argue in the following Chapter we need to know how to take the experience of victimization seriously. The implications of this 'race-spatial' analyis for policy makers need to be considered carefully. Racial harassment should be monitored and responded to by statutory agencies in a mode which addresses its specific historical and geographical contexts. From this perspective it should become possible to comprehend that racial abuse, intimidation and violence has a territorially destabilizing effect on its victims sense of security and quality of life in the social environment. It is considerations like these which are necessary if public agencies are to understand the entrenchment and dispersion (i.e. the spread) of racial harassment and intervene within the space of their jurisdiction.

# Notes

1. This comprises a number of approaches which attempt to supplement the analysis of pre-existing data sets or produce more specific analyses of data or official statistics than currently available.

2. Before comparing these statistics it was important to note the differences in their units of collation. It was the practice of the Housing department to collate numbers of different households reporting racial harassment, these were treated as collective cases rather than individual or isolated incidents like those recorded by the police. On this basis the Housing department figures usually concealed the fact that many households experienced more than one incident of racial harassment. According to the Housing department, between 1986-1989, 50% of households recorded by them reported more than one experience of racial harassment. The figures in Table 4.1 take into account recurring incidents (estimated as at least two) in order to provide an improved estimate of the actual number of incidents rather than households recorded by the Housing department throughout the period. It is these figures which are to be compared with those of the police.

3. According to Weber (1985:9) content analysis is a methodology which 'utilizes a set of procedures to make valid inferences from text'. The procedure adopted here is based on 'category counts'. This involves an analysis of text where particular words are assigned to various categories and the respective totals counted. The 'counting is based on the assumption that higher relative counts (proportion, percentages, or ranks) reflect higher concern with the category' (ibid.56).

4. 1987 is the year in which the Metropolitan police introduced their Force Order on racial attacks - see Chapter 2.

5. Both divisions are broken down into several numbered Home Beats, each of which is the patrolling terrain of a specific police officer (see Appendix 1).

6. This is the year in which the Housing department first began to record incidents of racial harassment reported to it.

# 5 Racial victimization : An experiential analysis

*Dhanwant K. Rai and Barnor Hesse*

> Many attacks on Asians and West Indians are attacks in
> the street when there is clearly no background of a prior
> argument or misunderstanding. In such incidents
> strangers may simply approach others and hit them, kick
> them, throw stones at them or even use knives and bottles
> to assault them.
>
> (Walmsley, 1986)

> research has only just begun to scratch the surface of the
> geography of racist violence and of organized resistance
> by black people.
>
> (Jackson, 1987)

> All victims have the right to specialist advice and
> support.
>
> (Mawby and Gill, 1987)

Asian and Black people have persistently been the victims of racial harassment in Britain (see Gordon, 1990a). Despite this the nature and reality of that experience continues to be questioned and disputed. Particularly alarming is the fact that the varied and connected experiences of racial victimization are all too easily forgotten in the welter of competing policy discussions and debates. But as should be evident the experience of racial harassment is uniquely traumatic principally because these apparently random incidents have a potentially life-long continuity. There is in other words little or no refuge from racial harassment where it has developed and become entrenched in the locations where people live, travel or work over a period of time. This is

158

particularly so where it continues to go unchecked and when support for the victims is often no more than a 'good idea' in the minds of agencies best placed to help but who are ultimately ineffective. What does it mean to experience constant and recurrent verbal abuse, damage to property, personal injury and even the prospect of death as a result of racial harassment? What is racial victimization? These questions are not usually subject to detailed analysis. But in the absence of posing these questions we risk diminishing the needs and rights of victims of racial harassment. In this Chapter we discuss the limitations of crime surveys and limited insights of existing research and argue that the victims of racial harassment should be understood *as* victims of crime. This brings us into conflict with the current field of 'victimology'. But it is within the context of social geography that we present an experiential analysis of the dimensions involved in racial victimization. We argue that the spread of racial harassment is also 'landmarked' by forms of *white territorialism* which in turn are a principal cause of incidents and events in particular places over time. We describe these experiences as *racial victimization scenarios*. This is the second dimension to the patterning of racial harassment. Finally we comment on the role of 'local' agencies in their response to victims of racial harassment, highlighting the importance of victims rights.

## Crime surveys, research and racial victimization

Crime surveys are now dominant in public policy analysis of general victimization. Emerging in the 1960s in the USA and in the late 1970s in the UK, initially they were designed to investigate and quantify the 'dark figure' of crime (i.e. the level of unrecorded crime). These surveys highlight the sort of crimes that go unreported and why, the experiences of victimization and the fear of crime. In the UK the British (National) Crime Survey, conducted by the Home Office was introduced in 1982 and followed up in 1984 and 1988. During the 1980s criminologists associated with Middlesex Polytechnic pioneered various local crime surveys. However, while crime surveys can provide firmer indications of the extent of particular crimes than is available from officially recorded crime statistics either nationally, regionally or locally; they incorporate a number of methodological problems which cast severe doubt on their capacity to 'measure' crime effectively. Walklate (1988:26) argues that crime surveys concentrate on conventional crime, that is, 'crime against the person (meaning for the most part "street crime") and crimes against property'. Other criminal activity which results in personal dehumanization (e.g. racial harassment, anti-Gay violence, domestic violence against women) is not usually considered in its own specific terms. Much of the reason for this lies in the incapacity of the crime survey to capture victimization experiences which are processual, that is, regular occurrences; they simply cannot quantify this. The cyclical and multiple features of particular forms of victimization are therefore not reflected in crime surveys. Genn (1988:90-91) suggests, 'this failure stems primarily from the general orientation of victim surveys and partly from the inherent limitations of the social survey method as a means of understanding complex social processes'. The British Crime Survey, for example, conceptualizes crime as a discrete event. Implicit in this characterization, argues Genn 'is potential victims as people who lead relatively crime-free lives which may, if they are unlucky be punctuated by becoming the victim of an assault, a burglary, a theft or some other crime'. This denies a reflection of the social reality of other forms of victimization. Even where conventional crime surveys have attempted to include these experiences, they have been confronted by the 'quantification' problem. For example the British Crime Survey, assigns a top value of 5 'discrete events' to recurrent crime in a victim's life. But this disconnects rather than connects a process.

Feminist research has been particularly critical of the traditional methodological approaches in crime surveys. Stanko (1985) argues that much of the violence against women is hidden from crime surveys, and suggests that the concept and reality of gender stratification has to be given credence to reveal its influence in women's lives. Many feminist writers (see Hall, 1985; Mama, 1990) have analyzed the reality of women's experiences through the formulation of focused questions which inquire into the range of male violence. Interestingly, the local crime surveys, initiated by the Middlesex Polytechnic criminologists, claim to recognize feminist criticisms and to have an approach which embraces the process experienced by the victims. But this apparent modification is negligible when we consider the status of racial harassment in their research. The criticisms of Sim et al. (1987) are relevant here. They suggest that the so-called 'realist criminology' under-pinning this survey approach conceptualizes 'crime (as) a particular problem in deprived inner-city areas; it is predominantly intra-class and intra-racial; it is a reflection of those most basic of capitalist values, individualism and acquisitiveness ..'. One problem with this approach is the idea that if crime goes unchecked, it will divide the working class community, it thus assumes a notion of homogeneity which is unsullied by victimization inscribed in differences of gender, race, sexuality, employment and so on. Specific victimization experiences appear to have no categoric, experiential identity in the local crime survey. This ignores for example the historical and geographical experience of violation encountered by Asian and Black communities in their encounters with 'white Britain'. It is not surprising then that local crime surveys can so easily trivialize the crime of racial harassment.

The second Islington Crime Survey (Crawford et al., 1990), provides a typical example of this. The research presents a detailed analysis of crimes in the London Borough of Islington but singularly fails to examine the nature of racial harassment. Instead it contains a vague gesture to its presence through a reference to 'racial tension' which itself is subsumed under the general category 'public abuse'. In effect the survey marginalizes and obscures racial victimization. This is perhaps all the more surprising given the high number of racial incidents recorded by the police in Islington during 1987-1989. We cite this simply because of the trend, developed in the latter part of the 1980s, when policy makers became increasingly influenced by local crime surveys. Although these surveys purport to examine crime in general they invariably *invisibilize* the specific crime of racial harassment. The point is there is no such thing as crime in general and specific experiences of victimization, demand specific consideration.

Nevertheless it is possible to derive from a small range of research some valuable observations on racial victimization. First there is the *range of its incidence*. For example, the Newham Crime Survey (1987) emphasized its *persistent nature*. It described how 116 victims reported 1550 incidents of racial harassment over a period of one year. Secondly there is its *impact on people's living conditions*. For example, the CRE report (1987a) on racial violence and harassment in housing, *Living in Terror*, described how the plight of victims is exacerbated when their homes, the traditional place of safety, are transformed into dangerous places to be. Thirdly there is the *traumatic experience of reporting racial harassment*. This was considered by the Home Office (1989:89):

> We have frequently been told that some junior police officers do not appear to appreciate that racial motivation can transform an otherwise apparently trivial incident into something that is particularly distressing for the victim. We have also been told of (police) officers who cause offence by dismissing as unfounded the victim's assertion that the incident was racially motivated.

This undoubtedly contributes to the large reservoir of under-reporting we discussed in Chapter 4. Fourthly, there is the *recurrent experience of victimization*. For example, the 1988 British Crime Survey (Mayhew et al., 1989:27) commented:

Afro-Caribbeans and Asians certainly reported many offences against them which they saw as having a racial basis. Being threatened because of race is very common; both Afro-Caribbeans and Asians were also often racially assaulted. For Asians, evidence or suspicion of a racial element in property offences is relatively frequent.

In addition the British Crime Survey noted that Asian and Afro-Caribbean people were more likely to become victims of crime than white people. Many of these experiences were conveyed in evidence to our Inquiry, however what became apparent through analysis is that the *experiential* content of racial harassment is patterned in social and *spatial* terms which mark it out as a distinct form of victimization. This has largely been ignored by victimological research which has so far failed to examine the extent of social variations in the experience of 'personalized' crime. In addition some of its more unhelpful concepts have filtered into the discourse of common sense which exerts its own influence on policy makers.

## The problem of victimology

The study of victimology (i.e. the relationship between the victim and the offender) is a relatively recent development (Walklate, 1988). Its origins can be traced back to the works of Menderson and von Hentig in the 1940s in the USA (Maguire and Pointing, 1988). These early works were primarily concerned with understanding why crime was committed. Attempts to explain the offender's motives extended to understanding the behavioural relationships between the offender and the victim. The analytical question which arose was: 'how did the victim contribute to the enactment of crime?'. This meant, studying the victim's behaviour. A series of misguided investigations followed. One system for understanding the victim's behaviour, developed by von Hentig, was constructed from a typology of thirteen categories, based on psychological and sociological variables which could be related to situations or persons. These categories included: youth, women, the elderly, immigrants, the depressed. Although they were not based on empirical evidence, von Hentig argued that people from any of the categories were more likely to create circumstances in which victimization occurred. Mendelson however went beyond these descriptive categorizations. He created six classifications and assigned 'values' to them. He introduced the notion of 'guilt' and 'innocence' in terms of the victims own complicity in their victimization. This was developed even further in the idea of 'victim precipitation', formulated by Wolfgang in 1958. The dominant logic of these early researches suggested absurdly that victims produced their own victimization rather than the converse. This is a legacy of misreading that continues to influence contemporary policy thinking. For example Kelly and Radford (1987) argue that notions of 'victim precipitated rape' and 'victim blaming' are clearly evident in studies of sexual abuse and domestic violence. These concepts not only reflect commonly held assumptions about sexual violence against women (e.g. the idea that 'women ask for it'), they also fail to take account of women's accounts of their experiences. A similar misreading distorts the diagnosis of racial victimization. Although this has generally been overlooked in the victimological literature it is common for racial victimization to be blamed on the fact that 'they' are here or 'they' are taking our jobs or 'they' refuse to live like 'us'.

Another influential development in victimology is the 'life style' model. This places personal victimization within a framework of life style or 'daily routines' in order to understand recurrent patterns of victimization. The model suggests people live within constraints, 'structural' (e.g. housing conditions, employment, etc.) and 'characteristic' (e.g. age, race, sex, class, etc.). Through adaptation to these constraints they construct a daily routine to their lives. It is in living these routines that they expose themselves to various risks of being victimized. These range from the time that people spend in public areas to the geography they share with the offenders (see Walklate, op. cit.). Smith (1986) discusses how variables in the life style model may be used as indices of risk: for example the size of the household provides a measure of the extent to which guardians are available to protect person and property; unemployment status provides an indicator (timewise) of exposure to risk. Arguably, the life style model also locates responsibility (the degree may be variable) with the victims (i.e. expose themselves to 'crime situations'). Although it may not be possible to alter to a life style of 'no risk' to victimization (e.g. people have to go to work, do shopping, engage in other daily routine activities) the life style model has influenced policy makers current ideas on 'target' hardening. This suggests the more difficult a 'target' is made, the less likely it will risk victimization. The 'target' referred to is confusingly interchangeable between person and property. Thus advice is available in Metropolitan police literature on crime prevention, to keep doors and windows secured with effective bolts - to harden the 'target'. The same idea is conveyed in advice to women (e.g. to avoid using isolated bus stops-see Home Office, 1991). Similar advice has also been made available to Asian, Black and other Ethnic Minority people, to reduce their risk of being racially victimized. The obvious difficulty is that the life style model, while providing a framework to establish a pattern in which property crime occurs, is unable to deal with specific crimes against the person because these have never been its focus. For example, domestic violence is a crime that occurs repeatedly in the home but the life style model can only encapsulate the public arena. Similarly, racial harassment, a recurrent crime with its own distinct dynamics and apparent random occurrences (see Chapter 4) cannot be explained simply within a framework of life style and daily routines. (A lot more might be gained by examining the life styles of the perpetrators of racial harassment.)

Although it may be argued that these victimological ideas, contain some plausible elements, they are nevertheless the source of two major deficiencies in current thinking on victims of crime. The first is a tendency to see crimes against specific persons (i.e. different communities) in the same terms as crimes against property or crimes for financial gain. At this point a second deficiency arises, this is the propensity to 'blame the victims' for their victimization. A great deal of policy analysis, whether concerning victimization or crime prevention, has reinforced these notions considerably. As Walklate (op. cit.:105) has argued in a slightly different context:

> It becomes difficult to envisage, for example, how concepts like 'victim precipitation' or 'life style' can be maintained. These concepts have been constructed with an individualistic bias. They need to be reconsidered in a form which locates victimization in a structural setting rather than an individualistic setting. This means that the explanations offered by victimology need to embrace a view that victimization can occur as a result of processes above and beyond particular individual action or personality.

While there is a need to expand and transform the conventional parameters of victimology, to cover variable and structural concerns, particularly where questions of personal violation or social dehumanization are major issues, this cannot be achieved solely within the confines of that discipline. Our analysis of the specificity of racial victimization suggests that additional perspectives are necessary to re-think the human experience of crimes which recurrently find expression in personal violations. This brings us to the terrain of 'social geography'.

# Geography and victimization

At this stage it is necessary to see how we can advance beyond the limited insights of existing research. We want to argue that ideas drawn from social geography are crucial to an understanding of the *constitutive experiential features* of racial victimization. In the previous Chapter we argued that racial harassment has a local geography (and history) which shapes the terrain for connected, diverse and recurrent *scenarios* of victimization over time. These important experiential contours are usually ignored by policy makers who have failed to perceive, let alone attach any significance to, overlapping patterns of racial victimization and their spatial forms of inscription. In this section we develop this discussion by arguing that a social geography of victimization needs to establish a sense of the relationship people are 'positioned' to have with their social environment and then move to question what makes people feel safe or threatens their idea of security.

## *Elements of a social geography*

How far the themes of victimology have begun to influence social geography is unclear, but a great deal of attention has been devoted to the geographical analysis of crime (Smith, 1986; Cater and Jones, 1989; Evans and Herbert, 1989). Despite its often exclusive reliance on legal definitions of 'offending' and the 'offender', which in turn lends credence to the individuation of 'crime' as a discrete event or criminality as a 'career', it is possible to tease out those elements that could inform (or point to difficulties in) a geography of victimization. Antecedents are the first pre-occupation here. Studies in the incidence of crime or delinquency had their geographical 'origins' in the so-called 'cartographic school'. This was pioneered in France during the mid-nineteenth century and subsequently imitated in Britain. As Cater and Jones (op. cit.:79) have noted, 'the sharp regional variations in offence rates disclosed by the early map makers supplied the first systematic evidence that criminality is space-specific'. It is at this point perhaps that the trajectories of a *potential* geography of victimization and an *actual* geography of crime diverge. As we shall argue they are contiguous rather than co-extensive analytical strategies.

Examining the background to the accentuation of geography in the analysis of crime reveals how conceptions of offending or breaking the law tend towards conceptions of 'space' or 'location' in which victimization occurs as a categoric event rather than an uneven, open-ended process. Consequently it is the spatiality of property (offences) rather than (offences against) the person which determines the criminological focus on victimization. In common with various strands in victimology, the social dimensions of a legal conception of property crime are applied inappropriately to a spectrum of crimes against the person. Arguably this has its roots in the urban ecological analyses of the Chicago school of ethnography in the United States during the 1930s. They spawned the other, more dominant strand in geographical approaches to crime. Particularly emphasizing 'spatiality' they developed an invariable focus on the 'areal co-variance between criminality and various aspects of the built and social environments' (ibid.:81). Leaving aside the difficulties of sustaining and defining an ecological analysis of the 'symbiotic' relation between crime and its environment (see Taylor et al., 1973:114), the general idea of environmental influence on the incidence of crime has continued to orchestrate the composition of many geographical analyses (see Evans and Herbert, op. cit.).

Within criminology generally much of the work undertaken has utilized what has been described as the 'opportunity/ motivation rubric' in analyzing the pattern and incidence of crime (see Cater and Jones, op. cit.:90). Increasingly geographers have emphasized the opportunity dimension in two aspects of space or the environment: 'distance' and 'architectural form'. The question of distance concerns the extent to which property crimes are committed near the offender's residence, where for example, information about potential targets may be readily available. Although this suggests that the 'geography of offences' is connected to the 'geography of offenders', it is recognized that the two are not necessarily isomorphic. Complimenting this approach the issues involved in architectural design and urban landscape draw attention to the extent to which the built environment determines the potential accessibility of a target to criminalization. The problem with both approaches for an analysis of victimization is that the social and spatial experiences of personal violations appear incidental to the concerns about property crime. A tendency to see the 'victim' as an adjunct to the 'crime' persists even when victimization is the acclaimed focus of study. For example, despite the mushrooming of victim surveys during the 1980s, it is instructive to note that 'the technique has not been extensively applied to the spatial patterning of victimization' (ibid.:104). As we have argued above victim or crime surveys have generally attempted to quantify the extent of crime incidents reported/unreported to the police and the extent to which different groups are victimized by crime. The crux of the analytical problem here lies with privileging the construction of 'crime' as a measurable, quantifiable entity and as a discrete category. The resulting statistical patina dissipates the 'actual' experience of victimization. Thus Kelly (1987:48) has argued that the victimization involved in sexual harassment must be seen as a 'continuum' because:

there are no clearly defined and discrete analytical
categories into which women's experiences can be
placed. The experiences women have and how they are
subjectively defined shade into and out of a given
category such as sexual harassment, which includes
looks, gestures and remarks as well as acts which may
be defined as assault or rape.

If we understand Kelly's concept of 'continuum' in spatial as well as
experiential terms then there is much in her observations that bear comparison
with other crimes against specific persons. Within this context the 'official '
category of crime is an insufficient basis for thinking about victimization. Not
only does it portray and skew the experience of personal victimization
(refracted through the dominant image of property crimes), as individualistic
and uni-dimensional. It obscures 'sequence and simultaneity' (Soja, 1989:28)
in victimization by reducing the spatialized continuum to the 'displaced' event.
The 'official' recognition of the victimization of Asian and Black communities,
women and Gay people provides numerous examples of the mystification of
the experiential and the spatial. With these ideas in mind then, we want to argue
that elements of a geography of victimization could emerge through two related
forms of analysis. The first would stress the role of 'space' (e.g. environment,
place) in the continuum of crimes against specific persons within the local
'ethnoscape' (Appadurai, 1990); and the second would examine the awareness
of these experiences through the concept 'spatial security'. The methodological
rationale of both analyses is encapsulated in Jackson and Smith's (1984:194)
contention that social geography should emphasize:

how people convey meaning to space as part of their
negotiated identity; how social interaction is
under-pinned by spatial differentiation; and, perhaps
most ambitiously, how space mediates between social
interaction and social structure.

It is within this context we make a number of theoretical remarks in the
following sections which may assist in developing useful tools of analysis.

*Local ethnoscape*

It is important to understand how particular demarcations of space (the street,
the estate, the neighbourhood), become embroiled in particular strategies of

167

'social dehumanization'. Analysis at this level therefore needs to distinguish '"people" variations with specific types of "people" at greater risk' (Herbert, 1989). But how can this be conceptualized? Appadurai (op. cit.:299) uses the term 'ethnoscape' globally to describe the 'landscape of persons who constitute the shifting world in which we live'. We can apply this equally strategically in a 'local' sense where, irrespective of long-term demographic transformations, (transient) permanence rather than (permanent) transience is the most striking characteristic of the everyday populace at any point in time. Thus for us the local ethnoscape which characterizes a neighbourhood or different regions of a city, consists of variously segmented population gatherings which 'landmark' a sense of 'place' both in relation to defining where 'we' are and to whom 'we' are. The local ethnoscape is constructed as permanence not simply through the recurrence of particular individuals 'here or there', but through the proportional repetition of particular categories of person (e.g. race, class, ethnicity, age, etc.) in the local geography of 'transient congregations'. These include public-transport populations, supermarket populations, residential populations, pedestrian populations, school populations, in short, any regular, 'landmarked' population gathering dispersed across an administratively bounded space. It is the immediacy and accessibility of these 'transient congregations' which for us defines the 'local' context. It is here that people see 'who' is around or 'who' surrounds them, here that people reflect (on) who they are and see reflections of themselves or their social 'differences'. This is the lived 'spacing' of 'community' where social encounters may reinforce or challenge ethno-margins and ethno-centres in the social landscape, where the power to dominate and the domination of power is variously expressed through the 'authority' of race, gender, sexuality, class and so on.

There are many different explanations for the emergence of specific victimizations (e.g. racism, sexism, homophobia). The question of ethnoscape is important because its fluidity and composition may enable us to understand how different (e.g. race, gender, sexuality and class) popular investments are engaged in struggles, in the production of 'imagined communities' (Anderson, 1983). Initially this may be a useful way of thinking about the spatialization of racial victimization. For example the 'multi-cultural society' (one image of the ethnoscape), has a quintessential contestability that 'marks' not only distinct regions and specific localities of Britain but the very idea of Britain itself. It is a precarious 'building block' of an 'imagined world' (Appadurai, op. cit.:298) in which the ethnoscape's 'non-white' constituents, (i.e. its margins) in the clusterings of day to day encounters, may be subjected to interrogation, disruption and violation. Elements of this racist logic have been amplified by Cohen (1988:28) where he writes:

The construction of the ethnic majority in Britain has
depended on the intervention of two key terms - people
and nation. One of the peculiarities of the English is the
way these terms have been coupled together as part of a
tradition of democratic resistance to the governing class
- whilst at the same time becoming actively racialised
and being used to marginalise ethnic minorities within
society.

The generality of this analysis, that is victimization predicated on the
contingencies of marginalization, can be extended to include other forms of
social dehumanization. It requires we recognize that the local ethnoscape is
embedded in a 'plurality of cultures and the multiplicity of landscapes with
which those cultures are associated' (Jackson, 1989:1). Its construction is
constantly a precarious mediation of innovation and conservatism. Populations
at greater risk of victimization may simply be those whose autonomy and
expressiveness of life style, simply by virtue of their 'different' social existence,
or assertion of self-determination, challenges and resists the oppressiveness of
dominant cultures within the ethnoscape and the latter's codification as
somehow representative of the 'people'.

*Spatial security*

People's awareness of their various (i.e. race, gender, sexuality) 'positionings'
within the local ethnoscape is obviously implicated in their comprehension of
personal safety. In this regard there is much to be learned from feminist research
in the area of violence against women which can point to how physical and
social space is conceptualized and negotiated in terms of security. Stanko
(1990) suggests that women devise routine precautionary strategies to limit the
every day possibility of violence. This involves women in the lived experience
of preparing themselves to anticipate male harassment and violence and
actively engages them in the negotiation of their own security. Stanko's (op.
cit.:6) description of this clearly has a wider, albeit differential application:

We gather experiences of safety and danger and come to
perceive situations as safe or as dangerous through our
own accumulated experience. We also come to
understand our own effectiveness in assessing likely
peril.

However, the capacity to 'negotiate danger' requires in many respects 'negotiating power' (ibid.:8). This suggests any adequate analysis should not ignore the wider unequal relations of power in 'society', in particular those of class, race, gender and sexuality. These are 'not mutually exclusive but interactive' (Hanmer, Radford and Stanko, 1989:6). For us this means while it is important to focus on specific forms of victimization, an analysis of people's awareness of spatial security must recognize the 'different' power relationships instituted in the socially constructed 'positionings' of people within the ethnoscape (i.e. society). Despite the undoubted advances of feminist research it has often failed to achieve this, for example Mama (1990:4) argues:

> Black feminists in the West have demanded that race, religion and culture be incorporated into the analysis of violence against women. In doing so they have begun to articulate an approach which challenges the ethnocentricism and essentialism of the approaches that have been generated by those Western feminists who have focussed too narrowly on patriarchy and sexual oppression, and therefore failed to consider class, racial and cultural oppression.

Specific forms of violation need to be seen in the wider context of connected and distinctive instances of social dehumanization. Where racial harassment is concerned, this is the basis of the analysis which goes 'beyond Anti-racism' (see Introduction). Only once we have grasped the relation of 'equivalence' (Laclau and Mouffe, 1985) between contested social differences can we begin to develop the focus of a geography of victimization.

In analytical terms a geography of victimization could also be resourced from a number of concepts recently developed by Giddens (1990). Although specifically designed for 'global' analyses, themes such as 'security versus danger' and 'trust versus risk' can be used to formulate ways of discussing peoples' spatial awareness of 'local victimization profiles'. These include the 'particular portmanteau of threat or dangers' (ibid.:100) which characterize various types of victimization. Understanding the extent to which different sectors of the population have trust or confidence in the social environment broadens the frame for analyzing the contextuality of victimization. It also reveals the social differentials in the quality of routine spatial security. Following Giddens (op. cit.:36) security may be defined as:

a situation in which a specific set of dangers is counter-acted or minimised. The experience of security usually rests upon a balance of trust and acceptable risk. In both its factual and its experiential sense, security may refer to large aggregates or collectivities of people - up to and including global security - or to individuals.

The desire for spatial security is quotidian, its attainment is premised on trust which in turn is routinized through reliability in the face of a continuum of social contingencies. However if, as Giddens (ibid.:54) suggests, trust is deployed in 'environments of risk' where varying levels of security are possible, the question arises, in what specific circumstances does trust palpably lapse? And how is this to be understood? These questions can be answered briefly by returning to the central theme of this book. It should be apparent from our analyses in previous Chapters (1-3) that racial victimization can so easily rupture the balance of day-to-day existence. By fragmenting the experience of living into a series of 'anxiety situations' it momentarily and persistently splinters the touchstones of social interaction. Resulting in what can best be described as 'spatial insecurity'. This characterizes the 'local' disruption people feel in their sense of safety or well-being and in 'the constancy of the surrounding social and material environments of action' (ibid.:92). Racial victimization is a particularly complex form of this disruption. Its analysis raises important questions concerning the racial experience of location.

*White territorialism*

If we accept that the general sense of local 'ethnoscape' and social settings within a bounded jursidiction is shaped by the interventions of diverse local populations, how then do we construe the particular sense of racially contested space which generates racial harassment? For us it is the relationship between white identity, racism and territory. This is what we need to explore in order to conceptualize the experiential or subjective impact of the logic of racial harassment, that is, its inscription in victimization. In other words we need to consider these issues in terms of the *relationship of the perpetrators of racial harassment to their location.* What then is the rationale of these recurrent forms of racist social behaviour in various places and locations over time? Bonnerjea and Lawton (1988:23) in a study of racial harassment in the London Borough of Brent provide an observation which is extremely relevant to our present discussion. They argue:

171

part of the attempt to establish the meaning of racial harassment requires the concept of 'territory'. *In particular it is white people's concept of territory which seems to be the problem.*

(emphasis added)

The concept of 'white territory' is relatively unexplored in much of the literature on racial harassment, yet its salience is evident in the connectedness of the victimization experiences. If racism generally exhibits a logic of social regulation and exclusion (see Introduction), then racial harassment in particular seems geared towards a territorial logic of expulsion, periodically accelerated by tactics of personal violation and even extermination (whichever is calculated to remove or eject the 'non-white' territorial presence). It is important to be clear about how we are thinking of territoriality, in one sense it is,

best understood as a spatial strategy to effect, influence, or control resources and people, by controlling area: and, as a strategy, territoriality can be turned on and off. In geographical terms it is a form of spatial behaviour. The issue then is to find out under what conditions and why territoriality is or is not employed.

(Sack, 1986:1-2)

In another sense the imperatives of territoriality should always be seen as a means to some end (see Smith, 1990). What then is the context and objective of 'white territorialism'? A rhetorical digression may be useful here: Consider the discursive resonances wrought by expressions like 'Pakis go home', 'go back to your own country', 'alien cultures swamping British identity', 'immigrants colonizing Britain', 'blacks ghettoizing the inner-city' or more recently 'Islamic fundamentalism sweeping the nation'. At least two things should be apparent from these spatial obsessions. Firstly there is heightened anxiety about these 'subordinate', 'other' populations resisting regulation and getting out of 'our' control; and secondly, there is a sense in which 'our' British identity (for 'our' read 'white') is under threat because 'our right' to dominate is being questioned; this is the expressive logic of the desire for racial exclusion. The point is, however disorganized or under-elaborated, the rationale of a cumulative racial harassment is the resistance to any diminishment in the authorial claims of a particular white identity to sovereign inscription in any layer of the social landscape or 'ethnoscape' in Britain. This is similar to Gilroy's (1987:48) observation that the 'black presence is thus constructed as

172

a problem or threat against which a homogenous, white, national "we" could be unified'. A subsiduary of this is the localization of racial victimization.

This emphasizes why the concept of 'territory' should be integral to the analysis of racial victimization. In particular it suggests that racial harassment expresses, in the eyes of its perpetrators, a sense of proprietorial relation to social space *as white territory.* This has been observed by other commentators. For example, Husbands (1982) in an analysis of racism in the East End of London during the period 1900-1980 observed that 'attacks tend to cluster in areas where black people form a small minority of the population, *but appear to be challenging the territorial preferences of whites'* (emphasis added). This also provides the background to Smith's (1989:162) discussion of the relationship between space and racial harassment:

> where such violence is particularly localized and intense,
> it may also be read as an expression of territoriality - as
> a popular means of asserting social identity, of defending
> material resources and of preserving social status. Racial
> attacks is (sic), from this perspective, a segregationist as
> well as an exclusionary practice, effected to keep or force
> black people out of particular urban neighbourhoods.

The linkage between territoriality, the assertion of an imperial white identity and racial harassment is a complex one, yet it is possible to argue that it is mediated by customary social behaviour among various individuals and groups in white communities who regard themselves in a racial or cultural terms to be *defending their space against change and transformation.* This persistently victimizes Asian and Black people, insofar as their cultures, demands, values and life styles are perceived as a threat to the exclusive dominance of white identities in the local ethnoscape or the social environment. It is only against this background that the complexity of racial victimization itself can be mapped.

## Racial victimization scenarios

Racial victimization is a complex phenomenon. In addition to its territorial imperatives and settings, our analysis suggests it points to many levels of experiences in a process that is always open ended. The actual incident may appear to be opportunistic from the perspective of the perpetrator (or even the researcher) but the impact on the victim is not transient, it cannot be dismissed as having a low probability of recurring. These are some of the characteristics of burglary victims or victims of street theft and may be termed the *simple* structure of victimization. In contrast, racial victimization, in common with other *crimes against specific persons* (e.g. violence against women, child abuse, anti-Gay violence) is not really carried out for personal financial gain, it seems to be an attempt to exert control over or violate the conduct and life style of the subject victimized. Typically this attempt at control or violation is exemplified through various forms of violence and abuse. In addition the different rationales involved in different types of crimes against specific persons are equally complex.

As we have suggested throughout this book the apparent random distribution of racial harassment incidents seem to have the sense of *deja vu* attached to them, particularly in the light of their persistent recurrence in particular locations. Also, it should be evident from the contextual analyses in Chapters 1-3 that the experience of harassment *as* victimization has various experiential dimensions. It is the patterned connection between these in the lives of the communities which are its focus, that for us invokes the image of scenario to describe what Asian and Black people are able to perceive in their locality even prior to so-called 'first hand experience' (see Chapter 4). This is the basis of the *complex structure of racial victimization.* We have attempted to identify at least four empirical dimensions in the construction of its scenario. Each is based on our contextual analysis of the scope of experiences in Waltham Forest.

*Multiple victimization*

Racial harassment may be experienced by Asian and Black people in a variety of verbal and physical violations which strike both person and their property. Many different forms of abuse may be experienced simultaneously by individuals and families. Often name calling progresses to physical assaults and damage to property, with severe consequences to the victims. In addition, it is fairly common for people to experience various forms of racial harassment in different places. We received evidence from school children of all ages, including those under five, describing their experiences, and from their parents who escorted them to and from school. Name calling from white peers in schools was frequent (many took this as a form of 'expected behaviour'). When walking on the streets between school and home, they were subjected to more verbal abuse and intimidation. Children also recalled in their evidence how their homes were racially harassed, for example racially abusive literature was occasionally pushed through their letter boxes. The potential for, if not actual subjection, to multiple victimization was a continual prospect. This *multiple*

174

victimization, with its *potential for escalation*, is in effect directed at whole communities, although it targets its victims at random.

## Cyclical victimization

Racial harassment is experienced by its victims as repetition. It has a cyclical quality, that is, victims are subjected to racial harassment over varying time periods, for example, every day, every week, every month, every few months or every few years. This cyclical feature of racial victimization also implies that within the time periods of its recurrence, it confronts different Asian and Black individuals and families at *apparently random moments*. Its impact can have profound long term psychological effects on its victims, these are often ignored or underestimated by the statutory agencies. Eventhough the persistent nature of racial harassment affects the whole family. For example for four years an African-Caribbean family experienced racial victimization from their neighbours. Stones, food, rubbish and excrement were thrown into their garden. The consistency of this victimization reduced the mother from a 'confident' person to a 'nervous wreck'. The effects on the children were equally devastating. Their two year old child developed skin rashes and their ten year old child continually asked his mother 'why don't they like us mummy?'.

In the evidence we received, verbal abuse, racial epithets like 'Wogs', 'Pakis', 'Black Bastard', 'Blackie', 'Golliwogs', 'Niggers', were described as continuous experiences. The overwhelming indication was that the victims grudgingly accepted this almost as a way of life for them. For example a teacher described how when an Asian parent was racially abused she said, 'don't worry, I don't want to make a fuss, it's always happening'. Asian and Black people in Waltham Forest were often subjected to physical assaults in public places, this included being spat upon, jostled in the streets, pelted with eggs and other items and even harassed by the police. The recurrence of life threatening racial attacks like arson left its victims profoundly distressed and anxious. A young African-Caribbean woman with small children was the focus of arson attacks despite moving house twice. The first time her flat was arsoned, 'it (the fire) wouldn't go out', and none of her neighbours helped. During another incident, her children were watching television when a sock soaked in petrol was set alight and pushed through her letter box. These horrifying experiences left the family traumatized. The children developed anxiety related problems (e.g. sleep walking and bed wetting). While the mother's concept of a safe property was transformed to include the possibility of escape as a major prerequisite. The cyclical features of racial victimization mean that Asian and Black peoples' fear of being harassed is extremely high, and the prospect of the crime actually taking place is almost equally high. While other forms of crime create genuine fear among people, sometimes high levels of fear, the actual probability of these crimes is often relatively low, even when under-reporting has been taken into account. In contrast the fear of recurrent racial victimization is often a product of *personal experience* in the surrounding locations.

*Secondary victimization*

The impact of racial harassment on its victims can have severe effects on the social behaviour of Asian and Black communities with regard to their social environment. Like any other crime, when it takes place, many Asian and Black people are inclined to report the incidents to the police and other statutory agencies. But, as we have seen, the response they receive is often less than helpful. The problems associated with reporting appear to be two-fold. Firstly there is the difficulty of actually persuading an agency like the Council or the police to consider a case in terms of racial harassment, and secondly, there is the issue of getting the agency to respond effectively. Both these problems present dilemmas which may lead to victims choosing not to report.

Our research revealed many examples of the frustrations felt when reporting traumatic experiences. These included instances where the victims had even identified the perpetrators to the police who still failed to take action. One family subjected to continual racial victimization from their neighbours frequently reported the perpetrators to both the Council and the police. The response of the police was to question the family's understanding of their responsibilities to the law, despite the family's willingness to give evidence in court. An intervention from Waltham Forest CRC to pressurize the police to respond produced the following comments in a letter from the Chief Superintendent:

> Rest assured that we will continue to keep the situation under review. In the meantime, perhaps Mr. Y could be encouraged to provide the police with some tangible assistance if he needs to call us to his premises in the future, he should be aware that his evidence and possible personal appearance would be necessary in any court proceedings. He seems reluctant to accept this fundamental requirement of the law at present.

Other evidence suggested the police were uninterested when called unless there was evidence of some physical damage. According to one witness, 'if we don't say yes, then the police don't bother coming out again'. Victims experiences of the Council were similar. Often they were simply not believed. One case described to us concerned an Asian woman who reported a racial attack to the Housing department. She was told by a Council officer, 'Asian people deliberately tell lies because they want to move'. Adverse comments like these discourage people from reporting. Often people were asked for extensive evidence. We were told 'the onus of proof is always on the victim'. This comes close to establishing a tacit precedent where victims are expected to undertake their own detective work to provide further evidence to substantiate their complaint. Despite this context, people did report to agencies and continued to do so repeatedly. It was more than evident that the role played by statutory agencies compounded the initial victimization.

*Spatial victimization*

It should be apparent that the previous dimensions of the racial victimization scenario, directly influence the relationship of Asian and Black peoples lives to their social environment. One result of this appears to be that Asian and Black people form *mental maps* of the distributions of racial harassment (see also Chapter 4). This suggests that people begin to perceive social spaces in 'racially' particular ways. That is, as locations which allow freedom of movement and those which inhibit; and locales which are 'no go areas' or are relatively safe to live. In this sense the movements of people are shaped by the *mental maps* they 'carry in their heads'. Not only do settlement patterns sometimes illustrate this, but the functional use of space is also affected. The cumulative effect of these perceptions, based on real experiences, creates conditions where Asian and Black communities adjust themselves to being forced to live in and contest an unsafe social environment.

The impact this has on Asian and Black people's life styles can be significant. Their social behaviour may be restricted in the local environment because they have to live with not only ineffective responses from statutory agencies when reporting their experiences, but the reality of the harassment recurring. Several witnesses described these experiences as: 'living under seige', encountering a 'total erosion of self confidence', finding themselves 'turning into nervous wrecks' and having their capacity to live 'normally' severely undermined. As a consequence the spatial mobility of people becomes restricted. Not only does this interfere with everyday life (e.g. going shopping, going to work, etc.), it also restricts access to the use of public facilities. Some people felt unsafe using public parks. For example, Sikh Sangat East in their evidence told us of situations where elderly people sitting in the parks and speaking in their own language were tormented with racial abuse like 'speak in English' and 'go back to your own country'. In addition they informed us:

177

> Children get verbally abused when playing in parks.
> Some members have talked about how they take their
> children to the park, white kids call them
> commonly'Pakis', subsequently parents do not take
> children to the park.

Even apparently innocent social activities like walking in the streets can be
intimidating and frightening. A group of Asian women informed us that they
only go out when it is absolutely necessary, for example, when accompanying
children to and from school, or to do the shopping. On these occasions they
went out collectively in small groups of twos or threes. In matters of
victimization, the social landscape is never neutral.

## The relevance of local agencies

In general we discovered very little service provision to victims of racial
harassment in Waltham Forest. In the evidence, it was clear that victims did
not know where to go for help or who could give effective assistance. A number
of community organizations confirmed this predicament. For example, the
Joint Council for Afro-Caribbean Organizations (JCACO) described 'the added
problem of the fact that it is not clear, to whom victims should or can report
racial harassment' while Walthamstow Constituency Labour Party (Lloyd Park
and Higham Hill Branches) stated:

> A common theme from those who feel that they have
> suffered racial harassment is their sense of isolation.
> There is no authority to which Asian families feel they
> can turn with confidence for help in resolving their
> difficulties.

Those who did approach some agencies, found themselves shunted around and
repeatedly attempting to consult an agency without any satisfactory help. In
Chapters 2 and 3 we analyzed the ineffective impact of the police and local
Council as statutory agencies, in this section we consider agencies in the
voluntary sector. Statutory agencies often fund voluntary organizations to fill
the gaps in local service provision. In addition voluntary organizations have a
legitimate role in putting pressure on statutory agencies.

The situation in Waltham Forest's voluntary sector was hardly encouraging. As we describe in later sections the Victim Support Scheme did not offer any specific service to victims of racial harassment; a similar neglect affected other agencies. For example the Citizens Advice Bureau was not only described as unhelpful but characterized as a 'military type regime' by one witness. Other witnesses described experiences of receiving inappropriate help (e.g. one was advised to take out a private prosecution and another was advised to seek help from our Inquiry). The CAB cited their lack of experience in dealing with racial harassment due to few enquiries and also commented:

> it would seem that the incidents of racial harassment reported to us are low for several reasons. For example, the Citizens Advice Bureau may not be seen to be as 'appropriate' for this type of problem as other agencies, such as (the) CRC, also a victim may feel that such crimes are insoluble, thus being deterred from seeking help altogether, finally many of the victims of this type of harassment may feel less able *for reasons of language and culture* to seek help.

> (emphasis added)

Leaving aside this inexplicable excursion into cultural explanations, our evidence suggests that what significantly deterred people from seeking help was that like other agencies the CAB did not offer a 'serious' service to victims of racial harassment. Other organizations gave similar explanations for not dealing with racial harassment. MIND, the organization that deals with people with mental disabilities, said they had no evidence to submit to our Inquiry as racial harassment had not arisen in the organization or been reported to them. While Waltham Forest MENCAP, who deal with children and adults with 'mental handicaps' wrote to say they had no reported cases of racial harassment. They suggested this was:

> because our agency specialises in giving information and advice on the area of mental handicap, benefits, services available etc.

Evidence received from Waltham Forest Association for People with Disabilities (WFAPD) suggested they were aware of a number of incidents of harassment of people with disabilities. They informed us that their representatives on various bodies sought 'to ensure that agencies which provide support or advice to such people are aware of the particular concerns disabled people may have in such situations, help they may need and of particular sources that help'. However they went on to explain that the cases they referred to:

> (had) not involved disabled people who are ethnic minority members of the local community. We feel however that such people may be particularly vulnerable to harassment.

The striking facts to emerge in the evidence from these and other specialist organizations in the voluntary sector are: an inability to understand racial harassment and its impact on victims or the role the particular organization could play in responding to the problem; a reluctance to acknowledge a responsibility for dealing with racial harassment; and a reluctance to countenance the existence of racial harassment either by publicizing what the organization could offer or by encouraging people to report incidents. It was particularly worrying that organizations which offered a specialist service (e.g. MENCAP, MIND, WFAPD), catering for the needs of people with mental and physical disabilities and advocates on their behalf, considered racial harassment to be a marginal concern in the lives of Asian and Black people. The absence of policies and procedures to deal with racial harassment and the sense of their 'waiting' to hear from victims implied that services from these organizations were dependent on the idiosyncratic views of the workers approached.

The only organization that dealt with cases of racial harassment in a significant way in the voluntary sector appeared to be the Community Relations Council (CRC). It offered limited practical advice and acted on behalf of victims when dealing with other agencies. Generally most community organizations did not offer a direct service regarding racial harassment, but acted as referral agencies. Apart from advising the police and the Council when they knew some victims would not approach these public agencies directly, it seemed there was little further help the CRC could provide. Perhaps it can be argued that funded organizations, which are specialist advice agencies should ensure their publicity clearly states what they can do for victims of racial harassment. If so this would require that their staff were adequately trained, aware of the need to address the issue and familiar with the role of other

180

agencies in providing additional specialized help (e.g. practical support). In particular, we would argue that local Councils should consider making this a part of the funding conditions, especially with regard to agencies like the Victim Support Scheme who have a clearly defined brief to help victims of crime (see later sections).

*Asian, Black and Ethnic Minority organizations*

The first point of contact for many Asian and Black people when seeking advice is often a relevant community organization. In Waltham Forest, these catered mainly for the specific cultural needs of the people they served. Some also provided a basic advice service in a sensitive manner and in appropriate languages. Many of these organizations were funded by the Council. Although they ranged from small grant aided 'support groups' run by volunteers to larger organizations with considerable salaried staff, the emphasis was usually on catering for the specific needs of their communities, and/or undertaking advocacy work. The evidence we received came from a variety of organizations. For example, the East London Harmony group met monthly as a support group to discuss racist incidents. They pursued these cases by putting pressure on other agencies to act. The Victim Aid Action group offered some initial advice, and referred cases to the Council and the police. While the Bangalee Women's Welfare Project wrote in their evidence that they 'Do not have the means to deal with cases directly'. This depicts the general response from many small community organizations. These organizations either provided a very basic advice service or did not deal with cases of racial harassment, referring them to other agencies (e.g. the police, the Council). A lack of resources in the Asian, Black and Ethnic Minority organizations put severe pressure on their ability to respond to the demands of dealing with racial harassment. The absence of an identifiable agency in the voluntary sector to deal with the problem, meant that these organizations, like many individuals who gave evidence, were *dependent on the Council and the police to take appropriate action.* This was often with fore-knowledge that very little would be done by them. Sikh Sangat East informed us that they advised people to go to the police but knew no action would be taken. The Joint Council for Asian Organizations, described specific experiences with the Council following referrals as entailing,'varying degree of responses depending on the advice of (the) person dealing with it'. While the Victim Aid Action Group stated: 'We have not seen any assistance available to victims of racial harassment in the Borough'. These were remarkable revelations. They confirmed that traditional advice agencies, like the local CAB and the Council's Aid Centre, were simply incapable of providing a response to meet the needs of the victims of racial

181

harassment. What is perhaps more significant is that no reference was made to the Council's telephone 'hotline' service on racial harassment, nor to the Victim Support Scheme. Asian and Black community organizations clearly seem to have been frustrated, under pressure and unable to help their communities effectively. This was in part due to the reluctance in the wider voluntary sector to take racial victimization seriously.

## Service provisions to victims of crime

In the UK, attempts to address the needs of racial harassment victims cannot be disentangled from the thinking which informs initiatives generally designed for victims of crime. Various forms of service provision exist for victims of crime. Although these are not based on any well defined victimological theory, it may be useful to consider van Dijk's (1988:166) work which suggests four 'ideologies' to describe the trend within the victims movement across different countries. He describes these as 'victimagogic' ideologies and defines them as ideologies 'about the best ways to give treatment, guidance or support to crime victims'. He argues they should be seen as objects for social analysis and research which could be used as a basis to develop a unified theory grounded in victimological research.

On the basis of van Dijk's four ideologies, it is possible to describe the provisions available in the UK. These can be categorized through the 'care' ideology, the 'rehabilitative' ideology, the 'retributive' or 'criminal justice' ideology and the 'abolitionist' ideology. The 'care' ideology emphasizes provision for victims of crime by the community, and generally perceives the problems they face as stress, psychological trauma or economic need. Victim Support Schemes provide this service in the UK. The 'rehabilitative' ideology, looks at measures which can 'treat' the offender. These can include victim-offender confrontations, in which the interests of the victim are often neglected. Here, crime is perceived as a conflict between two parties, the offender and the victim. Mediation schemes fall into this category. The 'retributive' or 'criminal justice' ideology encapsulates the idea that the offender must be punished according to the seriousness of the crime and the damage to society. Increasingly, there are moves to get the offender to compensate the victim. In the UK, this is reflected in compensation orders. Compensation is also available to crime victims from the Criminal Injuries Compensation Board (CICB). Finally, the 'abolitionist' ideology, favours the treatment of the offenders on the principles of civil law, arguing that the criminal justice system should intervene as minimally as possible. It suggests that mediation, reparation, aid to victims and crime prevention should be left to neighbourhood groups and other social networks. Some of this emphasis is currently found in the UK, particularly in crime prevention strategies (see Chapter 2). Below we discuss three structured provisions for victims of crime and consider whether they can meet the needs of victims of racial harassment.

## Victim Support Schemes

Initiated in the mid 1970s, Victim Support Schemes have been one of the fastest growing organizations in the voluntary sector. Their role is to provide short-term help for crime victims. They have four key features: they are independent organizations, employ full-time co-ordinators, rely on carefully selected and trained volunteers and are a 'front-line' crisis service agency. Most, but not all schemes are affiliated to the National Association of Victim Support Schemes (NAVSS), which was founded in 1979. The NAVSS co-ordinates the Victim Support Schemes, and publishes guidelines on their establishment. It also requires VSSs to have independent management committees which should consist of at least one representative from the police, probation or social services, a voluntary organization or church and scheme volunteers. The policies adopted by individual schemes determine their referral system (i.e. which crime victims they service). The exclusion of certain categories of victim is partly attributable to the result of police referral practices which are based on police perceptions of who needs the service. Generally victim support schemes are heavily reliant on the police for referrals (sometimes exclusively). But police referrals are not necessarily effective or efficient (Mawby and Gill,1987). Not only do the police act as *gatekeepers,* their representation on the management committees creates ambiguity in the 'independent' nature of the victim support schemes. They can have a disproportionate influence on the conduct of the schemes. Furthermore, where victims have suffered police harassment, the schemes may be reluctant to acknowledge such incidents and therefore not offer appropriate support. This is pertinent to Asian, Black and Ethnic Minority communities. Often these communities are reluctant to have dealings with the police because of their experiences, and would be apprehensive in seeking help from an organization that is seen to be so closely linked with the police.[1]

We are unable to comment in detail on the Waltham Forest Victim Support Scheme as they did not submit evidence to the Inquiry. Nevertheless, our own research indicated that the local Victim Support Scheme did not offer specific support to victims of racial harassment. There appeared to be no comprehension in the organization regarding the needs of victims of racial harassment and an undisguised reluctance to improve the situation. This was all the more remarkable given the organization's vehement opposition to the establishment of a 'hotline' telephone service in 1986 for victims of racial harassment (see Chapter 1). This suggested the scheme was unwilling to engage the issues involved in racial harassment and perhaps explained why the scheme as constituted was unable to offer a distinct and sensitive service to victims of racial harassment. In 1991 the scheme published a leaflet on racial harassment, this adopted a definition of racial harassment similar to that of the police.[2] It advised victims to take precautions to avoid victimization. The leaflet's advice was similar to that offered by the police on preventing property crime. It also advised victims of racial harassment to gather information about their perpetrators to help police investigations. There was no conception of the impact of racial victimization.

Interestingly, the scheme had ignored even the problematic recommendations from the NAVSS project report on racial harassment (see Kimber and Cooper 1991). This research examined how victim support schemes could provide an effective service to racial harassment victims. Based on three demonstration projects observed from 1988, regular evaluation was carried out until the production of the final report. The report's major conclusion was that 'racial harassment should become an essential and integral part of mainstream victim support work' (ibid.:89). It makes various recommendations on how this may be achieved, for example, training for staff and volunteers, designating specific workers to take a lead role, developing equal opportunities policies; and it offers pragmatic advice to victim support schemes on how to offer a relevant service.

The NAVSS report however presents a weak analysis. Firstly, in the elaborate process that each project went through to formulate a definition of racial harassment, they encompassed without distinction all communities except the (generally) majority (white) British population. The lumping together of all 'minority communities' fails to understand the specific racial victimization processes and the social impact on victims which may affect the nature of a relevant service provision. This also suggests, incorrectly, that racism is somehow experienced as a consequence of 'minority' status. Secondly, an extensive analysis of statistics in the report omits any clear findings which leaves us to question the validity of such work. An example of this is the information it presents concerning the year (in months) when racial harassment took place in the three Boroughs. Are we to think that racial harassment is seasonal? Thirdly, the report, recognizing the difficulties that victim support schemes have in obtaining referrals from and forming links with Asian, Black and Ethnic Minority communities, reflects on this in a peculiar way. It suggests 'the ways in which the "politics of race" are manifested at the local level is clearly a major issue for victim support schemes wishing to extend their work in the field of racial harassment' (ibid.:78). The researchers advise

184

that if the 'politics of race' is high on the agenda of local groups, then victim support schemes will find it difficult to form links with them. The logic implied here is unfathomable, what exactly is meant by the 'politics of race' and how can a high or low value be assigned to it? Generally, one of the main considerations of Asian, Black and Ethnic Minority communities is to challenge racial exclusion and it is inconceivable to think that the 'politics of race' will not be constitutive of their organizational agendas. By default this argument seems to recommend the position prior to the research. In analytical terms then the report makes very little contribution. But it is arguable, that its recommendations for victim support schemes could be useful in initiating or progressing work in this area. Whether schemes will implement these recommendations remains to be seen. If the example of Waltham Forest is anything to go by, the results may be disappointing.

*Mediation schemes*

A second form of community intervention has emerged in the form of mediation schemes. These are based on the belief that it is desirable to empower the community to handle its own conflicts rather than to have this responsibility arrogated by professionals. Although they deal largely with neighbourly disputes, some do extend their work to other sorts of conflicts (e.g. within families, between social groups, within organizations, etc.). The schemes are usually located in community bases, employing scheme co-ordinators and using volunteers from the local community to act as mediators in non-directive roles. Like VSSs, the volunteers are trained. Although mediation schemes may vary in their emphasis or practice of service provision, the technique employed can be generalized as follows. Usually one party will approach a mediation project and the details of the case will be taken by them if they think they can help, the second party will then be approached with the consent of the first party. The concerns of the first party will be conveyed to the second party and the project will attempt to mediate a settlement agreeable to both. Disputants enter into negotiations voluntarily, have to abide by the schemes rules and may abandon negotiations at any time. A settlement may be reached through the mediator, by both parties meeting face to face or not at all. The schemes vary in the number of mediators used, the number of meetings held with each party, availability of advice and support to one party if the other party refuses to enter negotiations, etc. Mediation schemes are relatively new in their formation, and there is little knowledge available about how racial harassment is tackled. It appears that where the mediators of a scheme think that a case of racial harassment can be dealt with in the comparable terms of a neighbourly dispute, then the case will be handled accordingly, while more complex cases would simply not be taken on. In effect the neighbour dispute is the problem *par excellence* that mediation schemes have been designed to resolve (Marshall and Walpole, 1985).

Where racial victimization is concerned, mediation schemes are inappropriate for two main reasons. Firstly, a relationship of inequality exists between the two parties. In cases of racial harassment, it is likely that the less powerful party (e.g. Asian and Black people), will be constrained to accept the best deal possible and not the most fair settlement, while the more powerful party may well concede as little as possible. The second main problem is concerned with how racial harassment is tackled. As we argued in Chapter 2 the police utilize discretion in dealing with racial harassment specifically as a crime. By defining racial harassment as a neighbourly dispute as distinct from a crime, the police may be influenced to treat these cases similarly by making referrals to mediation schemes. Asian and Black people may find that they are bargaining for their basic human rights in the mediation process. For both reasons, mediation schemes are wholly unsatisfactory forms of provision where racial victimization is concerned.

*Compensation to victims*

*(i) Compensation orders* We have discussed above schemes that offer support to crime victims outside the legal system. The provision available within the legal system is in the form of compensation orders. The Criminal Justice Act (1972) gave courts a general power to order compensation to be paid to victims by convicted offenders as part of their sentence. However, within a year, it was found that the use of compensation orders was made more widely in offences against property than where personal injury was involved (Rock, 1990:279). Problems in the computation of compensation for personal injuries contributed to their low use. Applications for compensation orders are the responsibility of the prosecution on behalf of the victim. Research by Shapland et al. (1985) found that often this was not done. As victims are usually not present in courts, and few know about the existence of the compensation orders, in most cases, victims did not receive any compensation from offenders. The Criminal Justice Act (1988) now requires the courts to give reasons where compensation orders are not made. This may be seen by some as a way towards improving compensation order awards. However, Duff (1988) argues that there are fundamental problems with the compensation orders which need addressing. He suggests that of the three relationships that exist in the judiciary system, between state and offender, victim and offender and state and victim, the criminal justice system is exclusively concerned with the state-offender relationship. As such, the system is concerned with deciding the appropriate

186

penal measure for the offender. Compensation orders take a secondary role and are adapted to fit in with the criminal justice system rather than being integral to its infrastructure. A number of difficulties arise here: firstly the criminal courts make compensation orders on the basis of what the offender can afford. The sum has to be a realistic amount and if payable by instalments, which should not last very long. Thus the awards are oftern 'meagre' amounts compared to the loss the victims may have suffered. Secondly where the convicted offender receives a prison sentence, they are almost never able to pay compensation because their source of income ceases, unless the order is to come into effect after the sentence in which case again, it has to be a realistic sum. Thirdly there are problems concerning evidential matters as awards are made whatever seems appropriate in the light of the evidence available. This poses particular difficulties in cases of personal injury. Victims are not usually present in the court and there is often no information available about the victim's loss. Criminal courts also find it problematic to compute compensation in these cases as their focus is on issuing penal sentences. Fourthly, victims have no right of audience in court to give evidence about their loss. Victims cannot apply for a compensation order to be made in their favour, nor can they appeal against a decision. Generally, the judicary is of the view that the criminal courts should concentrate on the 'state-offender relationship' and that the civil court can deal with the 'offender-victim relationship'. However in the latter system, legal aid is usually not available and for the victim to pursue compensation in the civil courts can be an expensive undertaking. Victims of racial harassment can rarely take advantage of compensation orders unless the victimization they are subjected to corresponds with some other offence triable in court. Racial harassment per se is not a criminal offence. We described in Chapter 2 the problems associated with the police in their recording and investigation of cases of racial harassment. Very few of these go to court. Even though the compensation order is less than a satisfactory arrangement for victims of crime its existence benefits some victims of crime. However for victims of racial harassment even this seems inaccessible.

*(ii)Criminal Injuries Compensation Board (CICB)* This was created in 1964 to provide state compensation to victims of violent crime (whether the offender was caught and/or not convicted). The government at the time accepted the principle that victims of violent crime should be eligible for some compensation for personal injury at the public expense (Rock, 1990:82). However the government also made it clear that the state was not liable for injuries caused to people by acts of others. The CICB provides ex-gratia payments based on strict criteria. It sets a minimum level of award below which compensation is not payable (for less serious injuries). It carefully scrutinizes any share of

responsibility of the victim in the commital of the crime. It also takes into account the 'conduct' of the victim, by checking previous convictions. Although the Criminal Justice Act 1988 has given victims a statutory right to apply for compensation, there is no right to sue the CICB to challenge the amount awarded or the refusal of an award. The service is 'discretionary' and not a 'right'.

The Board has been variously criticized, we discuss this here. The Board is limited to provide compensation to victims of violent crime only, and this Duff (op. cit.) argues is a fundamental problem. The 'victim-state' relationship is confined to a narrow conception of victims of crime, particularly to victims of violent crime (defined by the CICB). This Walklate (op. cit.) suggests is because governments can embrace greatest public 'sympathy' in this area and be seen to be doing something for the victims. Implicit is the 'notion of public responsibility and sympathy for the victim, suggesting that the state is not responsible but feels a sense of responsibility' (ibid.:114). The Board uses its discretionary power to assess eligibility of the claimant on the basis of their 'conduct' and 'innocence'. Although this may be a concern to avoid fraudulent claims, the idea embraces the traditional distinction between the deserving and the non-deserving found in the traditional welfare system model (see Williams, 1989). The CICB has the power to check the claimants past convictions, which will have a bearing on their award. The award may be refused or reduced depending on the severity of the convictions. The CICB also requires that the claimant, 'must be able to convince the Board that you were not in any way responsible for the incident in which you were injured' (CICB, 1990:para 6(c):28). The onus clearly lies with the victim to prove his/her innocence. Furthermore, the CICB has to be satisfied that the victim had informed the police about the crime at the earliest possible opportunity, and had co-operated fully with the police throughout the investigation of the case which can include making a statement, attending an identification parade, naming the assailant, attending court. Failure to comply with this requirement also prejudices the application. The most damning criticism lies in the fact that few victims are aware of the scheme's existence (Shapland et al., 1985; Walklate, op. cit.; Rock, 1990). Ironically, the largest single profession to claim compensation is the police (Rock, op. cit.). Duff (op. cit.:153-154) concludes:

.. it is possible for this broad and controversial discretionary power to exist because of the lack of definition of the state-victim relationship; there is no satisfactory theoretical premise which demands that crime victims be compensated and, as a result, there is no legally enforceable right to compensation. Furthermore, the fact that the only reason given for compensating crime victims is that they attract public sympathy demands that compensation be witheld from those who might be perceived to be 'undeserving'.

When we consider victims of racial harassment, we can immediately see a number of problems with the scheme. Asian and Black people often do not report racial victimization to the police because they perceive or experience the police as insensitive. This would clearly prejudice their application. The CICB's requirement for claimants to prove their innocence may pose problems for Asian and Black people in cases of racial victimization. We have seen in Chapter 2 how victims are often not believed by the police, and as the police view influences the CICB's decision, Asian and Black victims may well lose out. Finally, while knowledge of the CICB is generally absent in the public domain, this may be exacerbated in the Asian and Black communities.


## Mapping victims rights

Most legal systems are concerned with the prosecuting and sentencing of offenders while victims play a minimal role of giving evidence in courts. Although the effects of crime are suffered by the victims, their general neglect in the criminal justice system has led to the development of victims rights movement. As a result, movements in various countries across the world, some more organized (e.g. USA, Canada) than others (e.g. UK) have raised the issue of the victims rights. However it was not until 1985 that the General Assembly of the United Nations adopted a charter of victims rights. Waller (1988) comments that the charter, 'is an impressive landmark in establishing the need for action to provide equitable justice for victims across the world'.

The United Nations Declaration established four major principles for victims of crime:

(a) Access to judicial and administrative procedures (how victims should be treated fairly and their views considered).

(b) Restitution (payment for harm by offender to victim).

(c) Compensation (from government funds where restitution from offenders is not enough).

(d) Assistance to victims (need for support from agencies concerned with health and mental health care, social services, policing and justice).

The World Society of Victimology has campaigned for the implementation of these principles across the world. In 1987, it brought together a number of leading countries, including the UK to recommend improvement and expansion in victim assistance. However it was not until February 1990 that the UK produced a 'victims charter'. Before discussing this, we compare briefly developments in victims rights in the USA, Canada and UK.

*USA*

Although legislation exists in the USA to protect the interests of victims, two major pieces of federal legislation have had a considerable overall effect. These are: the Federal Victim Witness Protection Act of 1982, which promoted restitution by courts; and the Federal Victims of Crime Act 1984 which levied a special tax on federal offenders and enabled the use of fines to provide funds to federal states for the development of victim assistance networks and compensation programmes. This work continues to progress in many states in the USA.

*Canada*

Legislation exists in the form of Justice of Victims of Crime Act 1986 to implement the principles from the UN declaration. Many of the victim assistance programmes are based on 'needs assessment'. Regular surveys of victims needs are carried out and new services are created to fill any identified gaps. Most of the victim assistance programmes are located in police departments, based on the recognition that victims usually contact the police first.

In contrast to the USA and Canada, victim assistance is largely provided by volunteers from Victim Support Schemes usually funded by the Home Office and local authorities. The 1982 Criminal Justice Act gave magistrates the powers to order compensation from offenders to victims. Since 1964, state compensation has been available to victims of crime (see above for discussion of these services). Interestingly, the UK through its Victim Support Schemes has not pursued the USA or Canadian path of establishing more connections with the criminal justice system (Shapland et al., op. cit.). For example, victim assistance programmes in those countries enable victims to provide witness statements which may influence the sentencing of the offender. Traditionally the Victim Support Schemes have chosen not to intervene in the criminal justice system (Maguire and Corbett, 1987).

## Victims Charter ⬿

Rather belatedly in 1990, the Home Office published a 'Victim's Charter' subtitled - 'A statement of the Rights of Victims of Crime'. This document was hastily produced to coincide with the European Victims Day on 22 February. The Charter's attempts to raise victims rights as an issue fails miserably. Divided into three sections, developments, current services and a list of questions to consider to assess the standards of the criminal justice system, it makes no reference to the United Nations Declaration of the four principles established for victims of crime. The Charter provides no background information as to how it is 'linked' to the European system, except that it now has reciprocal compensation arrangements with four other European countries. While its claims to be 'A statement of the Rights of Victims of Crime' is confusing. Although some improvements have been made in the criminal justice system, when we compare these to the UN principles, the overall treatment of victims of crime seems inadequate. This can be seen if we consider it with reference to the four principles of the UN Declaration.

In relation to the first principle, access to judicial and administrative procedures, the Charter hardly attempts to comply. It fails to state clearly if this should be available as a right to the victim or as a discretionary information service provided by the police. It anything the emphasis seems to be on the latter, reinforcing police discretion.

As an interesting contrast the Government has made some improvements in the area referenced by 'restitution', the second principle of the UN Declaration. The Criminal Justice Act 1982, enabled victims to be compensated by convicted offenders. The problem with this however, was that compensation orders were infrequently used. To improve their usage the Criminal Justice Act 1988, required magistrates to give reasons if they had not considered payment from the offender to the victim in 'suitable cases'. The knowledge of this provision, however is not widely available.

If we consider the third principle, compensation, the Charter stipulates that the Government provides state compensation to victims of crime. Other than acknowledging the administrative difficulties, experienced by the CICB (e.g. long delays in payments and promising to increase staff to meet the backlog of work) it gives no consideration to structural problems in the scheme. A failure to tackle these problems will continue to offer a less than satisfactory service to victims of crime.

Finally, when we consider the fourth UN Declaratory principle, assistance to victims, the Government takes great pride in describing the Victim Support Schemes which 'offer comfort and practical advice'. The Charter gives information about the systematic increase in funding of these schemes from £1.5m in 1987/88 to over £2.5m in 1988/89 and approaching £4m in 1989/90, with an estimated £4.5m for 1990/1991. The Charter boasts that over 350 schemes cover England and Wales and over 10,000 volunteers are involved. However at an annual meeting of the National Association of Victim Support Schemes in 1991, the Director commented that the Government had failed to provide funding to some schemes and as a result they were experiencing financial difficulties. More significantly the Director announced, 'We are still waiting for improvements promised 18 months ago in the first victim's charter' (*The Guardian*, 26 July 1991).

The Government's attempts to consider the rights of victims have been resoundingly effete. It would not be surprising if a general withdrawal of the service provision emerged. The Charter is particularly problematic in so far that it offers no evaluation of statutory service provision and it provides no specification of the 'rights' victims can claim under the criminal justice system. Curiously the Charter poses a set of questions to consider in the improvement of the services. But there is no indication as to how the improvements will be considered and implemented. As well as failing to meet the exemplary criteria of the United Nations principles, the Charter is hollow in areas close to the interest of this study. For example, while it is encouraging to see the Charter make reference to the treatment of victims of rape and domestic violence and the progress made in this area, victims of racial harassment are conspicuously absent. The Charter fails to acknowledge their existence even when it refers to fair treatment:

Victims should always be treated fairly and without
adverse discrimination. Consistently with this, the
services will give particular consideration to victims who
are especially vulnerable such as children, victims of
sexual or violent crime, and those who are severely
shocked by their experience.

(op. cit.:8)

Once again racial victimization is submerged, beneath the surface of official
acknowledgement. By totally ignoring victims of racial harassment, the Charter
echoes the 'state of affairs' which results in a skeletal service provision (e.g.
Victim Support Schemes) and disparaging treatment by the criminal justice
system.


## (Neglected) needs of the victims of racial harassment

Given the scope of racial victimization outlined in this Chapter, we need finally
to consider the type of victim 'support' raised in our evidence as important in
terms of basic needs. In general terms the needs of victims of crime have always
been an area of neglect, this neglect has been compounded where victims of
racial harassment are concerned. For example, Shapland et al. (op. cit.)
conducted a major longitudinal study of victims in the criminal justice system.
They claimed that very little was known about what victims think despite the
rapidly expanding interest in victims. As an attempt to remedy this situation,
over a period of three years in Coventry and Northampton, they analyzed a
sample of victims from the initial reporting of the case to its outcome. They
considered the following offences: physical assaults; offences involving
physical violence and property loss; sexual assaults. Although the sample
contained a few Asian and Black victims, no reference was made to racial
victimization in the study. Despite this absence, the study's recommendations
do retain some interest and may be relevant to the needs of the victims of racial
harassment. Shapland et al. argue:

Victims should have an accepted role within the system
such that their contribution is acknowledged by the
professional participants. This implies that victims need
to be treated with care and respect by police officers,
prosecutors, court officials and compensation agency
personnel.

193

Their recommendations are made under five categories; (a) provision of information to victims about their case through the system; (b) a more thoughtful attitude towards the needs and difficulties of victims in the investigation and prosecution; (c) consideration for victims at courts; (d) compensation and (e) victim support services. Cooper and Pomeiye (1988) made similar observations when they assessed the needs of the victims of racial harassment based on the National Association of Victim Support Schemes project in Camden in 1986. They argued that the needs of the victims of racial harassment were similar to the needs of other victims of crime.

In our research, we were able to identify four categories of needs (see Figure 5.1 below). While three are significantly compatible with those discussed above, the fourth is equally important.

| | |
|---|---|
| 1. Action against perpetrators | *proper investigation of reported cases<br>*penalty/prosecution of identified perpetrators<br>*regular information about the progress of the case of victims |
| 2. Protection<br>    personal safety | *immediate intervention to secure personal safety of the victim e.g. injunctions, prosecution, alternative accommodation |
|     physical security | *immediate repairs to property<br>*provision of grants for security equipment |
| 3. Practical assistance and advice | *legal matters<br>*victims rights<br>*welfare rights<br>*insurance and compensation<br>*liaison with agencies |
| 4. Emotional support | *empathy<br>*counselling - sensitive, available in community languages, easily and safely accessible geographically |

**Figure 5.1: Needs of the victims of racial harassment**

It should be evident that these needs raise similarities with other forms of personal victimization (e.g. domestic violence and sexual assaults). However, needs are immaterial unless they are met with a strategic material response from responsive public agencies.

## Notes

1. A project report on racial harassment undertaken by the Polytechnic of North London for the National Association of Victim Support Schemes (Kimber and Cooper, 1991), based in three Victim Support Schemes, Camden, Newham and Southwark makes similar observations.

2. This was subsequent to the local publication of our research findings in 1990.

# Conclusion
# Towards a theory of safety

*Barnor Hesse, Paul McGilchrist, Dhanwant K. Rai and Christine Bennett*

> Any moment now the fabric would tear; someone would
> say I had no business there. And I would get up and either
> fight or run while the friendly beasts looked quietly on.
>
> (Suniti Namjoshi, 1988; 'The Blue Donkey Fables')

Throughout this study we have attempted to analyze the sequencing, simultaneity and situatedness of racial harassment and to consider forms of analysis useful in its comprehension. In many respects we have argued for the need to place 'race' in 'space' in order to illuminate the 'ethnicized' characteristics which appear in the construction of the social environment as a space of contested safety. A critical spatial analysis needs to augment an approach which takes us 'beyond Anti-racism'. One prevailing difficulty of course is that generally policy initiatives which have addressed issues of 'race' in Britain have tended to flow from a legislative discourse seldom free of the residue of 'immigrant problem' inflexions. Where racial harassment has arisen, the knee-jerk response has been to attempt to extinguish the so-called last flickers of an 'integration' problem occasionally inflamed by extremist turbulence. Although current analyses aknowledge a more widespread, more enduring problem, they have not moved far beyond this primary diagnosis. Consequently, the ways in which the social landscape may be constructed and contested in the name of white territorialism are racist implications which 'race relations' orthodoxy and traditional local government practice have failed to recognize. Yet recognizing the spatial and experiential contexts of racial harassment and its specific manifestations within bounded jurisdictions, is essential to understanding its operation and effects if policy is to be anything more than a makeshift fire blanket.

Similarly the characterization of racial harassment as neighbour disputes, or as random, rare occurrences are fundamental misreadings, which fail to see the connectedness of its incidence or impact (see Chapters 1 and 4). The procedural incoherences which flow from policy interventions are anchored in these misreadings (see Chapters 2 and 3). In short we argue that public agencies traditionally have not considered the extent to which they may themselves be negative factors operating in the contextual equation; their inability to appreciate this will tend to corrupt any solutions they may bring to the problem (see Chapters 2, 3 and 5). In fact statutory negligence is almost a patternable dynamic: Initially complacency permits an environment conducive to racial harassment; then an inept response to incidents fails to confront its effects; and in turn insensitivity compounds the pain of the initial experience. Recognition of these assorted problems requires policy solutions that are both strategic and systemic. If, as we suggest, the contextual contours of racial harassment are visible over time and across locations, it ought to be possible to establish a profile of the problem as it presents itself within the jurisdictions of the various agencies focusing upon it. A cartography of racial harassment is thus an essential prerequisite for the construction of any policy attempting to confront its entrenchment and dispersion within a given location.

Clearly the construction of policy is always a developmental process yet, paradoxically, it is not always conducted reflectively. It is essential that future policy on racial harassment does not reconstitute the shortcomings of the past. For this reason, in describing the conceptual framework within which policy formulations should take place, it will be necessary to analyse the ascendant model currently in place (the multi-agency approach). Following this we detail the strengths of our spatial conception, consider how and with whom it should operate and finally suggest a theory of safety which may provide an integral impetus.

## The multi-agency approach

It is widely recognized that individual public agencies by themselves are insufficient to facilitate a comprehensive impact on the various dimensions of racial harassment. We need to consider the implications this raises for combined forms of policy intervention. A fashionable policy response to co-ordinated action against racial harassment is flagged in the concept of the 'multi-agency approach'. For example, the Home Office (1989) in its 'Guidance for the Statutory Agencies' has argued:

Racial harassment needs to be addressed in a variety of social contexts, from a variety of angles, and by staff from a variety of disciplines, if it is to be tackled effectively. We have no doubt that the response to racial harassment would be greatly improved if all the agencies with a role to play recognise their responsibilities and took *unilateral* action (.....). But we also believe that it would be possible to improve the total response still further, both in relation to individual racial incidents and in relation to racial harassment in general, if agencies were to work more systematically together as part of a multi-agency (or multi-disciplinary) approach.

(emphasis retained)

This effectively means that a number of agencies that deal or should deal with racial harassment meet regularly to attempt to provide a co-operative agency response by sharing the responsibility for responding to the problem in line with their particular perspectives. This may involve monitoring the problem in specific geographical areas, or at particular stages in its development and generally working through the most comprehensive, collaborative response.[1] This idea is extremely plausible, but it is not without a number of acute structural problems. Research by Blagg et al. (1988:215) into inter-agency working practices, in a Lancashire town (Miltown) and two inner London Boroughs, has highlighted a number of these problems. They observed that different agencies do not start on equal terms, and that 'this inequality of power is an important factor in shaping the forms actually assumed in practice by inter-agency co-operation, liaison, collaboration, co-ordination or whatever term is preferred'. Inter-agency tension is intensified where objectives and goals are not clearly defined and there is a lack of clarity about what kind of contribution the agencies should make. Frequently areas of great uncertainty are encountered in multi-agency liaison. In one inner-London Borough, where a multi-agency forum had been meeting for five years on a monthly basis, the researchers found that the idea of agencies addressing the conflicts that existed between them was seen as a threat to the forum's very existence. They observed that 'the forum was an end in itself', and 'had reached a "cosy" stage of development where maintaining the coherence of the group itself, in terms of conflict-free face-to-face relationships between members, has come to be more important than identifying areas of conflict and attempting to remedy them'. The evasion of conflict was partly attributable to panel 'representation'. The research found, for example, that members were not delegated to represent their agency's policies in the forum, or to represent the forum's views to their agency. Other problems identified concerned the fact that issues were not necessarily seen in the same way by all the agencies. For example there were difficulties in agencies reaching agreement on a common focus *or perspective* for inter-agency work. The lead agency was seen to assume major responsibility and tended to dominate the forum.

Although there may be a number of advantages to be gained in the traditional multi-agency approach, the structural problems systematically undermine these. One concern is particularly important. Blagg et al.'s, research highlighted several problems in crime prevention multi-agency forums, which were invariably led by the police. They found that the police tended to off-load what they perceived as tedious problems (e.g. vandalism), to other agencies; did not provide requested information yet expected information from other agencies; and did not necessarily appreciate the *social* approach to crime prevention, preferring instead to focus on physical security measures such as better locks and doors. Moreover the agencies close association with a *police led forum* raised suspicions amongst the local communities regarding the exchange of personal information and a corresponding lack of public accountability.[2] In our view traditional multi-agency forums cannot be effective if they fail to address these problems and will fail to provide the strategic and publicly accountable form of co-operation amongst agencies which is necessary in any approach to tackling racial harassment. As we argue below redressing this is the key to developing a proactive perspective and response.[3]

## Model for policy co-operation in local practices

It is important to emphasize the *particular history and geography of racial harassment which gives rise to its contemporary spread in different locations,* that is its contextuality. This is necessary in order to develop a credible basis for collaboration among different agencies in a form of co-operative action against racial harassment. There needs to be clear agreement as to the nature of the problem *as a prerequisite of* any agreed jurisdiction-wide strategic responses. Indeed collaboration is only likely to be meaningful and enabling if it takes the form of a strategic co-operation. Sometimes the call for a multi-agency approach is invoked when matters like these are not even considered let alone resolved. There is a tendency for basic principles to be disregarded in the rush to collaboration. While the Home Office's 'Guide for the Statutory Agencies' is far from remiss in this respect (although their analysis differs markedly from ours) its uncritical insistence on a police-led, traditional multi-agency approach seems rather too 'rough and ready' when a more sophisticated and considered response is required.

There are at least two critical dimensions to our thinking here (which themselves need also to be the subject of discussion). The first arises from our assessment of the criticisms levelled at the traditional multi-agency approach where these have direct policy implications for redressing the spread of racial harassment. In our view there are at least *five minimum requirements for effective co-operation* between collaborating agencies, these are:

(a) Common objectives and perspectives for all the agencies represented in the collaboration.

(b) Equal and relevant status of 'representatives'.

(c) Clearly defined expectations and roles of the agencies.

(d) Clearly defined boundaries of confidentiality when individual cases and community issues are discussed.

(e) Establishment of a lead agency which is not also a domineering agency.

The second dimension is concerned with the means through which collaboration is established and the public status of that collaboration, in other words, the *accountability of co-operation.* If agencies and organizations throughout the statutory and voluntary sector are to be involved in action against racial harassment in a particular jurisdiction they will need to accept *ownership* of the policy impetus, this means they must be publicly involved in establishing and developing that impetus, as well as providing the requisite resources. Taken together these two dimensions represent the basis of what we would like to term an *agenda for policy co-operation* against racial harassment. We use Figure 6.1 below to illustrate how this could be developed to produce the basis for co-operative action against racial harassment in the London Borough of Waltham Forest.

**Figure 6.1:** **Agenda for policy co-operation against racial harassment**

It is important to appreciate that what we are proposing is not an initiative that 'starts from scratch'. Its premise is that there are various levels and types of agency/organizational developments already in existence (albeit relatively ineffective and unco-ordinated, see Chapters 2 and 3). Furthermore, despite the importance of attaining an effective Borough wide response in the long term, this should not be taken as a disregard of the necessity to develop specific policies and practices among various organizations, particularly the local authority, in the short term (see Appendix 4 for our recommendations in respect of Waltham Forest). What we are proposing here is a simple method of establishing a principled basis of co-operative action which is basically locational, that is it *starts from where we are.* Figure 6.1 sets out the key areas for initial development and co-operation through policy discussions. We place the weight of introducing these initiatives with the local authority simply because as an elected and all-purpose public agency it is best placed to command a spatial approach to its operational jurisdiction and has the resources which are relevant to sustaining broad policy developments. The objective of the Agenda would be to establish agreement with the police, Council departments, voluntary and community organizations, on the general policy objectives and the common strategic components of each agency's practical responses. According to our analysis, a social policy agreement like this, if it is to achieve any practical coherence, will need to be placed in a spatial context. This is the focus of the next section.

## A spatial approach to tackling racial harassment

The discussion in the previous section points to the importance of accountable collaboration and effective co-operation among various local agencies in order to have a systematic impact on racial harassment in a given area. The traditional multi-agency approach consistently fails to meet these criteria. Yet it is equally important that any collaboration between policy makers and public agencies is based on a clear perspective on *either the cause or the conditions of existence of the problem.* This requires the elaboration of what might be termed, a 'theory of safety'. Where racial harassment is concerned, this means emphasizing a *spatial approach.* In previous Chapters (see 1, 4 and 5) the analysis suggested that the *pervasiveness* of racial harassment in particular locales of Waltham Forest was an expression of *white territorialism.* This is a dynamic part of what we understand by the spread of racial harassment, over time and across locations. Its spatial implications are unmistakable. On the basis of their experiences, victims and potential victims of racial harassment (e.g. individuals from Asian and Black communities) construct mental maps which regionalize the Borough in multiple terms of relative safety. As this study had repeatedly insisted, combinations of inaction, ineffectiveness and indifference by both statutory and voluntary agencies have sustained the spread of racial harassment. In particular the neglect of action against perpetrators had ensured an omnipresent sense of insecurity in the social environment for Waltham Forest's Asian and Black communities. Each of these factors is part of a spatial pattern. It is virtually predictable. But as a pattern it also points to the possibilities for planning a credible response. Any effective developments in policy therefore must be informed by this *proactive perspective.*

In order to fully comprehend our approach it is worth considering how things look from a non-spatial point of view, that is the *random incident approach* which currently dominates the thinking of statutory agencies and policy makers. As we have seen this emphasizes the *quantification* of racial harassment, numbers, amounts and so on. It focuses mainly on the incident after its occurrence, which is usually perceived as random, sporadic, opportunistic, unpredictable and therefore not capable of being patterned (see Chapter 4). As a consequence, the search for some kind of pattern or explanation of racial harassment, implies a *reactive perspective.* One which dwells exclusively on identifying, after the event, racist or fascist groups and individuals who are 'known' to be racist (this seems to be the idea behind the police's notion of targeting 'racially motivated' crime). From this perspective the response of statutory agencies is problematic. Firstly, they can only react, a response is taken only after racial harassment occurs because this is perceived as a random event; secondly, there is very little action against perpetrators because *their individual intentions* rather than the *implications of their activities for white territorialism* are defined as the focus (unless of course they belong to a racist organisation); and thirdly the onus is inevitably on the victim of racial harassment not merely to report it, but *to prove it,* because statutory agencies (from this perspective), cannot *in the first instance* see the significance of the spatial dimensions of racial harassment. In order to explain this Figure 6.2 below illustrates how the phenomenon of the random racial harassment incident needs to be seen in terms of its spatial context.

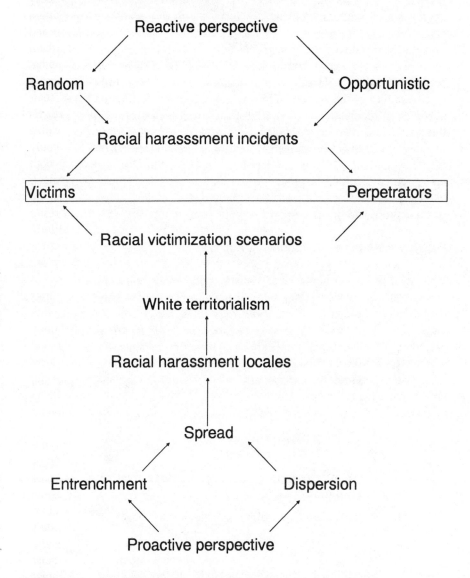

**Figure 6.2:  Racial harassment incidents in a spatial context**

It should be clear that what both perspectives have in common (see Figure 6.2) is a focus on the relationship between the victims and perpetrators of racial harassment (i.e. the victimological relation). Clearly where they differ is in terms of the context in which that relationship is understood. The reactive perspective with its individualistic bias sees only the random incident (or aggregates of random incidents) in terms of their amounts or their own particularities, that is *outside of any explanatory context*. In contrast the proactive perspective highlights the idea of racial victimization as a connected set of events, affecting communities over a period of time, experienced in particular locations persistently, that is, as a scenario. This is linked to a wider understanding of the spatial circumstances through which racial harassment becomes an incident. The point is that the reactive perspective is extremely limited. It is a perspective which is capable of revealing only the surface imagery of victimization and therefore cannot hope to facilitate anythng other than a precarious platform for a policy response. This has to be seen and understood in terms of the proactive perspective, since it is only a spatial set of understandings which can enable effective policy developments, agency collaborations and 'local' responses.

*Policy developments in a bounded jurisdiction*

What then is the starting point in a spatial policy approach to tackling racial harassment? In our view it is certainly the relationship between the victims and perpetrators of racial harassment *but only in so far as this is taken to be inextricably linked to the relevant social experiences of location.* This means considering the locational implications of specific incidents, the foreground scenarios of victimization and the environmental spread of racial harassment.In this sense then a socially *and* spatially relevant set of policy objectives could be formulated as follows:

* To respond to and tackle effectively reported incidents of racial harassment;

* To intervene in and challenge scenarios of racial victimization;

* To counter and eliminate the spread of racial harassment.

The first of these objectives is clearly the most immediate and practical; the second and third are designed for the development of corresponding medium-long term policies (see also Figure 6.2 above). These are not however, policy objectives which simply take the local authority or any other agency as initial points of reference, *rather it is the local jurisdiction as a whole which is the spatial point of departure for this approach.* This perhaps is a convenient place to cite the main difference between our study and some of the previous research. We have endevoured to focus on racial harassment not simply as a problem for the making or implementation of policy. If anything a significant drift in our analysis is towards the idea that *previous policy perceptions and developments have indeed become a problem for the people who experience racial victimization.* What also distinguishes our approach is Leigh's (1988:60) recognition that:

> A strategic plan which does not lead to action is not much use. It must also be sufficiently different from what has happened in the past to be setting a new direction. In judging its likely effectiveness people will expect to understand how one action relates to another.

This describes precisely the rationale we employ to move from general policy objectives to consider what we feel to be the three strategic components of policy responses to the issue of racial harassment in any bounded operational jurisdiction. These are: the development of a safe social environment; action against perpetrators; and support for victims. It is a combination of these responses which need to be considered by all public and voluntary agencies. First, however, the ideas involved in each need to be spelled out clearly.

*Developing a safe social environment*

In Chapter 5 we discussed briefly that aspect of racial harassment which expresses itself as *white territorialism* and how that contributes to an unsafe social environment for Asian and Black people. What then do we mean by safe social environment? This is difficult to sketch precisely but in general it is where peaceful co-existence prevails *among and between* various communities and where people feel secure in the knowledge that there are public agencies which *will* sustain and develop this. This invokes a pluralist principle of *safety*; every community or social group has a right to its social existence and cultural way of life within the law and to the extent this does not endanger the safety and security of other communities. The question of safety is particularly pertinent where crimes against specific persons are concerned. These mark out that complex range of personal violations which occur for no reason other than to denigrate or oppress people who belong to a specific marginalized community or subordinated social group (e.g. violence against women, child abuse, anti-Gay violence). Racial victimization is one of these social crimes. In general the planning of a safe social environment if considered in these safety terms, would note that where racial harassment is specifically concerned, this requires developing measures to counter-act the activities and effects of white territorialism.

### Action against perpetrators of racial harassment

This has now attained the status of an idea that is frequently espoused but rarely enacted in direct policy and practice. In addition its contribution to the development of a safe social environment and support for victims is sometimes obscured. It needs to be recognized that the persistence of racial harassment is owed less to the difficulties of its detection, or to the supposed reluctance of victims to report it, than to the degree to which it does not fully occupy that realm of public behaviours generally recognized as *proscribed*. If public agencies, like the police and the Council actually direct resources to action against perpetrators, it demonstrates publicly and immediately what quality of social environment is envisaged and what is regarded as unacceptable social behaviour. The primary aim of any strategy of action against perpetrators is not simply to punish miscreants, its substantial value lies in its deterrent effect. To take action against the perpetrator is to begin to challenge the traditions of racial harassment which exert a profound influence on a range of social interactions. The intention is to dissuade perpetrators from pursuing racial harassment because the likelihood of action against them is a *real prospect*; and also to stem some of the spatial implications of victimization (e.g. the build-up of 'no go' areas for Asian and Black people). The idea is to preserve a plural local sense of 'ethnoscape'.

### Support for victims of racial harassment

If the complex structure of racial victimization is properly understood (see Chapter 5), *only then* does it become possible to organize appropriate types and levels of response. Clearly the development of a safe social environment and action against perpetrators will have a role to play in combating the possibilities of racial victimization. But specific consideration also needs to be given to the *local* provision of immediate, direct and long-term responses once *victimization occurs*. Furthermore an absolute priority is the provision of public knowledge concerning the *actual* nature and *current* availability of advice, practical assistance and emotional support. The aim of victim support in this context is to ensure that immediate threats to safety are removed, to facilitate the appropriate support for the human consequences of racial victimization and to establish a basis for the victims confidence in their long-term safety. All this requires not only taking the experience of racial victimization seriously, but the issues posed by the general context in which forms of social dehumanization are enacted.

## Social dehumanization and the question of safety

Despite the extensive treatment of racial harassment in this study, it needs to be said that conceptualizing it in isolation, as a distinct social phenomenon, is a necessary but insufficient basis for understanding its institution. It is one thing to argue that it constitutes a social crime it is quite another to demonstate what is meant by this without an explication of its 'relations of equivalence' (Laclau and Mouffe, 1985) with other crimes against specific persons. This is what is required in order to reveal racial harassment as an instance of social dehumanization. We need to ask, what is the equivalential relation between personal violations 'like' racial victimization which enables us to refer to the generality of social dehumanization? At least one thing should be clear from our discussion of the 'local ethnoscape' in Chapter 5: where victimization and social marginalization co-incide we find the recurrent, antagonistic relationships which criss-cross the emergence and sedimentation of crimes against specific persons. The nature and direction of these 'anti-humanist' dynamics is resourced by struggles at the margins over the centrality and authority of particular experiences of living which are 'normed' and variously 'unmarked' by race, gender, sexuality and 'other different' social indentities. To put it simply, the 'silenced' aggregate, Asian and Black people, women and Gay people respectively 'threaten' the domination of the 'ruling general public', white people, men and heterosexuals respectively. While the desire to control and direct the outcome of personal qua social encounters, to retain the space of domination by reinforcing the space of marginalization, through gratuitous, persistent forms of abuse or violation, expresses the logic of social dehumanization. This is a social crime, yet what we mean by this still needs to be explained in a manner which takes us beyond the traditional legal concept of crime. Smith (1986:106) has suggested the possibility of a move 'towards the philosphical question of morality, redefining victimization in terms of social harm rather than in terms of the law as it is presently constituted'. However, more relevant to our approach is the 'curiously neglected' (ibid.) earlier work of Schwendinger and Schwendinger (1975) who provide a useful initial framework for our thinking about the concept of a social crime in terms of dehumanization.

Recognizing that there are 'socially non-injurious acts' which are defined as crimes and 'socially injurious acts' which are not construed as 'either civil or criminal violations' (ibid.:126), Schwendinger and Schwendinger argue that 'ethical criteria' like 'social injury', 'public wrong' (or social crime) need to be elaborated otherwise the narrow ethical standpoint of the legislature will prevail. They suggest the basis for this elaboration is the 'historically determined rights of individuals' (ibid.:132). A human rights criterion would mean not only ensuring the fundamental prerequisites for social welfare but also identifying 'those forms of individuals behaviour and social institutions which should be engaged in order to defend human rights' (ibid.:134). In so far as our conception of social crime is driven by a social policy impetus it will involve prioritizing different rights, hence our emphasis on dehumanization. But whatever the prioritization, Schwendinger and Schwendinger insist that the conditions which give rise to human rights violations should be a focus, they argue:

> the social conditions themselves must become the object of social policy and that it is not an individual or loose collection of atomistic individuals which is to be controlled, but rather the social relationships between individuals which give rise to criminal behaviour.
>
> (op. cit.:136)

An equivalent position is articulated by a great deal of feminist research on violence against women. For example, Jeffreys and Radford (1984:182) argue for a 'transformation of men's attitudes to women and to their own sexuality (which) would require the recognition for women of that most basic human right, the right to bodily integrity'. While in Gay literature the violation of human rights is described as the oppressive experience of 'traditional' social encounters with homophobia:

> Three main reasons for homosexual oppression emerge from the literature: first, that homosexuality poses some kind of threat to social stability; second, that homosexuality poses some kind of threat to the dominant view of gender and to generally accepted views on morality; and third, that homosexuality threatens sexuality, life style or status.
>
> (Crane, 1983:181-182)

208

Anti-Gay violence and violence against women, like racial harassment, in their various specific modalities are fundamental expressions of social dehumanization. Their avoidance is in Schwendinger and Schwendinger's (op. cit.:137) terms a basic human right: 'security to one's person' is a right which is more basic than others as a 'danger to one's health or life itself endangers all other claims'. The key problem for sustaining a theory of safety which can aspire to some form of policy recognition is not only the restrictive legal definition of crime, but the traditional social policy agenda 'consensus' which has excluded 'race', gender and sexuality as central policy concerns (see Williams, 1989). Nevertheless safety, as a potential social construction, should constitute the 'heart' of any policy approach. This should not be confused with the popular nostrums of crime prevention, disseminated by the Home Office and the police, which in their efforts to make the person invulnerable or the home impregnable may impart a sense of security to the wider community but cannot make inviolable the safety of specifically marginalized social groups. It needs also to avoid the simple idea that a 'place of safey' once located is a solution, as if 'safety is located geographically' (Stanko, op. cit.:12), when it is clear that these violations can occur anywhere. On the contrary, as is the case with racial harassment, a minimum social policy approach to the provision of safety needs to ensure that accountable and responsible public agencies place freedom from danger, risk or injury in the contested social domain at the centre and not the margins of their operational agendas. More importantly this should be accompanied by a social policy commitment which takes seriously the need to replace marginalization and dehumanization with pluralism and human safety. Needless to say, all this is beyond Anti-racism.

## Notes

1. Ostensibly this is the context of the ineffective police-initiated Racial Incidents Panel (see Appendix 5).

2. It is also worth noting that the Home Office suggests multi-agency approaches to tackling racial harassment should be led by the police.

3. Another limitation of the traditional multi-agency approach has been its non-strategic relationship with the voluntary sector and community organizations. This has allowed the voluntary sector to abdicate some of its responsiblity in tackling the problem of racial harassment. This particularly applies to agencies that provide a range of services from advice to specialized counselling and undertake development work in the communities. In Waltham Forest for example, most of

these agencies were funded by the local authority and virtually none had developed policy or practical responses to racial harassment. Here part of the problem could lie with the funding sources. Consideration should be given to making it a funding requirement for specific advice agencies, whose expertise is relevant to victims of racial harassment, to develop strategic responses. Without this, the often invoked support networks will generally not be available in the voluntary sector but confined solely to Asian, Black and Ethnic Minority organizations. Agencies like the CABs should offer a comprehensive advice service to victims of racial harassment.

# Appendix 1
# The London Borough of Waltham Forest

## Introduction

The following information locates the London Borough of Waltham Forest within the Greater London area and maps out the local government ward boundaries referred to in the preceding text. The size and distribution of the Asian, Black and Ethnic Minority population in Waltham Forest[1] is also sketched out. A brief description is given of the Borough's police divisions.

## Location

The London Borough of Waltham Forest is located in the north-east sector of London. It forms one of the outer boundaries of Greater London where it meets the County of Essex. Waltham Forest is surrounded by the following London Boroughs: Redbridge, Newham, Hackney, Haringey, Enfield and to the north, the County of Essex.

The boundaries of Waltham Forest are formed on the west by the Lea Valley and its chain of reservoirs, marshes and filter beds. These form a physical barrier with the neighbouring Boroughs of Enfield, Haringey and Hackney. Along this 13km border there are only five roads and three railway lines which form links with the rest of London. Remnants of Epping Forest remain in the north and east of the Borough where it abuts upon Essex and Redbridge.

## Constituencies and wards

Three major roads form the physical barriers which divide Waltham Forest into three Parliamentary constituencies. The North Circular Road and Forest Road form the boundary between the Chingford constituency in the north and Walthamstow constituency in the middle of the Borough. This boundary as well as being a physical one has also created a north/south divide in the

Borough. The Lea Bridge Road forms the limit of Walthamstow constituency and the start of Leyton constituency which continues southwards to the boundary with Newham. In this book, constituency wards are used as the main denominator of location. The wards are listed below in Figure A1.1 (see also Figure A1.2).

| Constituency | Ward |
|---|---|
| Chinford | Chapel End |
| | Hale End |
| | Endlebury |
| | Hatch Lane |
| | Chindford Green |
| | Larkswood |
| | Valley |
| Walthamstow | Wood Street |
| | High Street |
| | Lloyd Park |
| | Higham Hill |
| | St. James Street |
| | Hoe Street |
| Leyton | Cann Hall |
| | Leyton |
| | Leytonstone |
| | Cathall |
| | Grove Green |
| | Forest |
| | Lea Bridge |

**Figure A1.1 : Local government boundaries in Waltham Forest**

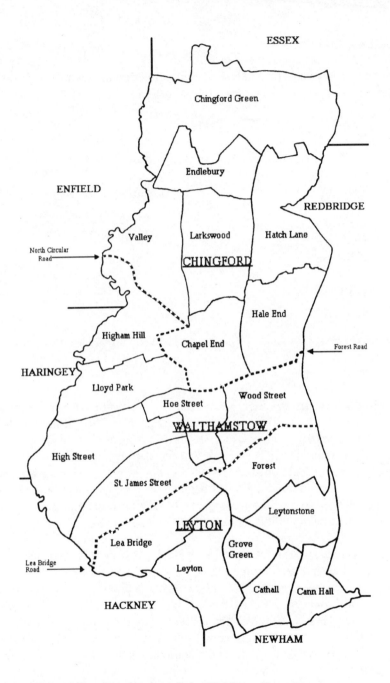

**Figure A1.2 : Map showing wards in Waltham Forest**

213

## Total population

The table below gives the total population figures for Waltham Forest in 1981, estimates for 1986 and a projected figure for 1991.

### Table A1.1

### Total population of Waltham Forest

| Year | Total population of Waltham Forest |
|------|-----------------------------------|
| 1981 | 217,058 |
| 1986 | 215,410* |
| 1991 | 216,260* |

*Estimate*

## Waltham Forest's Asian, Black and Ethnic Minority communities

*Population*

Nearly 86% of the Borough's residents in 1981 were born in the United Kingdon and almost 11% were born in the 'New Commonwealth' and Pakistan.[2] Comparing figures from data in 1971 it seems that between 1971-81 the 'New Commonwealth' and Pakistan populations increased at least 60% (there are some difficulties in comparison due to differences in definitions used). The Commission for Racial Equality estimated that the Ethnic Minority population of Waltham Forest, taking into account birth, death and in-migration rates, would total 44,000 at the end of 1986. Since 1981 the Borough has had one of the highest rates of annual increase (2.9%) in London of this section of the population. This is however lower than those districts outside London. The best available estimates for the Ethnic Minority populations in 1988 suggest that these communities form 25% of the Borough population, of this 22% are from 'New Commonwealth' and Pakistan and 3% belong to other communities, for example Turkish, Chinese. The percentage of the population in Waltham Forest who are of 'New Commonwealth' and Pakistani origin is the 11th highest nationally and the Pakistani community is the largest of any London Borough.

*Distribution*

The available data concerning the areas in which Asian, Black and Ethnic Minority people live comes primarily from the 1981 census data which classified people according to the birthplace of the 'head of the household'. This was done because many Asian and West Indian children[3] would have been born in the United Kingdom. The figures showed that over 20% of the total population in all the wards south of Forest Road (Walthamstow and Leyton constituencies), with the exception of Wood Street ward, were of 'New Commonwealth' or Pakistani origin. Wards with the greatest percentages were Cathall (31.5%) and Grove Green (nearly 30%) followed by Hoe Street and Leyton (both around 28%), Forest and Leytonstone (around 26%). By contrast wards north of Forest Road (Chingford constituency) had figures all below 12%. The lowest with 2-3% were Chingford Green and Hatch Lane.

*Countries of origin*

In 1981 of the population born in the 'New Commonwealth' or Pakistan nearly half were from East Africa or Asia and nearly 40% were from the Caribbean or the rest of Africa (many of the Borough's West Indians/Africans were born in the United Kingdom). Of the Asian population in the Borough nearly half came from Pakistan. The distribution of residents showed that although some areas had concentrations of both Asian/East African and Caribbean/rest of Africa (e.g. in Lea Bridge ward and Cathall ward), there were also some separate concentrations. The High Street/Hoe Street wards of Walthamstow and parts of Leytonstone ward have large numbers of Asian residents whereas areas of Leyton constituency (Cathall, Grove Green and Leyton wards) more often have Caribbean residents.

*Age profile*

The 1981 Census showed a high proportion of the Borough's young people lived in 'New Commonwealth' or Pakistani households - 29% of the total number of under 16 year olds. High Street and Grove Green wards had nearly 50% of their 0-4 year olds living in 'New Commonwealth' or Pakistani headed households and in Hoe Street ward nearly 50% of the 5-15 year olds lived in such households. The Pakistani/Bangladeshi group had larger proportions of young children in contrast to the Caribbean group who had relatively small proportions of children - this may however indicate that a proportion of Black households were headed by people born in the United Kingdom at the time of the 1981 Census.

The under 5s contained the highest proportion of Ethnic Minority members and this proportion declined through age groups as age increased. The vast majority of 'New Commonwealth' or Pakistani residents under 15 were born in the UK as were almost 30% of those aged 16-29. As time goes by more of the children born in the Ethnic Minority communities will have British born parents. The current Ethnic Minority elderly population totals under 1000 but could increase to almost 4,000 by the year 2001 which would be about 15% of the total population over 65.

## New arrivals in Waltham Forest

Between July 1988-August 1989, 368 people whose first destination was Waltham Forest (they may not have intended to settle in Waltham Forest) arrived in the United Kingdom. These 368 new arrivals[4] came from 37 different countries, the majority from South Asia (Pakistan, Bangladesh, India and Sri Lanka). Almost two thirds of arrivals from Pakistan and Bangladesh were women. Of the total, 50% were aged 16-34, a further 28% were aged 15 and under. The over 55s accounted for 14% of those arriving from South Asia. The most popular first destinations were Walthamstow (E17) 47%, Leyton (E10) 27% and Leytonstone (E11) 17%.

## Households

In 1981 there were 9,230 households in the Borough whose household head was born in the 'New Commonwealth' or Pakistan: 3,560 Caribbean households, 3,410 Asian households and 2,260 households headed by people from other countries.

The size of the household according to the 1981 Census, broken down by ethnic origin of the head of household, was for Caribbean headed households an average of 3.59 persons, with an Indian or East African head 4.36, with a Pakistani or Bangladeshi head 5.27 and with a head from any other birthplace (mainly UK) 2.45. The large size of some of these households was partly due to the younger age structure of these communities and hence a greater number of families with children.

In 1981, a larger proportion of private households in Waltham Forest were headed by someone born in the 'New Commonwealth' or Pakistan than nationwide. 6% of private households were headed by someone born in the Caribbean, 4.3% had a Pakistani/Bangladeshi head, 3.5% an Indian or East African born head and 3.7% had a head born in the remainder of the 'New Commonwealth' or Pakistan. Overall households with 'New Commonwealth' or Pakistani born heads made up 11.2% of the Borough's households. 9.7%

were Council tenants and 11.8% Housing Association tenants in 1981.

In the area south of Forest Road almost 1 in 4 owner occupied dwellings contained a 'New Commonwealth' or Pakistani household. Also in the south of the Borough, Afro-Caribbean households occupied the same proportion of public sector housing as white households (31%). Asian households occupied around 15% of public sector housing. This contrasted with the north of the Borough where 'New Commonwealth' or Pakistani households occupied a low proportion of public sector housing with the exception of Chingford Hall estate in Valley ward.

Of 21 estates, 13 had less than the Borough average percentage of population living in households headed by someone born in the 'New Commonwealth' or Pakistan. Those estates where these communities made up more than a quarter of the residents were Chingford Hall in Valley ward; Gosport Road and Boundary Road in St James Street ward; Beaumont Road and Oliver Close in Leyton ward; Avenue Road, Cathall Road and Norman Road in Cathall ward. 12 of the estates had above average percentages of Afro-Caribbean born residents and 7 had double the Borough average (Chingford Hall in Valley ward, Gosport Road and Boundary Road in St James Street ward, Beaumont Road and Oliver Close in Leyton ward, Avenue Road and Cathall Road in Cathall ward). By contrast only Oliver Close, Leyton ward and Norman Road, Cathall ward had more than the Borough average proportion of people born in the Indian sub-continent and East Africa.

The 1981 Census showed that 'New Commonwealth' or Pakistani households experienced above average levels of accommodation sharing and overcrowding. 42% of households were overcrowded (one or more person(s) per room) compared to the Borough average of 16%. Council estates in Leyton, St. James Street, Cathall and Valley wards were amongst the worst off on a number of indicators of relative deprivation. The Large Panel Construction estates[5] represent the most disadvantaged of the housing stock in the Borough. It was found that the number of Black and Ethnic Minority tenants was inversely related to the desirability of the dwellings (i.e. 47.8% of Black and Ethnic Minority tenants on the Boundary Road estate, St James Street ward and 27% of tenants of Avenue Road estate in Cathall ward were of Afro-Caribbean origin).

## Metropolitan police

### Metropolitan police district

The Metropolitan police district encompasses all 32 London Boroughs plus parts of the Counties surrounding London. The Metropolitan district is divided into eight numbered areas.

### Area 1

Waltham Forest lies within the Metropolitan Police Area 1 which also includes the London Boroughs of Islington, Haringey, Redbridge, Enfield, and parts of south-west Essex and south-east Hertfordshire. Area 1, from 1989, has been under the direction of Deputy Assistant Commissioner Walter Boreham, OBE who is based at Edmonton Police Station, London Borough of Enfield.

### Local divisions

Waltham Forest is split into two main divisions, Chingford and Leyton.

*Chingford* This division is subdivided into two smaller areas, Chingford and Walthamstow. There is a police station in each; Chingford police station at Kings Head Hill, E4 and Walthamstow police station in Forest Road, E17. Chingford division is under the direction of Chief Superintendent Stainsby (since 1991) based at Chingford police station.

*Leyton* This division has a police station in Leyton at Francis Road, E10 and a police station in Leytonstone at High Road, E11. Leyton division is under the direction of Chief Superintendent Nettleship (since 1989) based at Leyton police station.

### Home Beats

Each division is subdivided into smaller areas called 'Home Beats' which are the patrolling responsibility of a Home Beat officer. These are shown in Figure A1.3. The Home Beats do not necessarily coincide with local government ward or constituency boundaries.

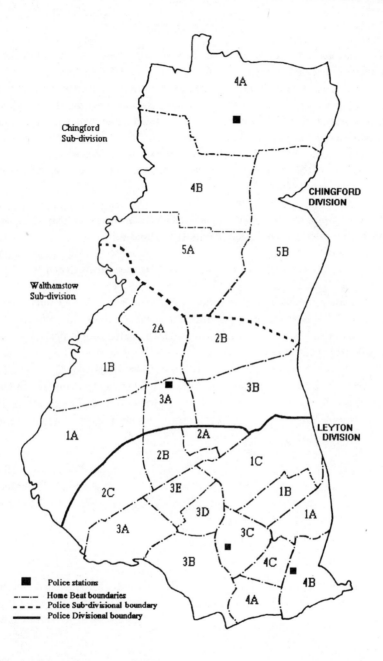

**Figure A1.3 :  Map of Chingford and Leyton police divisions showing Home Beat boundaries**

**Notes**

1. The information and data used has been drawn from a number of documents produced by the London Borough of Waltham Forest. A large proportion of this data has been extracted and analyzed from the 1981 Census conducted in Waltham Forest. The next collection of Census data took place in 1991, at the time of writing its data was unavailable to us. Various specific surveys and data collection exercises have been carried out since the 1981 survey and information from these have been used where appropriate. Where data has been collected under specific categories these have been used. This does not in any way imply that we agree with or support the use of all the terminology.

2. 'New Commonwealth' and Pakistan, includes countries in the Caribbean, Africa, India, Bangladesh, East Asia, the Mediterranean and Pakistan.

3. Children are those under 16 years of age unless specifically stated.

4. A new arrival is defined as someone who has been out of the United Kingdom for at least 12 months and has the intention of staying in the United Kingdom for at least 12 months. Students are included in this and those people normally resident here who have been abroad for 12 months.

5. Large Panel Construction is a method of construction using mainly pre-fabricated building panels.

# Appendix 2
# A note on research and methodology

The emergence of the Inquiry was the product of circumstances not usually associated with the style of Waltham Forest Council. In October 1987 the Head of the Council's Police Unit (renamed the Police Monitoring and Research Unit in 1990) prepared a report for the Police Committee entitled 'Policing Racial Harassment and the Development of Policy'. The report not only analyzed the role of the police but questioned the absence of a corporate Council response. Following this, the Head of the Police Unit drew up terms of reference for the establishment of an inter-departmental Council working party on racial harassment. This was initiated by the Police Committee and supported by the Race Relations Committee. Hence by March 1988, after the Working Party's first meeting, the Council's commitment to review its policy and co-ordinate its response seemed clear enough. Part of the Working Party's programme of work included the requirement to review the 'extent, patterns and locations' of racial harassment in the Borough. But one thing soon became apparent: this review could not take place without a prior thorough investigation of the nature of the problem in local experiences. Otherwise the development of Council policy would continue to rest on confused, distorted and inadequate understandings. It was in this context that the Police Unit developed proposals for the establishment of the Inquiry.


## Structure of the Inquiry

A panel was established on behalf of Waltham Forest Council in 1989 principally to support the research and to facilitate its 'public' dimensions (see below 'collection of evidence'). The composition of the Council Panel is set out in Figure A2.1 below:

221

| | |
|---|---|
| Cllr Neil Gerrard | *(Chair; Leader of the Council)* |
| Mr Barnor Hesse | *(Secretary; Head of Police Monitoring and Research Unit)* |
| Cllr Franklyn Georges | *(Labour Party)* |
| Cllr Mladen Jovcic | *(Conservative Party)* |
| Cllr Denise Liunberg | *(Labour Party)* |
| Cllr Bob Wheatley | *(Liberal Democratic Party)* |
| Mr Qadir Bakhsh | *(Head of Race Relations Unit)* |

**Figure A2.1 : Council Panel of Inquiry, 1988-1990**

The research for the Inquiry was carried out with strict regard to its terms of reference. These are set out below in Figure A2.2 .

1. To inquire into and comment on the extent, patterns and locations of racial harassment in Waltham Forest with particular regard to:

* the provision of Council services

* the role and involvement of the police

* the availability and support for victims of racial harassment

2. To produce a report with recommendations where appropriate, for the consideration of Council departments and other relevant agencies.

**Figure A2.2 : Inquiry's terms of reference**

The Inquiry adopted as its working or operational definition of racial harassment one formulated by the Commission for Racial Equality.

Racial harassment is violence which may be verbal or physical, and which includes attacks on property as well as the person, suffered by individuals or groups because of their race, nationality, ethnic or national origins, when the victim believes that the perpetrator was acting on racial grounds, and/or there is evidence of racism.

The Inquiry accepted that there is by now sufficient documented evidence to indicate that those principally disadvantaged and affected by racism at various levels of British society are Asian and Black communities. This is also the case where racial harassment is concerned. It was on this basis that the Inquiry requested local views, opinions and experiences to be submitted as oral or written evidence.

The Inquiry was co-ordinated throughout by a strategy team that provided research, analysis, development initiatives and administration. Following its launch and the initial public request for evidence on 7 November 1988, the panel heard oral evidence during the period, 23 January-26 February 1989. This was followed by another session of oral hearings, based on written evidence, which took place during 9 May-23 May 1989. From November 1988-August 1990 the Panel of Inquiry met on 19 occasions (excluding the time taken up by oral hearings).

*Methodology*

The method of a local Inquiry is increasingly being used as an attempt to involve the public at some level in the process of research into significant causes for public concern. The nature of this *action research* is usually exploratory, aiming to develop new initiatives, ideas, policies and generally raise public awareness. In other instances the objective is to explain or clarify the background to controversial events. Although there are broad similarities in the structure of different Inquiries, there is room for a wide variation in the particular methods chosen for the collection of 'evidence' (i.e. data), the development of analysis and the presentation of findings.

*Design* The terms of reference were drawn up to specify current gaps in knowledge necessary for policy development purposes. The Panel of Inquiry was used to publicize the seriousness of the need for local information (knowledge, experiences, documents) to assist in understanding and clarifying the issues. Two public meetings were organized to promote this. The Inquiry arranged for leaflets to be delivered to households thoughout the Borough, these constituted public requests for oral or written evidence. Local organizations were written to directly. An 'evidence guide', based on the terms of reference, was designed to simplify the process of evidence submission. The evidence guide contained a series of questions intended only as a guide to issues the Inquiry was interested in examining. Deadlines were made public for the submission of evidence. (Up to this point the local newspaper, the *Waltham Forest Guardian*, ran a weekly series of articles advertizing the work of the Inquiry). There were five types of evidence guides, whether for oral or written evidence. A general evidence guide, plus four specific guides for the Metropolitan police; Council departments; Housing Associations and voluntary sector organizations; Asian and African-Caribbean organizations. The specific guides denoted the target groups. In addition to the public solicitation of oral and written evidence, documentary research was carried out in each of the areas specified by the terms of reference and secondary analysis was undertaken on all the available locally compiled racial harassment statistics. The aim was to produce an incisive, contextual analysis of these areas in order to provide an analytical framework for understanding the submissions of evidence.

*Collection of evidence* There were various quantities and formats of evidence submitted from over 90 individuals and organizations, concerned with many issues both within and beyond the terms of reference. Only matters of direct relevance to the terms of reference were considered. There were two periods of oral hearings. Oral hearings I was for those who wished to submit oral evidence only. Hearings were attended by at least two Panel members, plus a researcher from the strategy team for the purposes of notation. Prior to the hearings each witness was contacted by a researcher who ascertained which areas (i.e. questions) of the evidence guide he or she wanted to cover. This was then conveyed to the Panel members prior to the hearing and the witness was questioned accordingly. All witnesses responses to questions were noted on sheets bearing the imprint of the particular question asked. All witnesses were asked if they wished to receive the handwritten copy of their evidence. Where this was desired it was complied with. All witnesses who were not representing an organization or who were not public figures were asked whether they were opposed to their names appearing in a list of those who had submitted evidence. Where this was indicated it was complied with. (It had been agreed previously that this criterion of individuals would not be named in the text.) Oral hearings II was based on a selected number of written submissions that required further clarification. In each case specific questions were sent to the individuals and organizations concerned, and hearings took place subsequently. (Although further questions were sent to the police, they chose to answer the questions in writing rather than verbally.)

*Analysis* All the evidence collected was specifically grouped and coded on the basis of its direct relevance to particular aspects of the terms of reference. A content analysis approach was adopted for exploratory purposes to identify recurring themes or perspectives which illustrated anything significant about the issues contained in the terms of reference and also in previous research. As a result of this process the analysis became more focused with clearer aims.

These were: to see what could be said about historical and geographical patterns in racial harassment both in Waltham Forest, and generally to detail the complex experience of racial victimization and the policy issues; to produce a comprehensive analysis of the investigative and policy problems in the polices' approach to racial harassment; to understand what precise developments and problems made the Council's role ineffective; and to attempt to outline a spatial analysis as a basis for the development of local policy initiatives against racial harassment.

# Appendix 3
# Oral and written evidence

This Appendix is an alphabetical list of witnesses who submitted oral and/or written evidence to the Panel of Inquiry.

Mr M. C. Afzal
Aid Centre
Mr Anwar; Waltham Forest Community Relations Council **
Asian Women's Parents' Group *
Bangalee Women's Welfare Project
Baptist Housing Association Ltd
Ms H. Banks
Beaumont Road Estate
Mr P. Boghal *
DAC W. Boreham; Metropolitan police Area 1
Black Teachers and Workers in Education
Mr P. Browning; Estate Manager,NALGO Housing Priority Estates Shop, LBWF **
Mr S. Bukhari
Ms N. Caesar *
Ms M. Canavan; Principal Personnel Officer,Works Department, LBWF **
Christian Action (Enfield ) Housing Association
Mr H. Cohen, MP
Consumer Protection Services, LBWF
Mr N. Cork
Mr L. Davis *
Downsell Infants School
Mr B. Dutt; Adviser, Walthamstow Citizens Advice Bureau **
East London Harmony
East London Housing Association Ltd
Family Housing Association
Ms J. Farmer
Mr M. Farooq *
Ms J. Fearon *

Ms S. Free; Borough Solicitor, LBWF **
Mr W. Furness; Director of Development, LBWF **
Mr M. Gordon; Co-ordinator, Afro-Caribbean Supplementary Education Service **
Mr A. Haouas *
Mr F. Hussain *
Mr N. Hussein; Association for Support of Asian Parents of Handicapped People *
Joint Council of Afro-Caribbean Organizations
Joint Council of Asian Organizations
Mr E. Kayongo *
Mr M. Khan
Mr N. Khan; Victim Aid Action Group **
Mr D. Knight *
Mr P. Knight; Director of Social Services, LBWF **
Mr M. Latif
Mr F. Lewis
Libraries and Arts department, LBWF
Ms S. Liburd
Ms J. Lomas; Acting Borough Solicitor, LBWF
London and Quadrant Housing Trust
Mr H. Malik *
Cllr N. Matharoo
Mr J. McIntosh
Mr J. Metcalfe
Metropolitan Housing Trust Ltd
Mr H. Mia *
Mount Carmel School
Muslim Women's Welfare Association
Ms J. Natai
Newlon Housing Trust
Nina West Homes Ltd
Pakistan Women's Welfare Association
Mr J. Patel *
Ms N. Patel
Mr M. Pearl; Assistant Director of Housing, LBWF **
Mr D. Philippos *
Cllr S. Pierpoint
Mr S. Playle *
Rushcroft School
Mr M. Sadiq Sheikh *

Samuel Lewis Housing Trust
Sanctuary Housing Association
Mr M. Shepherd; Chief Education Officer, LBWF **
Sikh Sangat London East
Solon Co-operative Housing Services Ltd
Mr D. Sparks
Mr G. Turner *
Mr Z. Uddin *
UJIMA Housing Association Ltd
Waltham Forest Association for People with Disabilities (Asian Advisory Group)
Waltham Forest Cameroonian and Friends Association
Waltham Forest Family Service Unit
Waltham Forest MENCAP
Wlatham Forest MIND
Walthamstow Labour Party (Lloyd Park and Highams Hill Branch)
Walthamstow School for Girls
Warden Housing Association Ltd
William Morris School
Mr A.Wilson; Assistant Director of Housing, LBWF **
Mr D. Wilson
Ms J. Wiltshire; Principal Personnel Officer, Recreation Services, LBWF **
DAC  P. Winship; Metropolitan police Area 1
Women's Koran Group *
Ms R. Younis

NOTE:  Eight witnesses (6 who gave written evidence and two who gave oral evidence) did not wish to be identified.

*Indicates witnesses who submitted oral evidence only.

**Indicates witnesses who submitted oral evidence in addition to written evidence.

# Appendix 4
# Recommendations arising from the inquiry into racial harassment

The Inquiry was asked to provide recommendations based on its analyses for consideration by Waltham Forest Council's departments and other local agencies. The recommendations contained here are provided in five sections. In our view they represent the basis for long term co-operative action.

## The spread of racial harassment in the Borough

1. That all agencies (in particular Council departments and the police) which receive complaints of racial harassment should record the place (e.g. housing estates, school etc.) and the location (e.g. electoral ward) of the incident(s) and make these statistics regularly available to the Council's Race Relations Unit.

2. That the Council's Race Relations Unit produce six-monthly reports based on an analysis of the information available (see Recommendation 1. above) and that this is publicized and disseminated widely throughout the Borough, to MPs, Councillors, voluntary organizations and members of the public.

3. That the Council either commissions or sponsors further research into the spread of racial harassment in the Borough which examines in more detail the entrenchment and patterning of racial harassment in:

(a) the Cathall and Leyton wards of the Leyton constituency;

(b) the Lloyd Park and Higham Hill wards of the Walthamstow constituency;

(c) the Valley and Chapel End *or* Hatch Lane wards of the Chingford constituency.

4. That in the short term (i.e. within three months of the Inquiry's publication) the Council publicizes its opposition to racial harassment and discusses the content of this Report in meetings held in each of the three constituencies of the Borough.

5. That in the medium term (i.e. within a year of the Inquiry's publication) the Council arranges in conjunction with relevant area based organizations at three monthly periods a consultative meeting in each constituency to discuss the local scenarios of racial victimization.

6. That the Council ensures the publication of a summary and review of the Inquiry in local community languages, braille and on audio cassette tape.

7. That the local newspapers are sensitive to the reporting of racial harassment and ensure that reports are not treated in a sensationalist or dismissive manner and that there is periodic reporting on the nature of the problem in the Borough.

8. That the Council initiates or sponsors the documentation of activities associated with racial harassment in the Borough each year through the production of publicly available annual monitoring reports.

9. That the Council monitors public statements made on behalf of the Council concerning its racial harassment policy developments to ensure that they are accurate and representative, and where this is not the case, that the Council publicly issues a retraction or an appropriate revision.

10. That the Borough's MPs be requested to support the introduction of a Racial Harassment Bill.

11. That the Police Monitoring and Research Unit ensure the widest distribution of the Inquiry's findings and contents by arrangement with appropriate publishers.

## Council policy

12. That the Council initiates the development of Borough wide co-operative action against racial harassment which ensures:

(a) safety from racial harassment in the social environment;

(b) action against perpetrators of racial harassment;

(c) support for victims of racial harassment.

13. That in furtherance of the above, the Council:

(a) prioritizes the work of its Racial Harassment Working Party in developing departmental specific and corporate policy regarding racial harassment in terms of a local co-operative action agenda;

(b) develops a framework for and subsequently initiates policy discussions with the police concerning the development of a local co-operative action agenda against racial harassment;

(c) develops a framework for and subsequently initiates policy discussions with voluntary and community organizations (including tenants associations) concerning the development of a local co-operative action agenda against racial harassment.

14. That within 2 years of publication of this Inquiry the Council publishes a document which details the policies, practices and principles of various agencies in the Borough in relation to an agenda of co-operative action against racial harassment.

15. That the Council recognizes as a special responsibility under Section 71 of the 1976 Race Relations Act the need to prioritize Council strategies against racial harassment.

16. That the Council's Police Monitoring and Research Unit arranges meetings with Chief and Senior Officers of the Council to discuss the policy implications of the Inquiry.

17. That the Council's Police Monitoring and Research Unit, monitors and evaluates the police's response to incidents of racial harassment.

18. That members of the public are encouraged to inform the Council's Police Monitoring and Research Unit of their experiences of the police response to racial harassment.

19. That the Council's Race Relations Unit monitors and evaluates the Council's response to incidents of racial harassment.

20. That members of the public are encouraged to inform the Race Relations Unit of their experiences of the Council's response to racial harassment.

21. That the Council's Chief Executive ensures that all the recommendations of this Inquiry are disseminated, developed, implementated and monitored where applicable or appropriate and reports to the Council within a year of the Inquiry's publication as to what progress has been made.

22. That the Council takes immediate steps and all necessary action to include a clause relating to racial harassment in the housing tenancy agreement.

23. That the Housing department amends the tenants handbook to make clear the Council's position on racial harassment and to indicate to tenants what to do if they are subject to racial harassment.

24. That the Housing department seriously considers using injunctions against perpetrators of racial harassment.

25. That the Housing department establish a temporary housing unit for the purpose of providing short term emergency accommodation for victims of racial harassment.

26. That Council departments ensure racist graffiti is removed within 24 hours of its discovery or reporting.

27. That the Social Services department monitor the incidence of racial harassment where it affects their clients in the context of the relevant Social Services area.

28. That the Social Services department formulate a policy responding to racial harassment which is supported by detailed practical guidance and incorporates measures for victim support and action against perpetrators

29. That the Social Services department initiate the development of support schemes or provisions for victims of racial harassment.

30. That the Education department develops courses or seminars for the Borough's schools and colleges which present and explain the Council's response to racial harassment.

31. That the Borough's schools and colleges provide a counselling service to pupils who have been racially harassed.

32. That the Borough's schools and colleges develop clear policies on dealing with perpetrators of racial harassment including the possible use of expulsions.

33. That the Borough Solicitor produces a report on available civil and criminal legal remedies which can be used by the Council in a policy against racial harassment with particular reference to legal action against perpetrators and legal powers to assist victims of racial harassment in both the public and private sectors.

34. That the Borough Solicitors department develop expertise and experience in the use of injunctions against perpetrators of racial harassment.

35. That solicitors in the Borough Solicitors department are trained specifically in the use of legal remedies in the context of racial harassment.

36. That the Development department monitors and develops a response to racial harassment in the context of planning and building applications, enforcement cases and public consultation exercises.

37. That the Department of Personnel in conjunction with the Race Relations Unit devise a training programme on the implications of racial harassment for service delivery and the rationale of a policy response.

38. That all relevant front-line Council staff receive training on addressing the implications of racial harassment within three months of their appointment.

## Police response

39. That the Home Office review the operation of the 1987 Metropolitan police Force Order on racial attacks and make public the contents of that review.

40. That the Metropolitan police take seriously the views of victims of racial harassment and have particular regard to the locale of reported victimization.

41. That the Metropolitan police devise a specific training programme for police officers in the investigation of racial harassment crimes.

42. That Chingford and Leyton police in conjunction with the Council devise a publicly accountable procedure for monitoring the attitude and satisfaction of victims of racial harassment to the police response.

43. That the Metropolitan police emphasize both in publicity and practice their intention to take action against perpetrators of racial harassment.

44. That Chingford and Leyton police should prioritize action against racial harassment as a divisional priority.

45. That Chingford and Leyton police seriously consider the use of independent criteria of assessment as specified in this Inquiry in relation to divisional objectives on racial harassment.

46. That Chingford and Leyton police publicize any successful actions undertaken against perpetrators of racial harassment.


## Victim support

47. That the Council and the police investigate all reported cases of racial harassment and make it clear that the onus is not on the victim to prove his/her victimization.

48. That the Council set up a professional counselling service across the Borough on racial harassment that is easily accessible, sensitive and able to provide gender and ethnic matching should this be required by the victims.

49. That the Council, the police and agencies in the voluntary sector clearly state in their publicity the services they offer to victims of racial harassment and how victims can take up that service.

50. That the Council makes it a funding condition to relevant advice agencies that they provide an advice service on racial harassment, and should monitor and evaluate their performance at annual grant renewals.

51. That the Council provides financial compensation to victims of racial harassment in the public sector for the damage to their property.

52. That the Council provides protection and support services to victims of racial harassment to alleviate the immediate dangers and fears they experience (for example, emergency accommodation, allocation of telephones).

53. That the Council provides an accessible and easily available language interpreting service to victims of racial harassment and to other agencies.

54. That the Council initiates the co-ordination of service provision in the statutory and voluntary sector for victims of racial harassment and address any identified gaps in the service.

55. That the Council establishes a complaints procedure regarding its services to victims of racial harassment and provides clear guidelines on the investigation of complaints.

56. That the Council develops proactive work on racial harassment by establishing formal and informal support networks for victims through its departmental community development work.

57. That the Council reviews Waltham Forest Victim Support Scheme to determine what measures can be taken to render it appropriate for use by victims of racial harassment.

58. That the Council develop in conjunction with specialist advice agencies an effective response to racial harassment in private sector housing and the small business sector.

59. That the Council's Racial Harassment hotline is discontinued in its present form and that a more comprehensive pro-active scheme is developed in consultation with local Asian, Black and Ethnic Minority community organizations.

60. That the Council's Race Relations Unit arranges on a regular basis meetings between Council departments and voluntary sector agencies to discuss and monitor services to victims of racial harassment.

# Appendix 5
# Waltham Forest racial
# incidents panel

One of the recommendations of Lord Scarman's report on the Brixton Disorders in 1981 was the establishment of 'consultation' between the police and the community in each London Borough. The main purpose behind this was to create a structural basis for dialogue. The Police Liaison Consultative Group in Waltham Forest was established in 1985 with representatives from members of the local police, the Council and community organizations. In January 1986 the Consultative Group established a Racial Incidents Panel (RIP) to look specifically at racial incidents in the Borough. The record of the RIP since 1986, however, is a dismal account of the way in which mute consensus and organizational flacidity undermine the best intentions of essentially police led crime prevention initiatives.

Initially the terms of reference formulated and agreed by the Consultative Group for the RIP, covered the following areas: assessing the extent and nature of alleged racial incidents; increasing the confidence in the community about the police's and other agencies' response; and suggesting improvements in these responses and promoting good practice. The RIP membership was taken from the Consultative Group with the police's local Community Liaison officer (CLO) acting as an adviser. In its early meetings the CLO also acted as the servicing secretary of the Panel. Towards the end of the first year of Panel meetings it became clear that to fulfil its role more information and input was required from Council departments in particular Housing, Education and Recreation Services. At this point also, representatives from the Council's Housing department and the Racial Harassment Advice Service were invited to the meetings. However, at the end of 1986 the RIP appeared to be uncertain as to its role in outreach work and casework on racial incidents. 1987 brought a period of change within which, only three meetings were held while the administration of the RIP transferred from the police to the Council's Secretariat. In 1988 its terms of reference were expanded by the Consultative Group to include the role of 'community interveners'. This provided the RIP with an additional responsibility, namely to act as a mode of intervention in the event of threatened or actual serious racial incidents. This additional role required members to liaise closely with the local police in monitoring current trends, attend places of disturbance, prevent or minimize racial incidents and campaign through local youth and community centres to encourage peaceful co-existence. This change potentially gave the RIP a more proactive remit but it appeared also to arouse concern amongst some members as to their actual role in these potentially dangerous situations. The police's view however was that they would not be expected to undertake this alone and that part of their role would also be to inform the police of racial harassment incidents or complaints even if the complaints were against the police.

At a meeting on 19 April 1988 the RIP recognized their first pattern of racial attacks based on police statistics. According to the minutes of that meeting almost 2/3 of suspects were juveniles, 70% of victims were of Asian origin and 70% of juvenile suspects cautioned did not come to the notice of the police again. Ironically at a subsequent meeting the CLO after presenting the police's racial incidents report commented that there appeared to be no particular pattern to the incidents he had reported. However, it was apparent that the RIP still hoped to identify parts of the Borough more subject to racial harassment than others.

It is clear that the RIP was an initiative through which the local police attempted to raise the profile of its activities with regard to racial harassment in the Borough. Here too, however, developments on the surface belied the swamp of inactivity into which a lack of direction could lead an apparently promising initiative. Thus, at the time of writing, very little constructive progress had been made in reference to any of the RIP's terms of reference. That the RIP continued to meet was evident, that it was capable of registering a sense of achievement was less so.

Throughout its existence the RIP encountered a number of concerns that it persistently failed to resolve or address. The RIP's membership, for example, was a continual problem. Initially, attendance at meetings merely fluctuated, eventually this diminished considerably and could not be reinvigorated by the recruitment of new members. The attendance of the Council's Racial Harassment Advice Service Co-ordinator (an officer from the Race Relations Unit) for a short time seemed to provide some direction and focus, but what remained vague was how directly the RIP were involved in the cases reported to it.

The RIP's principle failing, is that it produced virtually no analysis of the extent and nature of racial incidents in Waltham Forest. Although statistics were presented regularly by the police and the Housing department, these were not subjected to a thorough analysis and there was no follow up to any conclusions about the pattern of racial harassment in the Borough. Admittedly to have done so may have required more extensive research and investigative resources but there appears to have been no discussion in this context. It was perhaps indicative of the RIP's deficient sense of purpose or analytic function, for example, that it did not require from the police any more detailed information about the location of reported incidents than the Home Beat area. Not only would the numerals and letters which denote divisional Home Beats have been, at best, obscure to anyone without a working knowledge of how they related to the police's geographic sub-division of parts of the Borough, but any patterns or correlations which may otherwise have been evident between type, time, or exact place of incidents were made invisible by this cryptic identification. How was it possible for the RIP even to begin to discern spatial patterns of racial harassment if it could not pinpoint where incidents were taking place? The 1990 guidelines on racial harassment appeared to concede the existence of a functional cul-de-sac down which RIP's seem predisposed to travel, where it stated 'They should not be allowed to become bureaucratic, simply a monitoring function'. However, police confidence in the existing 'multi-agency' approach appears unshakeable, in spite of the problems exemplified by RIP's.

An approach to assessing the police response to racial incidents seemed to be a task that the RIP was singularly unable to tackle, to the extent that this did not even appear to have been considered a relevant objective. At every meeting the CLO reported on the nature and progress of recorded incidents. But there was no critical questioning or comprehensive evaluation of what the police *actually* did or whether the victims were satisfied with the police response. Without these assessments it would be impossible for the RIP to make any recommendations as to improvements or good practice.

The relationship of the RIP to its 'community interveners' was extremely unclear. Even assuming the value of this approach it was questionable whether members of the RIP would have had the training, experience and ability to undertake a role which involved delicate, sustained and impartial negotiation. Moreover it was noticeable that the RIP had at some of its meetings been presented with cases of racial harassment referred to it from RIP members or outside agencies. But its role as a co-ordinating body for dealing with cases of racial harassment was haphazard and ill defined. It could request the police or Council to take action and monitor the response and follow-up but beyond this it had no procedures or personnel to deal with individual cases.

In theory the idea of a RIP to monitor and assess racial incidents in the Borough has several merits: it could keep the issue on the public agenda, required the police and Council departments to be aware of the issues and provide a forum in which these could be discussed. However, in practice it simply had not achieved anything, a fact reflected in perennial problems of its membership's attendance at its meetings. This failure may have been symptomatic of the police's lack of conviction about the problem of racial harassment in the Borough or even an unfamiliarity with the strategic nature of policy development. This might explain why the RIP had become almost bureaucratically purposeless and why it was only the last ditch insistence of senior police officers present at the Police Consultative Group meeting on 8 February 1990 which prevented the RIP from being disbanded.

# Bibliography

Anderson, B. (1983), *Imagined Communities*, Verso, London.

Appadurai, A. (1990), 'Disjuncture and difference in the global cultural economy' in Featherstone, M., *Global Culture*, Sage, London.

Ball, W. and Solomos, J. (eds.) (1990), *Race and Local Politics*, Macmillan, London.

Bauman, Z. (1991), *Modernity and Ambivalence*, Polity Press, Cambridge.

Benyon, J. and Solomos, J. (1987), *The Roots of Urban Unrest*, Pergamon Press, Oxford.

Blagg, H., Pearson, G., Sampson, A., Smith, D., Stubbs, P. (1988), 'Inter-agency co-operation : rhetoric and reality', in Hope, T. and Shaw, M. (eds.), *Communities and Crime reduction*, HMSO.

Bonnerjea, L. and Lawton, J. (1988), *No Racial Harrassment this week - a study undertaken in the London Borough of Brent*, Policy Studies Institute, London.

Bottomley, K. and Pease, K. (1986), *Crime and punishment:interpreting the data*, Open University Press.

Brantingham, P. and Brantingham, P. (1984), *Patterns in Crime*, Macmillan.

Brown, C. (1984), *Black and White Britian - the third PSI Survey*, Gower, Aldershot.

Burrows, J. and Lewis, H. (1988), *Directed Patrolling : a study of uniformed policing*, HMSO.

Camden, London Borough of (1988), *Racism in Camden Housing*, London Borough of Camden.

Cater, J. and Jones, T. (1989), *Social Geography*, Edward Arnold, London.

Cohen, P. (1988), *Multiracist Britain*, Macmillan, London.

Commission for Racial Equality (1987a), *Living in Terror - A report on racial violence and harassment in housing*, CRE.

Commission for Racial Equality (1987b), *Racial Attacks : A survey in eight areas of Britain*, CRE.

Cooper, J. and Pomeyie, J. (1988), 'Racial attacks and racial harassment:Lessons from a local project' in Maguire, M. and Pointing, J. (eds.), *Victims of Crime:A New Deal?*, Open University Press.

Crane, P. (1983), *Gays and the Law*, Pluto Press, London.

Crawford, A., Jones, T., Woodhouse, T., Young, J. (1990), *Second Islington Crime Survey*, Centre for Criminology ; Middlesex Polytechnic.

Criminal Injuries Compensation Board (1990), *Victims of crimes of violence - A guide to the Criminal Injuries Compensation Scheme*, HMSO.

Department of the Environment (1989), *Tackling Racial Violence and Harassment in local authority housing: a guide to good practice for local authorities*, HMSO.

Duff, P. (1988), 'The "victims movement" and legal reform' in Maguire, M. and Pointing, J. (eds.), *Victims of Crime :A New Deal?*, Open University Press.

Ekblom, P., Simon, F., and Birdi, S. (1988), *Crime and Racial Harassment in Asian-run small shops: the scope for prevention*, HMSO.

Evans, D. and Herbert, D. (1989), *The Geography of Crime*, Routledge, London.

Fielding, N.G. (1988), *Joining Forces - police training, socialization and occupational competence*, Routledge.

Forbes, D. (1988), *Action on Racial Harassment - Legal Remedies and Local Authorities*, Legal Action Group and London Housing Unit.

Forum for Initiatives in Reparation and Mediation (1989), *Working through Conflict - Annual Report 1988-9*, FIRM.

Genn, H. (1988), 'Multiple Victimization' in Maguire, M. and Pointing, J. (eds.), *Victims of Crime:A New Deal?*, Open University Press.

Giddens, A. (1990), *Consequences of Modernity*, Polity, London.

Gilroy, P. (1990), 'The End of Anti-racism' in Ball, W. and Solomos, J. (eds.), *Race and Local Politics*, Macmillan, London.

Gilroy, P. (1987), *There ain't no Black in the Union Jack*, Unwin Hyman Ltd.

Gordon, P. (1990a), *Racial Violence and Harassment*, Runnymede Trust.

Gordon, P. (1990b), 'A dirty war:The new right and local authority Anti-racism' in Ball, W. and Solomos, S. (eds.), *Race and Local Politics*, Macmillan, London.

Gordon, P. and Newham, A. (1986), *Different Worlds - Racism and Discrimination in Britian*, Revised edition; Runnymede Trust.

Gould, P. and White, R. (1974), *Mental Maps*, Pelican Books.

Greater London Action for Racial Equality (1989), *The Metropolitan Police Anti-racial harassment campaigns 1989 - an assessment: policy implications for the future* (August), GLARE.

Greater London Council (1984), *Racial Harassment in London*, GLC.

Gregory, D. and Urry, J. (eds.) (1985), *Social Relations and Spatial Structures*, Macmillan.

Grimshaw, R. and Jefferson, T. (1987), *Interpreting Police Work - policy and practice in forms of Beat Policing*, Allen & Unwin, London.

Hall, R. E. (1985), *Ask any woman*, Falling Wall Press.

244

Hanmer, J., Radford, J. and Stanko, E. (1989), *Women, Policing and Male Violence*, Routledge.

Herbert, D. (1989), 'Crime and place:An introduction' in Evans, D. and Herbert, D., *The Geography of Crime*, Routledge, London.

Hesse, B. and Hill, V. (1989), 'Doing it to death', *Legal Action,* (October).

Hill, M. and Bramley, G. (1986), *Analysing Social Policy*, Basil Blackwell.

Home Affairs Committee (1989), *Racial attacks and harassment-Second follow-up to the Home Affairs Committee's Report in 1986*, HMSO.

Home Office (1991), *Practical ways to crack crime-The Handbook*, fourth edition, HMSO.

Home Office (1990), *Victim's Charter:A Statement of the Rights of Victims of Crime*, HMSO.

Home Office (1989), *The Response to Racial Attacks and Harassment: guidance for the statutory agencies*, HMSO.

Husbands, C. (1982), 'The East End Racism 1900-1980', *London Journal,* 8, 3-26.

Institute of Race Relations (1987), *Policing Against Black People*, IRR.

Jackson, P. (1989), *Maps of Meaning*, Unwin Hyman, London.

Jackson, P. (ed.) (1987), *Race and Racism - essays in social geography*, Allen & Unwin, London.

Jackson, P. and Smith, S.J. (1984), *Exploring Social Geography*, George Allen and Unwin, London.

Jefferson, T. and Grimshaw, R. (1984), 'The Problem of Law Enforcement Policy in England and Wales: The case of Community Policing and Racial Attacks', *International Journal of the Sociology of Law*, May.

Jeffreys, S. and Radford, J. (1984), 'Contributory negligence or being a woman? The car rapist' in Scraton, P. and Gordon, P. (eds.), *Causes for Concern*, Penguin Books, Middlesex.

Jones, G. and Stewart, J. (1983), *The Case for Local Government*, George Allen & Unwin, London.

Kelly, L. (1987), 'The Continuum of Sexual Violence' in Hanmer, J. and Maynard, M. (eds.), *Women, Violence and Social Control*, Macmillan Press.

Kelly, L. and Radford, J. (1987), 'The Problem of Men:Feminist Perspectives on Sexual Violence' in Scraton, P. (ed.), *Law, Order and the Authoritarian State*, Open University Press.

Kimber, J. and Cooper, L. (1991), *Victim Support:Racial Harassment Project-Final Report*, Community Research Advisory Centre, The Polytechnic of North London.

Laclau, E. and Mouffe, C. (1985), *Hegemony and Socialist Strategy*, Verso, London.

245

Layton-Henry, Z. (1984), *The Politics of Race in Britain*, Allen and Unwin, London.

Leigh, A. (1988), *Effective Change*, Institute of Personnel Management.

Lustgarten, L. (1986), *The Governance of Police*, Sweet and Maxwell, London.

Luthra, M. and Tyler, A. (1988), 'Left in the dark on racism', *Guardian*, 7 September.

Maguire, M. and Corbett, C. (1991), *A study of the Police Complaints System*, HMSO.

Maguire, M. and Corbett, C. (1987), *The Effects of Crime and the Work of Victims Support Schemes*, Gower, Aldershot.

Maguire, M. and Pointing, J. (eds.) (1988), *Victims of Crime: A New Deal?*, Open University Press.

Mama, A. (1990), *The Hidden Struggle - Statutory and Voluntary Sector Responses to Violence against Black Women in the Home*, London Race and Housing Research Unit, London.

Marshall, T. and Walpole, M. (1985), *Bringing people together: mediation and reparation projects in Great Britain*, Home Office.

Mawby, R.I. and Gill, M.L. (1987), *Crime Victims - Needs, Services and the voluntary sector*, Tavistock Publications, London.

Mayhew, P., Elliot, D. and Dowds, L. (1989), *The British Crime Survey*, Home Office Research Study 111, HMSO.

Metropolitan police (1990a), *Working Together for Racial Harmony*, Metropolitan police.

Metropolitan police (1990b), *Chingford divisional report 1990*, Metropolitan police.

Metropolitan police (1990c), *Leyton divisional report 1990*, Metropolitan police.

Metropolitan police (1989a), *London Racial Harassment Action Guide*, Metropolitan police.

Metropolitan police (1989b), *Memorandum by Metropolitan Police in Racial Attacks and Harassment - Second Follow-up to the Home Affairs Committee's Report in 1986,* Metropolitan police.

Metropolitan police (1989c), *Chingford divisional report 1989*, Metropolitan police.

Metropolitan police (1989d), *Leyton divisional report 1989*, Metropolitan police.

Metropolitan police (1988a), *Chingford divisional report 1988*, Metropolitan police.

Metropolitan police (1988b), *Leyton divisional report 1988*, Metropolitan police.

Metropolitan police (1987a), *Chingford divisional report 1987,* Metropolitan
     police.
Metropolitan police (1987b), *Leyton divisional report 1987*, Metropolitan
     police.
Metropolitan police (1986a), *Force Appraisal September 1986*, Metropolitan
     police.
Metropolitan police (1986b), *Chingford divisional report 1986*, Metropolitan
     police.
Metropolitan police (1986c), *Leyton divisional report 1986*, Metropolitan
     police.
Metropolitan police Commissioner (1990), *Annual report for the year 1989*,
     HMSO.
Metropolitan police Commissioner (1989), *Annual report for the year 1988*,
     HMSO.
Metropolitan police Commissioner (1988), *Annual report for the year 1987*,
     HMSO.
Metropolitan police Commissioner (1987), *Annual report for the year 1986*,
     HMSO.
Metropolitan police Commissioner (1986), *Annual report for the year 1985*,
     HMSO.
Metropolitan police Commissioner (1985), *Annual report for the year 1984*,
     HMSO.
Metropolitan police Commissioner (1984), *Annual report for the year 1983*,
     HMSO.
Metropolitan police Commissioner (1983), *Annual report for the year 1982*,
     HMSO.
Metropolitan police Commissioner (1982), *Annual report for the year 1981*,
     HMSO.
Miles, R. (1989), *Racism*, Routledge, London.
Nanton, P. and Fitzgerald, M. (1990), 'Race policies in local
     government:Boundaries or thresholds' in Ball, W. and Solomos, J. (eds.),
     *Race and Local Politics*, Macmillan, London.
National Association of Victim Support Schemes (1989), *Working for victims
     of crime - Annual report 1988-1989,* NAVSS.
Newham, London Borough of (1987a), *Metropolitan police racial harassment
     campaign*, Police and Community Safety Unit.
Newham, London Borough of (1987b), *A survey of crime and racial
     harassment in Newham*, Harris Research Centre.
Ramdin, R. (1987), *The making of the Black working class in Britian*,
     Wildwood House, Aldershot.

Roach Family Support Committee (1989), *Policing in Hackney 1945-1984*, Karia Press.

Rock, P. (1990), *Helping Victims of Crime*, Oxford University Press.

Sack, R. (1986), *Human Territoriality*, Cambridge University Press, London.

Schwendinger, H. and Schwendinger, H. (1975), 'Defenders of order or guardians of Human rights?' in Taylor, I., Walton, P., Young, J., *Critical Criminology*, Routledge, London.

Scraton, P. (ed.) (1987), *Law, Order and the Authoritarian State*, Open University Press.

Seagrave, J. (1989), *Racially motivated incidents reported to the police*, HMSO.

Shapland, J., Willmore, J. and Duff, P. (1985), *Victims in the Criminal Justice System*, Gower, Aldershot.

Sim, J., Scraton, P. , Gordon, P. (1987), 'Introduction: Crime, the State and Critical Analysis' in Scraton, P. (ed.), *Law, Order and the Authoritarian State*, Open University Press.

Smith, D. M. (1990), 'Introduction' in Chisholm, M. and Smith, D. M., *Shared space, divided space*, Unwin Hyman, London.

Smith, S. J. (1989),*The Politics of Race and Residence*, Polity, Cambridge.

Smith, S. J. (1986), *Crime, Space and Society*, Cambridge University Press, London.

Soja, E.W. (1989), *Post- modern Geographies - the re-assertion of space in critical social theory*, Verso, London.

Solomos, J. (1989), *Race and Racism in Contemporary Britain*, Macmillan, London.

Stanko, E. (1990), *Everyday Violence : how women and men experience sexual and physical danger*, Pandora, London.

Stanko, E. (1985), *Intimate Intrusions:Women's experience of male violence*, Routledge and Kegan Paul.

Taylor, I., Walton, P., Young, J. (1973), *The New Criminology*, Routledge, London.

Thompson, K. (1988), *Under Seige*, Penguin, London.

van Dijk, J. (1988), 'Ideological trends within the victims movement: An international perspective' in Maguire, M. and Pointing, J. (eds.), *Victims of Crime:A New Deal?*, Open University Press.

Walker, I. (1985), 'The fires of racial hatred', *Observer Supplement*, 22 September.

Walker, M (1990), 'A place of safety' - *unpublished interview with Thora Rose*.

Walklate, S. (1988), *Victimology - The victim, and the criminal justice process*, Unwin Hyman, London.

Waller, I. (1988), 'International standards, national trail blazing and the next steps' in Maguire, M. and Pointing, J. (eds.), *Victims of Crime: A New Deal?*, Open University Press.

Walmsley, R. (1986), *Personal Violence*, Home Office Research Study 89, HMSO.

Waltham Forest, London Borough of (1990a), *Borough Trends 1990*, L.B. of Waltham Forest.

Waltham Forest, London Borough of (1990b), *Housing Investment Strategy 1990-91*, L.B. of Waltham Forest.

Waltham Forest, London Borough of (1990c), *Survey of Afro-Caribbean Households in Waltham Forest in 1989*, L.B. of Waltham Forest, Social Services Dept, May.

Waltham Forest, London Borough of (1989a), *Ethnic Minority Communities in Waltham Forest: A Review of available statistical information*, L.B. of Waltham Forest.

Waltham Forest, London Borough of (1989b), *PAU Information Note 89/3: Recent Estimates of the size and characteristics of Ethnic Minority Communities*, L.B. of Waltham Forest.

Waltham Forest, London Borough of (1988), *High Rise System Built Housing -past, present and future*, L.B. of Waltham Forest, Council estate improvement team.

Waltham Forest, London Borough of (1986), *Survey of Ethnic Minority Businesses*, L.B. of Waltham Forest, Dept. of Development.

Waltham Forest, London Borough of (1981), *Borough Trends Supplement - 1981 Census Small Area Statistics*, L.B. of Waltham Forest.

Waltham Forest Police Monitoring Group (1985), Bulletin and newsletter, May.

Waltham Forest Police Monitoring Group (1983), Bulletin and newsletter, May.

Weatheritt, M. (1986), *Innovations in Policing*, Croom Helm in association with The Police Foundation, Kent.

Weber, R. (1985), *Basic Content Analysis*, Sage, London.

Williams, F. (1989), *Social policy: A critical introduction*, Polity Press, London.

# Index

252

253